WINGBEATS II:

Exercises & Practice in Poetry

WINGBEATS II:
Exercises & Practice in Poetry

Edited by
Scott Wiggerman &
David Meischen

🐈 **Dos Gatos Press** 🐈

Austin, Texas

Wingbeats II:
Exercises & Practice in Poetry
© 2014, Dos Gatos Press
ISBN–13: 978-09840399-5-1
Library of Congress Control Number: 2014939679

The editors wish to thank the poets who generously allowed their poems to
be used as examples in the *Wingbeats* exercises; and—most important—the
teaching poets who submitted exercises for this book.

First Edition
14 15 16 17 18 19 20 5 4 3 2 1

Cover Design: Kristee Humphrey
Manufacturing: OneTouchPoint Ginny's

Dos Gatos Press
1310 Crestwood Rd.
Austin, TX 78722
www.dosgatospress.org

Poetry is what you find
in the dirt in the corner,

overhear on the bus, God
in the details, the only way

to get from here to there.

~ *Elizabeth Alexander*

I read the line over and over
as if I might discern
the little fires set
the flames of an idea   licking the page

~ *Natasha Trethewey*

Table of Contents

III. The Role of Repurposing

IV. Structure & Form

V. The Power of Words, Names, Numbers

VI. Complicating the Poem

Acknowledgments

Index of Contributors

Alternate Table of Contents

Working with Others

Voice or Persona

Variations on Narrative

Incorporating Research

Nonlinear Approaches, Nonlinear Poems

For Poets Seeking a Challenge

Revision

Mining Memories

Exploring the Senses

For the Beginning Poet

Note: These exercises work especially well for students in the early stages of writing poetry, though we recommend them to all poetry writers, regardless of level of achievement. Please note, too, that many young poets, including K–12 students, would be capable of tackling even the most challenging exercises in *Wingbeats II*.

Chapter I:
Jump-Starting the Poem

A poem can be said to have two subjects,
the initiating or triggering subject, which
starts the poem or "causes" the poem to be
written, and the real or generated subject,
which the poem comes to say or mean,
and which is generated or discovered in
the poem during the writing.

~ Richard Hugo

Alan Birkelbach

The World Is Ending in Ten Minutes!

You, along with the billions of people on this planet, have been told that culture and society as we know them are about to end. The end is inescapable; most of humanity will not survive. The end might be an invasion of aliens. It might be sunspots. It might be giant tidal waves. Doesn't matter. You know it's coming. The disturbance is on the horizon and heading your way. You are sitting on your patio with a beer, a pen, a pad of paper, and a container to stuff your last words into. What are you going to write?

Rationale

A poet rarely has the luxury of time to wait for the muse. This exercise demands that the poet produce *now;* its primary purpose is to train the mind to write on demand. But there are two important concerns to consider. First, because you have a hard stop built in—ten minutes—you are limited to approximately one hundred words. Second, you must decide how to approach your last ten minutes. Will you write your last love letter, a thank you to Mom and Dad, a query to God, a "seven stages of death" poem? Or will you step outside of self-indulgence and write about larger issues? Remember: these are your last words. If by chance a later civilization finds your container, do you want yourself remembered, or do you want your words, your experience, remembered? Are you maudlin, whiny, strong, wise, accepting, or struggling?

Procedure

I. This exercise works best in a group—for purposes of comparison. Each participant gets a pen, a pad, something to drink, and something to store the poem in. For the sake of the workshop, it can be an unmarked envelope. Or a Mason jar. Or a cheap metal thermos from a dollar store.

II. The instructor sets a timer and tells the participants when to start. When the ten-minute timer signals time, the participants must set down their pens whether they are finished or not. All participants will stuff their poems into their containers and seal them. And then the world ends. Kablooey.

III. While bugs are sorting through the rubble outside, the instructor passes out the containers, mixed, to all participants. Each person who submitted a poem gets a poem. It might be his or her own—or not. Participants are asked to consider the following questions:

- What route did the poet take in the poem you are reading? Do you think the route she or he chose was the easy way—or the hard way?
- Did the poet actually sign his or her name to the poem? Why or why not?

IV. Participants read the poems aloud and discuss how individual writers responded to this challenge. The following questions are useful:

- What was the hardest part of the exercise—the time/size constraint or the decision about the direction of the poem?
- Do you think it's important that poetry might be one of the last items that humankind generates? Or would it be better if we were known for our science or architecture?

Note: For purposes of comparison—and to stimulate discussion—William Stafford's "At the Bomb Testing Site" is readily available online and in multiple anthologies. (See also Keith Ekiss' exercise "The World Without Us," page 56.)

An Example

This haiku sequence is my response to the ten minute prompt:

> The journey of a
> thousand steps stops here. Oh look.
> Just past me. A hawk.
>
> It is good I have
> read all my books. They would have
> been lonely unused.
>
> As the wind starts I
> remember her kiss. Right here.
> On my cheek. Eyes closed.
>
> ~ *Alan Birkelbach*

Alan Birkelbach, a native Texan, was the 2005 Poet Laureate of Texas. His work has appeared in journals and anthologies such as *Grasslands Review, Borderlands, The Langdon Review,* and *Concho River Review.* Recipient of a Fellowship Grant from the Writers' League of Texas, Birkelbach has been nominated for Wrangler, Spur, and Pushcart prizes. A Distinguished Poet of Dallas and a member of The Academy of American Poets, he has twice been a featured reader at the Texas Book Festival and has spoken at schools and colleges across the state.

Getting Unstuck: Ten Warm-Ups

Dancers, musicians, visual artists, opera singers, athletes, and actors share two things in common: they all warm up, and they all practice. Poets, we can benefit by joining them. Try these quick exercises, use some of the variations to them, or invent variations of your own. Give yourself extra points for word play, sonic elements, a final *real* poem (as opposed to just an exercise), and unique/interesting combinations. Post this sign:

There is No Such Thing as Writer's Block

I. Playing Games

Write a poem giving directions for how to play a childhood game. You might begin with prose as you doodle ideas, but transform it into a poem, please. Revise as needed until you achieve a poem that readers gradually recognize as an extended metaphor. Our epiphany—and yours: the poem is not about a game, but something else you have not named.

2. Freezing in Here

Scope out what's in your freezer and make a list of 6–8 items. Write a poem that includes some or all of these, your intentions for them (hanging them up as a frieze?), or why you forgot about them. Or write a poem about something amazing/strange/unexpected you discovered there. Maybe it isn't food. Remember, you can *make stuff up*. (And maybe clean out the freezer). Next time: write a recipe poem, maybe for something you cannot/would not eat.

3. Boxes

What size? What shape? What for? Some boxes are not containers. Some hold delight; some hold sorrow; some are hidden. Maybe your belching boxer has a box of bones; maybe Bach had boxes as a bachelor. Stretch as far as you can, playing with the idea of a box—not Pandora's. Being sensible is not required, nor is using alliteration.

4. Internally Yours

Write a page of rhyming words, exploiting all the spelling variations you can think of. Do it on the patio with some iced tea. Do not fret about bare spots in the grass. Just muddle along, enjoy the day, then go back and add another column. Fill the page. Then circle an interesting selection of rhyming words (not *moon–June*, please!). Aim for more unique combinations like *quiet–riot* or *cheese–knees*. Use the circled words in a poem. You may use them anywhere you like *except* at line endings. Eventually, fill out the lines to conjure a poem and cut any words that do not belong. You will recognize them easily. Don't you love it that a poem tells us when it's finished?

An Example

Semi Colon

a pair of dots, spotty dots, gotta lotta tottle dots—
or sometimes flighty innards, partially plumbed
sore as a mummy's torn tummy, glummed and forlorn.
Returned to health, a chummy bum might hum, or slam
each sentence with shots of flimflam, humdrum semaphores.

~ *Sandra Soli*

5. Imagine This!

Improvise a page about a place you have never been. No fair cheating. Let it eventually become a poem. Cut out the rambling. Include street names, a person, something to eat, perhaps a myth about the place. Conjure specific details. Don't use the obvious (Parisian Eiffel Tower). Stretch yourself. *Make it up.* My example: "Dora Evelyn Thaw in Pisa Before Her Husband Commits Murder." My inspiration: Lawrence Thornton's novel, *Imagining Argentina*. Marvelous details, and the author had never been there in his life.

An Example

Dora Evelyn Thaw in Pisa
Before Her Husband Commits Murder

Inside a thumbprint of sun
I am waiting for you
on Hotel Francesco's terrace,
the afternoon winding down
like a clock whose churchkey
has been lost.

Piazza dei Miracoli's tourists
screamed in my direction, cameras

clicking—yes, Floradora herself,
the girl who sparkles dust
motes in the Rialto's whirring dark.

I played the coquette, as expected,
smiling postcard smiles, happy
in stunningly graceful poses
but today I am tired, Harry.
My poor feet!

Lucky Floradora is worn out,
I tell you, from razzle-dazzle.
Their Field of Miracles in the wrong
shoes. Hurry back, can't you?

Now the scented Gauloise
(careful, don't damage the manicure)
from the silver case
you chose at the corner shop
on Via Santa Maria,
my new initials engraved
even before you proposed.

You were so sure of me—
unlike Stanny, though some said
I was not the first to perform
in his red velvet swing.

The pinch of gossip (flick ashes here).
He knew I loved expensive toys.
Even Garbo could lust for
the future I have yet to imagine:

Star of the courtroom drama,
a million dollars, a million readers
binging on the news of murder,
our divorce, the greedy scrambling
for tarnished mementos I once touched.

~ *Sandra Soli*

6. Poetry with Ease / without Ease

Down to essentials! Let's move from syllables to the basic component of language: a single letter of our alphabet. Write a poem or paragraph using the letter *E* in every word. Work about twenty minutes. The first time will be a bit slow. Next, write a poem or paragraph in which the letter *E* is forbidden—make it illegal. Repeat the warm-up exercise several days in a row. Notice that your brain cooperates much faster now, supplying new legal words to replace the illegal words you may have thought of first. Mix up the exercise by choosing an *A* or *O* in a later session. This exercise will challenge you to stimulate brain synapses and find words to satisfy the rule you selected at the outset. Extra prize points for trying the exercise with the letter *I*—a tough challenge! Go ahead, give yourself a star.

An Example

Reverie

The bees dream:

                elite fields,
          plentiful pollen,
     sweet nectars,
                extravagant reaches.

The bees dream,

                their knees covered,
         legs enveloped,
     necks smeared:
                delirious excess.

The bees keep dreaming:

                yellow pleasure,
         heavenly zeniths—
     east, west,
                pesticide-free.

~ *Scott Wiggerman*

7. Slinky

Remember the toy that traveled end-to-front, repetitively coiling its way down the stairs? Consider a line-building exercise that uses the same technique. Begin with a line. Use one or several of the line-closing words to begin the next line. Repeat at will. If you can coil back to the beginning, so much the better. Or not. Writing a Slinky is a line-building game, so enjoy yourself—no stress allowed. (See also Laure-Anne Bosselaar's exercise "Repetition & Cadence, or Repetition *for* Cadence," page 61.)

Note: I want to credit Dara Wier's poem "Apology for and Further Explanation of an Attempt to Divert Accusations of Equivocation," enormous fun to read and an opportunity for poets wanting to practice line work.

An Example

Poem Made of Bad Words for Poems

There are words I love.
I love you. There you are.
You are loving the words too, saying them.
Saying them there, the words.
Words love the saying of love there.
There, where love is and words are, too.
Too, I give you these words.
Words are what they are.
They are saying *Love. Give.*
Give love there, where you love them.
Love them, the words. Say them.
Say them where? Why?
Why, Love, where love is. There.

~ *Sandra Soli*

8. Let There Be Music (♫ ♫ ♫)

Grab your baton and conduct musical passages within poems while reading them aloud. In your own writing, consider not only vowels and consonants, but also duration and pitch. Think of syllables as musical notations, using eighth notes, quarter notes, half and whole notes—even a corresponding rest (pause). Mark up a poem's syllables as though you were working with sheet music; focus on stressed and unstressed syllables as you work. Next, think of a short song you know well. Substitute other words for the song lyrics, choosing words with the same rhythm and duration. Read your new words aloud, perhaps to another person. Can your partner recognize the original song?

9. Steals

You've probably enjoyed **transpositions** (making a poem by using someone else's words) and **translitics** (fake translations) as poetry-generating exercises. Consider ways you can add to your arsenal of legal theft techniques. Open a collection of stories by Chekhov, Poe, or García Márquez. Fish for a title or first sentence of a story. Close the book and freewrite an improvisation. When revising the raw material, you can erase the stuff you stole—or perhaps call the poem "Stolen from Edgar." Or not. Next time, copy six titles from a bookshelf. Choose one or combine several, then begin. After twenty minutes, something will start happening. Be open to variations.

10. Poet's Superpower

Stretch your creative thinking mode by taking us into the realm of your secret superpower, whether it be elemental transmutation, telekinesis, or perhaps one of the more common dream phenoms, the ability to fly. Don't tell us it's a dream; just let us experience it with you. Use this exercise as a reminder: every poet's greatest superpower is language. (See also Lee Ann Roripaugh's exercise "Poetry Superpowers vs. Poetry Kryptonite," page 104.)

An Example

Flying

Are we not all Icarus, in our heart of hearts?
~ *Peter Spear*

She watches herself climbing
the steepest balcony tier,
stretching her neck.

A dark-breathing audience,
the tide she might swim in
some other time, does not expect

this surprise, the trick of flight
as she steps into a puddle
that began a circle of penlight.

Hey look, someone yells, *Look up!*
That woman thinks she's a swan.
Can you reach her?

Chaos. Everyone surging up
from their seats, transformed
as the notion of air or swan light.

Nascent ceiling fans. The idea
they need most to believe:
her neon beak a sun, rising.

~ *Sandra Soli*

Sandra Soli, writer and editor, facilitates workshops throughout the Southwest. Her poetry, short fiction, and photographs have appeared widely in such journals as *Ruminate, The New York Quarterly, Southern Poetry Review, Naugatuck River Review, The Grove Review, SLAB, Cross Timbers,* and *War, Literature, and the Arts.* She is a regular reader at Oklahoma's Scissortail and Woody Guthrie Festivals and enjoys collaborative projects with artists in many disciplines. Honors include the Eyster Poetry Prize from *New Delta Review,* an Oklahoma Book Award, and two nominations for the Pushcart Prize. Soli currently serves on the board of Oklahoma's Center for the Book. Puns and poets, equally outrageous, are her delight.

Junk Drawers: Tools & Rules

developed this exercise for a summer writing conference with a theme of "under construction." I decided to focus on tools, everyday kitchen tools, items that are commonplace in everyday life, but things we often overlook, take for granted. This is the rationale behind many of my poems: to take the stuff of ordinary life, hold it up to the light, let it shine.

Procedure

I. Prepare

I use Karla Huston's "Dogma for the Junk Drawer" as a model. Wendy Morton's "A Drawer Filled to Overflowing" also makes an excellent model.

Dogma for the Junk Drawer

I believe in the tangled hank of string,
the tail that snakes over a small box
of pretty flower greetings waiting
to be mailed. I believe in the slant-tip
marker, its thick sick smell,
the small sharpener, broken points
of lead collected in corners.
I believe in an old menu with coffee stains
and sandwiches like Boney Billy and The Narmer,
the chewed roll of black tape,
stained wine corks smelling faintly of grape.
Playing cards with shuffled edges, the lazy
red dice with white dots. I believe in the box
of tacks and Bulldog hangers, in the needle-nose
pliers and small claw hammer—
in unfinished work, the dimples in the wall
and bent nails. I believe there is a way
to fix what is broken, a way to make use
of the useless. I believe if you dig deeply,
you will find what you need.

~ *Karla Huston*

I use visual aids: a collection of well-worn 1950s kitchen memorabilia from my mother's kitchen and my husband's mother's kitchen: a gravy separator, a pastry cutter, a potato masher, a flip-top can opener, etc. I recommend using anything quirky you find in your own kitchen drawer. These gadgets might not seem necessary, but they can spark some excellent memory pieces.

II. Write

My method is simple and low-tech. After I introduce the subject, discuss a sample poem or two, and open things up for discussion, I let students have at it. My remarks include many of the same things other writer-teachers say:

- Keep the pen moving.
- Banish the inner editor, the one who says, "This isn't good enough."
- Don't be dismayed if what you write seems really bad. Keep writing. Don't be afraid of a lousy first draft.
- Don't think. Write. Believe poetry will come bubbling up from the well.
- Skip lines as you go. You can use the space later for crossing out, drawing arrows, etc.
- If you're on a roll and can't find the right word, use a blank. If you think of three or four words or images at the same time, use them all, separated by slashes. If you can't think of where a line is going, but you have rhythm and momentum going, use blanks to fill out the line. Keep going.
- Think of the line as a unit of breath.
- The image is the beating heart of a poem; Tu Fu's student had it right when he said, "The right images are like being alive twice." Use all five senses; then tap into the river of memory, the sixth sense. Use the focus of a camera lens, allowing it to zoom in on one square inch.

Twenty minutes is a good space of time for adults, ten for high school students. I bring a kitchen timer along, so that we use our time wisely. And I write along with the group.

III. Revise

I break for ten minutes, asking students to look over their work, searching for a line where the rhythm really works; I suggest revising other lines to match it. If the piece is just not working, I suggest circling images/lines/phrases that show potential. Something new may start from these. I also tell students that now they can put their critical hats back on and take a good hard look.

Are there parts that aren't working? Flabby? Clichéd? Too general? One of my teaching mantras is "Specific is terrific." Good old Anglo-Saxon words are more concrete than their fancy Latinate cousins. I quote Stephen King: "The road to hell is paved with adverbs"—to which I add adjectives. I suggest circling modifiers and challenge students to see how many they can excise. I quote Mies van der Rohe—"Less is more"—and ask students to see what they can part with.

This is part of my practice, too. First, I try to amass a body of material. Then, like a sculptor, I chip away at it, chisel it down. I ask students to listen for the poem's inner music—not necessarily words that rhyme but words with sounds that play off each other. Can the music be enhanced?

Finally, what if you took off the first three and last three lines—throwing out the eggshell to make an omelet? How would the poem work now?

IV. Discuss

Taking turns, we read our work aloud. I remind students that this is not a competition. *But* when you hear a poem and think, "Gee, I wish I'd written *that*," think about why that is. Make notes. Go home and write your poem again, trying out whatever it is you liked in other poems—voice, tone, narrative style, or other features. These are exercises, not finished pieces. The *real* poem that comes out of a workshop is the one whose author keeps working, draft after draft, until she or he gets it right.

We don't offer critiquing but comment instead on what we see working in each poem. After all, it's a *work*shop. So what parts—specific images, lines, music, rhythm—are working well? I encourage all to keep working, to keep reading, and to send me poems after the session is over.

Sometimes, the work produced is dazzling. Sometimes, what happens is journeyman's work. Who can say why this is? It's a mystery.

For me, writing is going on a journey, one where you don't know the final destination. I agree with Robert Frost: "I have never started a poem yet whose end I knew. Writing a poem is discovering." There are folks who can write fully finished, easily published pieces in a twenty-minute prompt session—my hat is off to them—and there are others, like me, who will go home with just one tiny trembling image. If the last line is what comes to you, then start there. There's no one way to do this. Poetry happens at the intersection of magic and moonlight. The important thing is to get that first draft down—and then keep going.

Example Poems

Litany of the Desk Drawer

I believe in the dark desk drawer,
nubs of erasers too worn
to rub anything out, pencils
too short to be sharpened, nibs
of pens, screw-top tips, odes
to penmanship in a time
of keyboards, paper clips
that have lost their *u*'s, slips
of paper with illegible words,
brass fasteners, three-hole punches,
stamps in former denominations,
gummed reinforcers, those little
life preservers, snips of lead, pencil
shavings, staples that have slipped
out of line, mucilage, with its slit
mouth glued shut, all of this, here,
in the tomb of the no-longer-used,
where even the smallest scrap
can somehow be of use.

~ *Barbara Crooker*

Litany of the Crock

Praise the stoneware jug holding wooden spoons cracked
and worn, stirrers of batter, gravy, pasta. Whisks
waiting to marry oil & vinegar, sugar & cream. Mallets
eager to tenderize meat. Spatulas strong enough
to separate the thinnest cookie from its silver tray.
Rubber scrapers waving their hands, saying, "Use *me*.
Use *me*." The flat sail of the separator cleaving
lean meat from liquid fat. The dented mesh strainer,
where pesticides are washed away. Below them,
in the floury dark, rests my mother's rolling pin,

creator of crusts so flaky they could have tempted
Adam, made him fall. In a world filled with counters
of polished granite in kitchens where nobody cooks,
let us praise this container of clay holding the homely,
the unlovely, the used-up, and worn. Praise tools
that work without batteries or electricity. Praise
the work of our hands.

~ *Barbara Crooker*

Barbara Crooker is the author of four poetry collections, including *Gold* (Cascade Books, 2013); *Line Dance,* winner of the 2009 Paterson Award for Literary Excellence; and *Radiance,* winner of the 2005 Word Press First Book competition and a finalist for the 2006 Paterson Poetry Prize. Crooker has had poems in numerous publications, including *The Green Mountains Review, The Christian Science Monitor, Nimrod,* and *The Bedford Introduction to Literature.* Her poetry has been read on the BBC, the ABC (Australian Broadcasting Company), and by Garrison Keillor on *The Writer's Almanac;* she has read in the Poetry at Noon series at the Library of Congress. Her awards include the Thomas Merton Poetry of the Sacred Award, three Pennsylvania Council on the Arts Creative Writing Fellowships, fifteen residencies at the Virginia Center for the Creative Arts, a residency at the Moulin à Nef, Auvillar, France, and a residency at The Tyrone Guthrie Centre, Annaghmakerrig, Ireland.

Beyond Story: Moving a Poem from Concrete Image to Revelation

A narrative poem tells a story. And like any story writer, the poet must take care to set the scene and to develop the central image around which a poem resonates or reveals its meaning. Remember that every line of a good poem works to prepare the reader for the closing line or lines, the moment of epiphany or revelation, the *Ahhh* moment.

Preparation

In preparation for writing your own poem, read "The Gift" by Li-Young Lee. Note that the central metaphor in Lee's poem is a physical object, a splinter. An alternate poem might be Ruth Stone's "Air," in which the physical object is a blue shirt.

The Gift

To pull the metal splinter from my palm
my father recited a story in a low voice.
I watched his lovely face and not the blade.
Before the story ended, he's removed
the iron sliver I thought I'd die from.

I can't remember the tale,
but hear his voice still, a well
of dark water, a prayer.
And I recall his hands,
two measures of tenderness
he laid against my face,
the flames of discipline
he raised above my head.

Had you entered that afternoon
you would have thought you saw a man
planting something in a boy's palm,
a silver tear, a tiny flame.
Had you followed that boy

you would have arrived here,
where I bend over my wife's right hand.

Look how I shave her thumbnail down
so carefully she feels no pain.
Watch as I lift the splinter out.
I was seven when my father
took my hand like this,
and I did not hold that shard
between my fingers and think,
Metal that will bury me,
christen it Little Assassin,
One Going Deep for My Heart.
And I did not lift up my wound and cry,
Death visited here!
I did what a child does
when he's given something to keep.
I kissed my father.

~ *Li-Young Lee*

Procedure

I. Make a list of memorable moments that revolve around an object. Whether from past or present, choose an object that resonates with you, that carries emotional weight, either positive or negative, that you remember because it evokes a bookmark moment in your bank of memories. Your subject need not be dramatic to readers; in fact, it may be insignificant to all but you.

II. Now it's time to do some freewriting. Be *really free:* Allow your images to roam, to scatter, to take wild leaps. As you write, use as much sensory detail as possible—sight, sound, smell, taste, touch. The senses allow writers to take readers along on a shared journey. Anything goes! The goal is to put your critical self in a dark cellar and open the door to freedom and possibility.

Consider the associative movement of the following piece of freewriting, the memories that surfaced from writing about an object that was important to me as a child:

> My father took me to his office one Saturday when I was four or five. An accountant, he had a bit of work to do and shuffled many thin sheets of blue-lined paper across his oak desk. The narrow lines were covered with rows of

penciled numbers. It was the early fifties, and I remember watching the fours and nines, and the lovely number eights flow from the point of my father's pencil quickly across the page. It seemed this language was as mysterious as the musical notes inside the heavy rectangular cover of the book my aunt opened above the piano keys before she played. In fact my father was always humming under his breath, songs like "Blue Moon, keep on a-shining in June" while he wrote the rows of numbers.

Then suddenly I saw a new object on the corner of his desk. Next to a palm-shaped, sky blue bowl holding paper clips, a little iron dog sat on its haunches. Apparently, he had been watching my father too along with me, or so I thought as a four-year-old. "Go on, take it," my father said. "Just a trinket from a client." I didn't know the word client, but no matter. I carefully lifted the little body. It was cool in the palm of my hand. I closed my fist around the hips, legs, shoulders, snout, and even the hanging ears which were all tucked tightly to the cast iron body. He (I always thought of the little dog as a boy) became a best friend I could close in my palm. I can't tell you the car trips he took in the old, un-air-conditioned Corvair. He sat on the felt deck just above the back seat, buffeted by the wind like me and my brother, except we had hair that criss-crossed our faces and stung. A good part of the time the iron dog slept in my open hand, which I shaped into a cradle, or sat on the back deck, little round eyes studying the states of Louisiana, Alabama, Tennessee, all the two-laned roads up from New Orleans to Rock City then back down to Florida. My father wore what he called Hawaiian shirts on vacation, good-time shirts with maroon flowers and green leaves the size of hands. Unlike the father who wrote songs with numbers, he drank Jax beer from the cooler in the trunk, threw the empty cans along the side of the road. They would clink on the pavement behind us, and for a few seconds sounded as if they were trying to catch up. We stopped at strip motels with rooms shaped like narrow shoe boxes and doors that opened directly onto strangers loading or unloading suitcases in the parking lot. By then my father was drunk as a hoot owl. That was what my mother said before she ushered us to bed.

The writing itself—the *free* in freewriting—pursues an object that *may* be an image in a poem I eventually write. I have no way of knowing whether the iron dog will be included in the final poem. It may have served to move me into a subject about which I had no idea I needed (or wanted) to write. What I discovered is that I have something important to say, perhaps about my father, my relationship to him, or perhaps about my mother or myself.

Notice also that memories of the iron dog led to memories of car trips with the dog as a companion, that these led to images of my father's vacation shirts, then images of beer cans tossed along the roadside, and finally to what my mother said about my father at bedtime. There is material here for a poem, too, moving from grounded details—the cooler, the empty cans clinking, the shoe box motel rooms, my mother's hoot owl comment—to a revelation that is implied by the closing lines.

If I use this freewriting as a springboard to poetry, I do not know where the poem might take me or even whether the poem will be one of affirmation or regret, of joy or sorrow. But if I trust the details, the process, the movement toward understanding, the poem will not let me down.

III. Write a first draft of your poem. As with freewriting, let yourself move forward *without knowing* the next turn. Crumple up the road map and throw it away. Remember the cliché, "No surprise to the writer, no surprise to the reader." Writing is discovery, awakening. Through it we learn more about our relationship with self, with others, with things—our relationship with the greater world. Good, honest writing reveals the self to the self. Along the road to discovery, if you listen closely to your unconscious, you will learn your own best methods of accessing the symbols that define your experiences.

Tips

It is also important to develop habits that help you access the unconscious. One writer might retreat to a quiet room with a glass of wine, while another prefers music and still another finds that reading admired poems helps him or her enter the world of language and sound, of simile, metaphor, symbol. The most important act is simply listening. And as one listens, one writes. A poem may go through many revisions in the effort to find its way to the finish line—to a moment of epiphany that reveals a truth to both reader and writer.

An Example

Bed

Outside Concepción, Honduras, a man
walks the scorched edge of a deserted
road with a bed on his back.
He carries it like a second set of bones,
his own or those of someone he loved.
Barefoot, bent from planting maize
and beans, the man's back curves

to meet the rack of rods and springs.
Perhaps he found the bed, his first,
dumped by the side of the road,
or he is leaving or going to a woman,
or a child survived or died in this bed.
Perhaps he made a world once in this bed.
We cannot see desire or loss on the man's face,
know only that he seems determined
to bear the weight of it.

~ Christine Dumaine Leche

When I wrote the first line of this poem, I had no idea where the man—or the poem, for that matter—might go next. I quite literally was sitting in a bus riding through the Honduran mountains when I saw a man carrying a mattress spring on his back. He was deeply bent from the weight of his task. The poem is simply speculation about what the bed might mean to the man, why it mattered to "bear the weight of it."

Christine Dumaine Leche is author/editor of *Outside the Wire: American Soldiers' Voices from Afghanistan* (University of Virginia Press, 2013), a collection of writings by active duty soldiers to whom she taught classes in Afghanistan through the University of Maryland–Europe in 2008–09. Leche also taught soldiers in Bosnia (1997–2001) and Kosovo (2007). A recent finalist for the Rona Jaffee Award, she has won the Academy of American Poets Prize, the Deep South Writers Competition, and the Lena Todd Poetry Prize, among others. Her poems have appeared in numerous publications, including *The Massachusetts Review, Nimrod,* and *Rage: Female Genital Mutilation in African Society.* Leche holds a Ph.D. in Creative Writing and 20th century American literature from the University of Louisiana; she currently writes poetry and teaches at Austin Community College.

Sentimental Immunity: The Animal Poem

This exercise, which I often use in advanced workshops, works best when the writers have had enough experience to be able to sidestep cliché. It's directive enough to yield an element in common from everyone, but it's open enough to accommodate both the poet who can't step on a bug to the poet unmoved by the source of that morning's bacon.

Preparation

Read three or more masterful poems in which an animal appears, and if you're working with a group, have a conversation about each of them. These can help inoculate you against sentimentality while awakening greater awareness of your subject matter and jogging your own catalogue of animals. Animals have made memorable appearances in poetry, sometimes as the central figure, sometimes as part of the scenery. The animal may signify something other-worldly, bring a message from the dead, or remind readers of their animal nature. The animal may awaken—or numb—human compassion.

Whether you're working alone or with a class, the poems suggested below can help start the conversation your poem wants to have with existing poems:

- "We Had Seen a Pig" by Marvin Bell
- "The Moose" by Elizabeth Bishop
- "Self-Deliverance by Lion" by Lucie Brock-Broido
- "A narrow fellow in the grass" by Emily Dickinson
- "With Animals" by Mark Doty
- "Parsley" by Rita Dove
- "The Skunk" by Seamus Heaney
- "The Bear" by Galway Kinnell
- "The Intruder" by Carolyn Kizer
- "Encounter in August" by Maxine Kumin
- "The Wellfleet Whale" by Stanley Kunitz
- "Animals Are Passing from Our Lives" by Philip Levine

- "Commercial Leech Farming Today" by Thomas Lux
- "Canis" by Cleopatra Mathis
- "Canoeing with Alligators" by Naomi Shihab Nye
- "Milk the Mouse" by Michael Ryan
- "For I will consider my cat Jeoffry" from *Jubilate Agno* by Christopher Smart
- "Burying an Animal on the Way to New York" by Gerald Stern
- "Ode to Chicken" by Kevin Young

These poems model a multitude of approaches. Kizer, Kumin, Kunitz, Nye, and Stern examine moments where the wild and domestic collide. Bell, Levine, and Young contemplate the eating of animals; Levine employs an animal speaker. In Bishop, Dickinson, Heaney, and Mathis, the animal is the catalyst for change in the human observer; for Heaney and Mathis, this change marks a turning point in a relationship. Nye and Lux use wry humor—and the actual animal is absent. Brock-Broido, Smart, and Kinnell invoke extreme perceptions of animals to help us understand the human. Dove and Ryan's animals are peripheral presences that facilitate the exploration of human cruelty to other humans. Brock-Broido, Dove, and Lux's poems are linked to information you can search for in a library.

Once you start looking for poems with animals in them, you'll find that they are abundant. A terrific resource is the Poetry Foundation's online search tool, which has an Animals category under the subject heading Nature, with literally hundreds of animal poems.

Here's an excellent model in its entirety:

Canis

It was a small comment, wasn't it, about who they were
—that last year on the dunes when all the town talk
was of coyotes, prairie wolf in search of an ocean,

those footprints instead of rabbits surrounding the shack
or half-sunk in the cranberry bog
just off the path. They heard the howling somewhere

behind their backs as they walked out past midnight,
singing at the top of their lungs:
abandon me, oh careless love—although they knew

the coyotes knew exactly where they were. No surprise
to either of them when they wailed unusually close
and loud on a moonless night after an argument,

this time a mean one about the dogs. For God's sake,
the dogs, how much trouble they were to him,
their feeding and whining and constant

need to go out, no matter how wet or cold. And so on
till silence set itself between them, holding stiff
as each turned away to bed. But the coyotes just outside

started up their merciless lament, as if
the entire genus called them, had bound the tribe together
in protest for their brothers. Hours they heard the keening,

both of them sleepless, that rising, falling
complaint in their ears—until he couldn't bear it, he said
I'm sorry, I can't do this anymore, and she in a rush

of understanding the exact suffering fit of it, jumped up
and closed the offending one window's
half-inch crack, and just like that

in the dead center of a moan, the coyotes
stopped their noise; what I mean to say is
the wind stopped making that heartbroken sound.

~ *Cleopatra Mathis*

In this poem Mathis captures a pivotal moment at the end of a marriage, using
dog, wolf, and coyote imagery to dramatize the human struggle far more ef-
fectively than any summary or explanation could. Much of the poem's power
depends on its restraint in the use of adjectives—and their even harder-to-use
cousins the adverbs—which almost always put the sensory or factual meaning
first: "constant," "sleepless," "rising, falling," "close," "loud."

Only after a number of such descriptions does the poem take the liberty
of using "heartbroken," which by then the reader can embrace, having experi-
enced the canine presences—and human conflict—first through the senses.

Procedure

I. Look for an animal that speaks to you. Go beyond the obvious candidate, such as a pet, from whom it can be hard to get distance (though if it must be a pet, a long-dead one may be easier to invoke effectively).

- A class or an individual can go looking in the real world, taking a walk while on the alert for animals to which we don't normally pay much attention—pigeons, squirrels, cats in windows, service dogs, insects, images of animals in ads, even roadkill.

- You might think about the role of animals in everyday routines: the animals that provide foods in the supermarket, the centipede you'd rather not meet when you turn on a light at 2 a.m., or references to animals in the naming of sports teams or descriptions of human behaviors.

- Look to art, history, news, imagination. Visit a gallery or museum and look for an animal image that speaks to you.

- Think about animals your grandparents knew long before you were born; consider the symbolism of your Chinese zodiac animal; recall a creature-heavy picture book you read as a child or to a child; take a nonhuman perspective while reading or watching the news.

II. Free-associate. Write a first draft that's allowed to be as terrible as it needs to be. It may be fragmentary—words written all over a page with no sentences. Let your mind wander from one association to the next. I find that paper and pen are the best tools at this stage, but feel free to work electronically if that's better for you.

III. Refine the free association. For me, this means going through the embarrassing first draft and underlining or circling the bits that have potential. It can take a day or two away from the first draft to be able to see these. Adapt this step to your own favored process.

IV. Revise. Re-draft as often as needed to find the poem's form—and the animal it wants. You might find yourself switching animals or editing the animal out entirely. But for this prompt, press on until you get an animal poem, even if the animal makes only a cameo appearance.

Variations

- This exercise can be made more specific, requiring that the animal have a connection to the writer's ancestors, or that the poem employ idioms around an animal (a slang dictionary can be handy).

- Restrictions can be helpful. You might specify that the poem *not* be in the voice of the animal—or not be in the voice of a human observer. It may also be helpful to designate whether the poem can be a riddle.

- For a class, try asking that a particular animal appear in particular circumstances, and see what happens. When I asked a fiction and poetry class to include a lobster in a car, they produced lobsters real, inflatable, and metaphorical, some being driven home from a fish market, some riding as full-fledged passengers.

- After discussing the example poems, ask students to jot one or two animals they think worthy of exploration, then hand their list to the person to their left, so that everyone ends up working with someone else's animal.

Tips

- It's probably a good idea, at least at first, to avoid animals in purely pathetic situations—marked for euthanasia at the shelter or en route to becoming chicken nuggets—unless the poem can find an approach that has more ambiguity than villain versus victim.

- Excessive beauty or cuteness can turn against you as well; descriptive language can become your enemy. If portraying the animal starts to get out of hand, focus on nouns and verbs.

- Look for the middle ground, the gray areas, of your thoughts and emotions; start experimenting with those doubts rather than your convictions.

An Example

Friday Afternoon

I am greeted by a dead pig
sprawled on my kitchen table.

My father has finished
slicing its fatty underbelly so that
its body blankets the table.

Abuela has cut off its feet,
tucking them away in the freezer
to save for stew.

My mother has bathed its cold
pink skin in lime adobo
that lingers in my kitchen
like stale perfume.

I stop in the doorway
to let out a shriek
while the dead pig
my family pampers
stares at me

with its mouth open wide
as Kevin O'Brien's toothy grin
when he renamed me
Dora the Explorer.

My father removes the cigar from his mouth
to ask, "What? You've never seen a dead pig before?"

~ *Mariel Fernandez*

Adrienne Su has taught creative writing at Dickinson College in Pennsylvania since 2000. Recipient of an NEA fellowship, she is the author of three books, *Having None of It* (Manic D, 2009), *Sanctuary* (Manic D, 2006), and *Middle Kingdom* (Alice James Books, 1997). Her poems appear in anthologies such as *Asian American Poetry: The Next Generation, The New American Poets,* and *Best American Poetry 2013*.

One More Mask:
Exploring the Theater of Poetry

Mask-making is an exercise I conducted the first day of a weeklong poetry workshop at Jens Jensen's wooded retreat, The Clearing, at Ellison Bay, Wisconsin. Because it came up so early in the week, and so unexpectedly for the students, this exercise functioned as a kind of ropes course in creating a poem from a new speaking voice, ending in laughter and surprise. It also led us to think imaginatively and critically about who gets to speak in a poem—and the effect our choice of speaker has. (See also Veronica Golos' exercise "Becoming Another: The Persona Poem," page 100.)

Phase I: Preparatory Discussion

Start by reading a variety of mask poems:

- "The Girl Scouts Earn their Cosmetics Badge" by Robin Chapman
- "We Wear the Mask" by Paul Laurence Dunbar
- "The Poem as Mask" by Muriel Rukeyser
- "Aztec Mask" by Carl Sandburg
- "Mask" Maxine Scates

I. Discuss who is speaking and who is wearing a mask in each poem. Talk about the use of persona masks; archetypal, mythic, fictional, and contemporary icons as speakers; and first-, second-, and third-person narrators as variations of masks in poems. Talk about the issues that arise in the use of persona/mask poems and appropriation of voice.

II. Ask about and discuss Halloween masks worn as children.

III. View and discuss masks and their cultural function, for example:

- recognizable personae in ancient Greek Theater
- the stock characters of Commedia dell'Arte in the Italian Renaissance's improvised plays (only the lovers unmasked!)
- the Major Arcana of the Tarot deck
- the Jungian archetypes of roles and the transitional events of birth, death, separation, initiation, marriage, and displayed/hidden sides of the self

Note: You can find a variety of images by googling Masks on Google Images, including the masks of other cultures in ritual and dance—Igbo, Kwakiutl, Mexican, Balinese; Indonesian shadow puppets; Hopi Kachina dancers. . . .

Phase II: Mask-Making

Keeping in mind the preparatory discussions, the goal is to make a mask that can be held in the hand with the materials at hand.

Materials can include any or all of the following: stiff paper plates, gallon milk jugs cut in half and gessoed, traditional Halloween eye masks, very stiff poster board paper in a rainbow of colors, colored markers, acrylic paint, water and brushes, feathers, sequins, ribbons, yarn, wrapping paper, manila envelopes to use as backing, tongue depressors or popsicle sticks, non-toxic paper glue, stapler, see-through tape, utility knife and cutting board, scissors, needle and thread. Improvise from whatever you have on hand!

Mask-making can get messy, so cover tables with newspaper. Set up a cutting station with healing board; a painting station with brushes, water, apron, palette plate, and tubes of acrylic; put out several baskets of scissors and glue.

Have fun!

Phase III: Drafting a Poem

Late afternoon or evening assignment: Draft a poem that speaks in the voice of your mask. The next morning, have participants read their poems with masks in hand. Expect knockout performances!

Variations

- Instead of making a mask that can be held in the hand, have students make one that can be worn over the face, and have them read their poems with masks on.
- Prior to starting Phase II, include a brief visit to a Dollar Store (or its equivalent), where students may pick up cheap non-traditional materials for masks.

Examples

A mask can lead to serious reflection, as with Judy Roy's poem about Kilroy. The materials themselves, reminders of childhood play, can also evoke whimsy in the mask-making process—and in the poems they elicit—as with Janet Leahy's playful use of rhyme. Or the mask might move a writer beyond whimsy, as with Sandy Stark's dream-like visions.

Reaching for Immortality

Kilroy was here, they scrawled
on World War II tanks and ships,
on fighter planes and concrete walls
from Boston to Berlin, Omaha Beach to Iwo Jima,
wherever a GI might need to assert
I am still alive
I am still
I am

Kilroy was here, they drew,
a face to hide behind,
round eyes, long nose,
a suggestion of fingers.
A brotherhood of boys,
terrified, triumphant,
making their mark.

~ Judy Roy

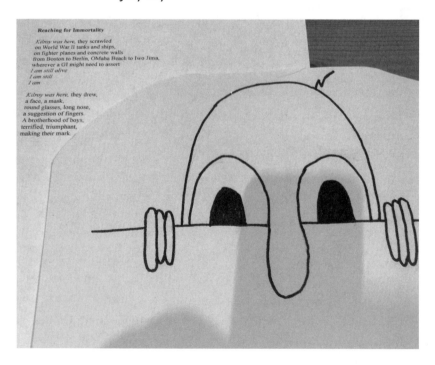

Seeds of Protest

I found reverie with the bee
and the prairie and Emily

That was long before living
in Innisfree
with Will and his hive
for the honey bee

Then Ferlinghetti came across
the sea
We drank the *Irish Mead* of liberty
smoked metaphor and simile

Feathers of protest he laced through my hair
I joined the protest with vigor, with flare

~ *Janet Leahy*

Note: Janet Leahy's poem (above) goes with her mask on the preceding page.
Sandy Stark's mask (below) goes with her poem on the facing page.

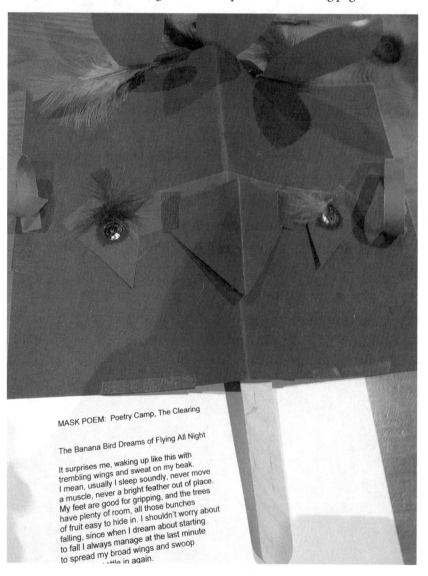

MASK POEM: Poetry Camp, The Clearing

The Banana Bird Dreams of Flying All Night

It surprises me, waking up like this with
trembling wings and sweat on my beak.
I mean, usually I sleep soundly, never move
a muscle, never a bright feather out of place.
My feet are good for gripping, and the trees
have plenty of room, all those bunches
of fruit easy to hide in. I shouldn't worry about
falling, since when I dream about starting
to fall I always manage at the last minute
to spread my broad wings and swoop
...ttle in again.

The Banana Bird Dreams of Flying

It surprises me, waking like this with
trembling wings. I mean, usually I sleep
so soundly, never a feather
out of place. But recently I've dreamt
of flying all night.

It starts with hovering low, then
suddenly spiraling toward an oddly
yellow sky. Even the bananas glow
as I pass them, then disappear as I try
to grab some in my sharp beak.

I have to find them again, all
those bright yellow bananas, and this goes
on and on until the Second Brightness,
the rising of the Banana Sun, when all
the other birds in the jungle wake and sing
a Chorus of Expectation for Bananas, oh woe
to the one who does not fetch and deliver them.

And what gods assigned this role to me?
I'd rather be a humble hummingbird, tasked only
with sipping nectar and singing short,
rhyming poetry.

~ *Sandy Stark*

Robin Chapman is the author of nine books, most recently *One Hundred White Pelicans* (Tebot Bach, 2013), a collection of poems about climate change; and *Dappled Things* (Paris: Revue K, 2013), a portfolio collaboration with photogravure artist Peter Miller pairing twenty-three of her poems with his gravures. Chapman has recent work in *Alaska Quarterly Review, The Cortland Review, Prairie Schooner, Nimrod,* and *Wilderness.* Recipient of a number of book awards and the Appalachia Poetry Prize for 2010, she teaches week-long poetry workshops at The Clearing, a Wisconsin folk school, and Bjorklunden, Lawrence University's retreat center, in Door County, Wisconsin. She lives in Madison, Wisconsin.

The Foodie Response:
Pushing through Writer's Block

I am often asked about writer's block, and people are surprised by my answer:

I don't believe in writer's block.

We all have times when we just can't get the words out or when we write a poem, the results dismay us so we crumple it into the trash can or delete the file. This is a natural part of the craft. Just like anything you tackle in life, poetry takes experience; it takes *practice*. But how can you turn writer's block into practice?

I work at poetry three to five hours every day. This doesn't mean that for three to five hours I am *creating* poetry; it means that for three to five hours a day, I am working at the *craft* of poetry. If I have nothing new in my head to work on, I pull out previous work and begin editing. I devote some time to reading other poets' work. Or I work on deadlines for sending poetry out or on upcoming poetry projects. The administrative side of poetry takes more time than we like, but for those who want to be published, it must be done.

Still, there are times when a poem is somehow stuck. Don't stump yourself thinking, *Oh no, writer's block.* Instead, think, *Okay, how do I get words out of my head and onto paper?*

My suggestion is to read. Pull out your favorite poetry book. Personally, I never travel without a few of my favorites, my constant companions, just for these times. The poems I love are marked, underscored, and dog-eared so that I may come back to them time after time after time. Marginalia usually surround the words. My books are used, worn, written up, and I find I can't exist without them.

When writer's block strikes, I recommend a dual strategy:

1. Think about poems you love and food you love.
2. Let the combination draw you into words.

Procedure

I. Food Poems

What is a food poem that you absolutely *love*? Start with that one. Let's look at one of my favorites.

French Toast

Pain perdu: lost bread. Thick slices sunk in milk,
fringed with crisp lace of browned egg and scattered sugar.
Like spongiest challah, dipped in foaming cream
and frothy egg, richness drenching every yeasted
crevice and bubble, that's how sodden with luck
I felt when we fell in love. Now, at forty,
I remember that "lost bread" means bread that's gone
stale, leftover heels and crusts, too dry for simple
jam and butter. Still, week-old bread makes the best
French toast, soaks up milk as greedily as I turn
toward you under goose down after ten years
of marriage, craving, still, that sweet white immersion.

~ *Anna Krugovoy Silver*

I come back to this poem time and time again. Why? I like how the author describes *pain perdu* in such delicious detail, then ties it to her deepest sensual desires. This poem reaches inside and stirs something primal; it connects my innermost thoughts and feelings by way of something so simple—stale bread. Yes, I am a foodie, but the poem gives me a direct emotional response.

Here are some other food poems that might help get you started:

- "Green Chile" by Jimmy Santiago Baca
- "Osso Bucco" by Billy Collins
- "A Display of Mackerel" by Mark Doty
- "Blackberry-Picking" by Seamus Heaney
- "The Gospel of Barbecue" by Honorée Jeffers
- "Applesauce" by Ted Kooser
- "American Milk" by Ruth Stone
- "This Is Just to Say" by William Carlos Williams

II. Food Poem as Springboard

What do you love about the poem you've chosen?

- Content, length, style, imagery, form?
- After you've read the poem, what does it make you think or feel?

- Does the poem make you feel as if you're tasting food? If so, how?
- Does the poem spur memories? If so, explore them.

Jot your answers and start there for your poem.

III. Food as Springboard

Think of a favorite food, a favorite dish, a favorite recipe.

- Why do you love it?
- What tastes are involved—salty, sweet, sour . . . ?
- What time of day do you eat it?
- Is it seasonal or made just for celebrations?
- What memories do you associate with it?

Think of times when you enjoyed this food.

- Who were you with? What were you doing?
- Did someone make it for you or did you make it for yourself?
- What are the other senses—the way it smells, feels, the crunch, the way it fills your stomach?
- For an immersion experience, prepare your food item. Make notes during the process. Make notes as you eat. Serve the dish to others. Ask questions. Make more notes.

An Example

Indian Summer

The summer my son graduated college,
he and his girlfriend packed up both houses,
rented a U-Haul, moved to Austin,

only to find themselves back home
when the landlord's homeowner's association
evicted them after just a few weeks.

They arrived, embarrassed, proud heads down,
moving boxes back to their room upstairs,
my husband grumbling about age and responsibility—

my husband, who had no childhood to mourn,
who began taking care of his mother at thirteen,
who never had a home to go back to.

But I felt it in my bones—that Indian Summer,
that deep September swelter blurring all lines
between blessings and curses—

felt a strange sensation that this was somehow a gift
for my men, out on the back porch, sharing whiskey,
though neither one knew it, neither one realizing

two childhoods of hurt were healing in those last hot days.
I made a feast of steak and squash and summer corn,
tossed soaked cobs on the grill.

I doubt they'll remember this time,
when they both believed their world was ending,
but in the short, dark winters to come,

they'll talk about the sublime crop that summer—
best corn of their life—the perfect mix of rain and heat,
how they've never tasted anything so sweet.

~ *Karla K. Morton*

Food is connected so personally to so many events in our lives. It's such an intricate part of our lives that it makes a good catalyst for a poem. Pull out your favorite food poems; study the greats. Fix yourself a snack.

Karla K. Morton, 2010 Texas Poet Laureate, is the author of nine collections of poetry, including *New and Selected Poems,* her contribution to the TCU Texas Poets Laureate Series. Described as "one of the most adventurous voices in American poetry," Morton is a Betsy Colquitt Award Winner, twice an Indie National Book Award Winner, the recipient of the Writer-in-Residency E2C Award in Seaside, Florida, a two-time Pushcart nominee, and a nominee for the National Cowgirl Hall of Fame. With fellow Texas Poet Laureate Alan Birkelbach, Morton established an ekphrastic collaborative touring exhibit titled *No End of Vision: Texas as Seen by Two Laureates,* pairing photography with poetry. Her work was recently featured—with seven other prominent authors—in *8 Voices: Contemporary Poetry of the American Southwest* (Baskerville, 2012).

Things:
A Brainstorming Game for All Ages

Years ago, after a poetry reading, a man from the audience, wishing to express appreciation, handed me the gift of a glass eye, dropping it into my hand with a belly laugh. You, too, can generate poems—and perhaps strange gifts—by playing the Things game. The goals of this exercise are to practice focus, to generate ideas for poems, and to trust the improvisational process.

Preparation

I. Prepare and cut out game pieces prepared on slips of paper. Each slip will contain a category of things such as those on the facing page. (For a start, you could photocopy the facing page and cut the items apart.)

You can devise an intricate list, depending upon the age of the group (Things from the Sixteenth Century, Things in a Detective Novel . . .). Supply other topics as desired. Variations acceptable? Of course!

II. Place your game pieces in a decorative tin or box; mix them up.

Procedure

I. Each writer chooses a slip at random, being sure to keep his or her selection private.

II. The game is most fun as an interactive guessing game. Someone begins, naming a list of items in the things category; the group has to guess aloud what is on the slip of paper. Using this method, the responses get very loud!

The *It* person recites a list—*green beans, Pennzoil, Wolf brand chili*—and keeps adding to the list until someone guesses the winning answer: Things That Come in Cans.

III. The person guessing correctly begins the next list, perhaps this one: *light poles, billboards, cows, fences.* Winning answer: Things You See from Car Windows.

A more difficult list: *baseballs, measles, a falling star* (Things to Catch). Or opposite choices: *rabies, the flu, a grenade* (Things Not to Catch).

IV. Players can make notes for later writing. Or just have everyone begin a poem that emerges from the most interesting results.

THINGS IN A KITCHEN DRAWER

THINGS IN THE REFRIGERATOR

THINGS THAT GO BUMP IN THE NIGHT

THINGS YOU CAN'T LIVE WITHOUT

THINGS NO ONE USES ANYMORE

THINGS IN A CANDY STORE

THINGS FROM THE _____ CENTURY

THINGS IN A DETECTIVE NOVEL

THINGS IN A CHEESY ROMANCE NOVEL

THINGS IN A HOLLYWOOD ACTION MOVIE

THINGS THAT MAKE YOU LATE

THINGS THAT COME IN CANS

THINGS THAT COME IN THREES

THINGS YOU CAN SEE FROM CAR WINDOWS

THINGS YOU DO NOT DESERVE   THINGS YOU DESERVE

THINGS IN THE GLOVE BOX   THINGS IN THE GARAGE

THINGS YOU FORGET   THINGS YOU REMEMBER

THINGS YOU DO FIRST   THINGS YOU DO LAST

THINGS WITH BUTTONS   INVISIBLE THINGS

THINGS A DOG WOULD SAY   SILENT THINGS

THINGS PEOPLE LIE ABOUT   THINGS YOU PRACTICE

THINGS INSIDE OTHER THINGS   THINGS YOU LOSE

THINGS YOU STAND IN LINE FOR   THINGS THAT BREAK

THINGS THAT DISAPPEAR   THINGS ON A MAP

THINGS TO CATCH   THINGS NOT TO CATCH

Variations

The process also works as an individual exercise. Select game pieces at random or, more simply, fill a legal pad with a list of things, using something different from the list each time; perhaps set a timer for fifteen minutes and write. The thing category often becomes your title. By the way, the game is great for long car trips. You can make up silly categories without any slips of paper at all; other passengers in the car guess the answer from things listed aloud.

An Example

Things You Don't Ask

Barroom piano plays "Smoke Gets in Your Eyes"

This party was like all the others
until the man made of eyeballs:
ordinary except for the pupils,
one large as my thumb, and round,
the other tightly slit,
a vertical cat's eye.

He walked into my stare
as into half a bright light,
me trying to say Hello
without What's wrong with your eye—
hoping he'd mention it,
you know, Fine weather
we're having, my eye was shot out
by Cupid, Stupid—

or The kids brought me a glass eye
for Christmas.

I keep it in the refrigerator
to surprise my mother-in-law;
or Nice to see you but your torso
is upside down due to my eye—you do
see a difference, don't you?

Actually, my eyes are considerably
better than average. Far-fetched?
No, mismatched. I expect you imagine me
in some pain, but the eye isn't damaged
at all: a mere variation, not a new phylum.

Hey, there's the girl I eyed earlier,
sharp outfit (tie-dyed!). Perhaps she's wondering
about my eye—and that woman staring, hoping
to look like she's not—BLUE! They're BLUE!

Have a drink, what's your sign,
who are you seeing these days?
Yeah, my mother used to tell me
they'd stick that way, too—
but you can't believe cock-eyed stories
like that, now can you?

(Piano flourish)

~ Sandra Soli

This performance poem began with the Things game and ended with the most unique gift I've ever received. Oh, the glass eye guy? He said the poem was the first he had ever heard that so clearly expressed how it feels to be stared at in public.

See page 11 for a biography of **Sandra Soli.**

Scars:
Getting Under the Skin

Recently my sister showed me the scars from her double mastectomy. She has two white half-moon scars on the top of her implants and two on the bottom bracketing the new breasts like smiles. Teaching a creative writing class at a local community mental health center, I have also been thinking about psychological scars—and the many ways in which the wounded recover and thrive. Both scars from physical accidents or surgeries and scars from psychological wounds can be starting places for a writing exercise that is transformative for both writer and reader.

Though this exercise can stir up painful memories, it can also be exhilarating. The physical scars on our own bodies or on the bodies of others can take us many places. They can jump-start ideas that help us heal and reflect. It is in the healing or recovery that we learn to understand if not appreciate our scars.

Preparation

Have students think about scars by reading and discussing the "Scars" section of John Unterecker's poem "Hospital" and "Lines" by Dan Beachy-Quick, provided here.

Scars

That little scar I'll never see on the left underside of my heart
or the almost-closed arteries opening and closing like baby mouths
or the good artery, a tiny flow talking about tomorrow. . . .

Strange in the garden, watching two boys wrestle in long grass,
their wheelchair friend in zebra-striped pajamas watching the wrestling,
all three in the hungry shade of a magnolia.
Binoculars:
The boy in striped pajamas' dense shouts: shouting, shouting:
"Quit it, you cocksuckers! They won't even let you *walk* on the grass.
        Quit!"
They are hidden by the magnolia. I cannot hear them.
The long magnolia branches wrestle like boys' white arms and legs.

That scar in the groin: hernia. Punched hole in the groin: heart catheter.
The new scar throat to belly.

Now they have helped the zebra boy back into the wheelchair
and, pushing him up the hospital ramp, take turns bumping shoulders.
"Quit it, you pricks! Do you want me thrown out of the place?"

I listen to my casual heart beating veins into arteries; then I approach
the zebra and his friends.

In Africa, wildebeest, impala, warthog gather at the waterhole, nudging
shoulders.
The gaunt flat-topped trees cast lion shadows,
vultures circling. Where are the sabre tooth tiger, the mastodon?

I think of America cemented coast to coast, white jet-trail scars for sky,
a loveliness of footprints jumbled on spring grass.

~ *John Unterecker*

This poem is a narrative anchored in the particulars of a specific place and
time. A man who has had heart surgery observes three adolescent boys in the
garden of a hospital. The poem begins with a scar the narrator can't see, a sur-
gical scar on his heart. Without this opening, what follows might seem light
or even trivial—two boys wrestling while their friend admonishes them to
behave. But the narrator's awareness of his scarred heart—his own mortal-
ity—casts a shadow here. And as the boys roughhouse, the narrator returns to
the subject of scars:

That scar in the groin: hernia. Punched hole in the groin: heart catheter.
The new scar throat to belly.

Following this blunt reminder, the narrative returns to the boys, but one of
them is in a wheelchair.

What might his injury—his scars—be? Finally, the narrator makes the
kind of leap that only poetry allows—from a boy in zebra-striped pajamas and
his shoulder-bumping friends to African animals gathered at a waterhole and
a reminder of the mortality of all creatures: "vultures circling. Where are the
sabre tooth tiger, the mastadon?" And then another leap, to an image of the
narrator's country with "white jet-trail scars for sky" and a reminder of fleet-

ing youth that also brings us, full-circle, back to the poem's opening scene—
"a loveliness of footprints jumbled on spring grass."

Lines

The lightning struck him and left a scar.
The wind stopped blowing and the wheat stood up.
Self-tensed self, who is this I that says I?
I had a scar in the shape of lightning
That split in half when I opened my mouth.
The sun just a circle of heat in the sky
Throwing absence in the shape of clouds
Down on the field. Another life placed
In the middle of the life I called my own.
A lesser god commanded the front: return.
A little god knocked about in the germ.
The third person put me outside my own sphere.
A small god chanting lightning in the synapse.
Wind blows the wheat down. He calls it prayer.

~ Dan Beachy-Quick

This poem develops as a series of associative leaps. It opens with lightning and
the scar it leaves, perhaps in a wheat field, during a thunderstorm, with wind.
The first leap comes in the third line, with a question about identity. Poems al-
low—they encourage—these kinds of leaps. Lines 4 and 5 return to scars and
lightning. Lines 6–8 return to a field, perhaps the wheat field where the light-
ning struck as the poem opened. Lines 8–12 really jar us out of narrative con-
tinuity, as if shocked out of narrative by lightning, which is where the poem
returns—but to the brain's lightning, electrical impulses "in the synapse." And
then back to the wheat field. And prayer.

Procedure

I. I often start by telling about one of my own scars and have each student, if
willing, tell us the story behind one of her or his own scars. This step can even
come before reading and discussion of the poems by Unterecker and Beachy-
Quick.

II. Students freewrite about one or more of their own scars or the scars their
peers have spoken of. The scar is a jump-start. Students may use the scar to

tell a story as Unterecker does. Or they may use the scar as a springboard into metaphor and associative leaps, as in Beachy-Quick's poem.

III. Students share their work in small groups or with the entire class.

IV. Students shape their work into poems, using Unterecker and Beachy-Quick as models.

Variations

Possible variations include having students write about particular wounds and subsequent healing. They might write about an injury of some kind and the healing or recovery that comes afterward. The chosen injury need not be physical; students might write about a psychological or heart wound. Students might write about loss and recovery; they might follow a movement from sorrow and lamentation to joy and praise. (For another approach to poems that focus on scars, see Victoria Redel's "Memory, Periphery, & Then Some," page 307.)

An Example

Sun Healing

All the traumas fold in on themselves,
Opening later to new seasons. Thin white
Scar on my forehead. My
Spiritual third eye sees. Early infant falling.
Tumor removed. Grandfather's
Bargain with God. Him taken that month, me
Living on. My thighs pump
A pink bicycle up a slight grade.
Gearless, unnerved by gravity, my
Selves then and now know blasphemy for the universe.
Scar, a white beam of light. Cleansed in river water,
I am in no prison. I speak clearly of
Blood, revenge and forgiveness, how it takes
Miracle medicine to heal our wounds, fade our scars.
Before I began to sing, I was crazy with the past,
With the drowning of Egyptian horses. Today I
Blow softly into silver flutes. This is the true story.
I would steal wild mustangs, rampage

Borders with dances, gallop, leave a red cloud of dust.
I am learning a dangerous astrology of unity. We are each
Baptized in starlight and magic. Our names
Light up what's dark.
My new name is mixed blood and mine.
Scars renamed. I walk down to the local courthouse,
Erase what was put upon me without my consent.
I have grandmother's Pueblo eyes. We are illuminated,
Cyclic. Rivers of clear blue mountain water run over scars.
We are all waiting for a persistent sun chasing a
Wounded moon. We know it is coming to light us all.

~ *Sheryl Luna*

Sheryl Luna received the Andrés Montoya Poetry Prize for her first collection, *Pity the Drowned Horses* (University of Notre Dame Press, 2005). This volume was a finalist for the National Poetry Series and the Colorado Book Award. Luna's second collection is *Seven* (3: A Taos Press, 2013). She has received the Alfredo del Moral Foundation Award from Sandra Cisneros, as well as fellowships from Yaddo, the Anderson Center, Ragdale, and CantoMundo.

A Little Bit of Soul: Narrative Medicine

Ever get tired of a pair of shoes you once adored? Maybe you put them in the closet when they seemed worn out. A few years later stressed leather is all in vogue, and they are definitely that. You pull them out, give them a good cleaning and pair them with something else trendy or eclectic, and they have a new place in the world, greeted with welcome by your admirers at work, saving you some cash you could use elsewhere. Language—and our perception of it—has multiple lives as well.

In this exercise, you will revive language that has been labeled as broken, worn out, cliché. Or you will find poetry in criticism that wounds.

Procedure

I. Create a list of three ideas, notes, or issues that you find bothersome or insulting. Mull over the list for the sake of source material.

As poets, when what we do has been criticized, misunderstood, misread, or oversimplified, we can easily become offended. Yet there is ripe material for poetry in statements unfair to the genre or to our work within it.

For example, writing recently in the *New York Times Book Review* Paul Rudnick supposes, "Like a bore at a cocktail party, most poems discuss only the weather, their feelings and that little gray bird they saw on their way to work." This statement led to a discourse in social media among poets who, like me, began an instant round of parody in response.

II. Write to give the list new life, new purpose. Anchor this act of reincarnation in the specifics of place, time, and sequence.

Maybe it is criticism in general that is the worn-out wounding. The next time you hear critical language you feel is baseless, that arises out of misunderstanding, sort through the criticism for items that you question. Write to find the poetry in them, allowing the language to invoke a counter truth.

After reading Rudnick's review, for example, I could think of few poems I had read lately that dealt with the three items he singled out—weather, the poet's feelings, an observed natural detail ("that little gray bird"). A little bit of soul invoked the next morning in the application of this exercise brought about the short poem that follows:

Morning Review

for Rudnick

The Mississippi kite holds the branch
towering over water, 'neath pillars of loose clouds

making me a bit dreamy and less concerned
with the *New York Times* and Americana's loss
of love for letters and poetry.   Is it real, they say?

Only if experimental!   The experiment here in witness,
repose, wondering if in some curtailed twist of ether
you or I could become the kite, the cloud, the water.

If so, would a column mean much
        to the horses I forgot to mention?

~ Allison Adelle Hedge Coke

An Example

Someone I deeply admired suddenly criticized me sharply for an instance he did not witness but heard through me and then another version based in rumor. The criticism included three assumptions: 1) that the speaker's approach was superior to mine, 2) that I had been disobedient, and 3) that the rumor itself was valid. Rather than argue, allowing a personal issue to fester, I turned instead to this exercise, letting the wound inspire a poem. As I share a canoeing background with the individual who criticized me, a canoe seemed the vessel to carry the misunderstanding to a higher place. This is the result:

Eddy Lines

for JS

In transgressions
migrating song to stone,
au courant   your flint sparks
question each turn
waving over azimuth.

Brother, allow me to backpaddle, offer
bearing,   boil,   berry break—brace—
least we broach C-2.

In the chine,
a quail covey
awaits release,
as Passenger Pigeon
and Carolina Parakeet
long over yaw
from foreigner squall—

Sternpaddler, you
call for reason
when sometimes
water just is and
the path we bear upon it
simply running
rock garden,   reading water,
quartering or purchasing
avoiding pitch, pivot, portage
for the freedom here.

Beyond the lob tree
a mouth opens.
We both go there
one after another.
First you, me.
Then me, you.
Our dugouts surely
best what lapstrake we make
sur le voyage.

Smoker ahead,
this yoke may come in handy
despite shuttle duty.

One day
Kevlar may be essential
to offset keening.

For now, it's the cut of it,
the lean and what boldens
each of us, singularly,
in the gradient.

I'll feather, you ferry,
until eddy lines
we cross apart
and yet together
through this art,
dead reckoning.

Perhaps, one day,
mapping courses
for one another, lest
we forgive odds,
make mutual course,
loose branches so
some might follow
more easily.

~ Allison Adelle Hedge Coke

Notice that the poem breaks free of the original misunderstanding, that a reader need not know who said what about whom, that an insult can turn into a poem that does not return the insult.

Allison Adelle Hedge Coke serves as field faculty for the University of Nebraska M.F.A. Program and Naropa University; she is a Visiting Writer for the University of Central Oklahoma and the University of California, Riverside. In the fall of 2014, she will take a Distinguished Writer position at the University of Hawaii. Hedge Coke is a literary activist working with disaster relief, incarcerated youth, elders, and various alternative populations in need. She founded and directs the annual Literary Sandhill Crane Retreat & Festival at the migration epicenter. Her books include *Dog Road Woman* (American Book Award for Poetry); *Off-Season City Pipe; Rock, Ghost, Willow, Deer; Blood Run;* and *The Year of the Rat. Burn* (Mad Hat) and *Streaming* (Coffee House) are both forthcoming in 2014. Recently edited anthologies include, *Effigies* (Salt/Earthworks, 2009) and *Sing: Poetry from the Indigenous Americas* (Sun Tracks, 2011). *Effigies II* (Salt/Earthworks, 2014) will be her ninth edited volume.

When Good Advice Turns Bad

This exercise provides practice in negative thinking, something we poets need to be good at. We don't want to say what's been said before. We don't want to impart ideas that everyone already embraces. We need to look at things from different angles, to embrace the controversial and the weird, to shake it up a bit. We want to fan the fires. We want to make some trouble.

Throughout our lives, we are given pieces of advice. Do this. Do that. Don't do this. Don't do that. Here is your opportunity to go against behavior you've been advised or even compelled to conform to.

There's a tradition in poetry for this approach. The speaker in John Donne's "A Valediction: Forbidding Mourning" counsels his beloved not to miss him while he's away from her. Charles Baudelaire in "Be Drunk" argues not in favor of sobriety but against it. In "Do Not Go Gentle into That Good Night," Dylan Thomas advises his father not to accept death but rather to fight against the inevitable. This strategy of taking a contrary position can be liberating, exciting, and surprising—for both the poet and the reader.

Here's a poem I wrote in response to the advice that we should see the doctor regularly—the last thing I want to do. My poem argues just the opposite of the accepted wisdom.

You Should Avoid Doctors

Because they find something you don't
want. That's their job, finding trouble. They impose
music you'd never choose, a paper gown, a cold room,
then force you to disrobe and uncover
information you've hidden for years—
you're overweight, or under, need more exercise,
less caffeine, and everything you love
is dangerous. You've never been this exposed.

You cough and breathe, cough and breathe.
They listen to your heart, a cold disk placed
on chest and back, alarm on their faces, suspicious
of this and that, as if your heart were a criminal,
which often it is.

They misread the flutters, leaps,
and flips as disease—myocardial infarction,
atrial fibrillation, endocarditis—when you know deep
in your heart that it's fear you feel and you awake each day
not with joy but despair, heartachy, heartsick, heartbroken,
like some cheesy country western song.

So what
can a doctor do? Cut it, stitch it,
repair it? Reach in with his fist and rip out
the organ? It's already gone. And the pain
you feel is the phantom kind as when
a leg's blown off after stepping
on a landmine, and even years later the fugitive
limb still throbs to the beat.

~ *Diane Lockward*

Procedure

I. Choose a piece of good advice to refute. You might choose one of the following:

- Chew with your mouth closed.
- Don't make waves.
- Play by the rules.
- Eat your vegetables.
- Be polite.
- Keep your elbows off the table.
- Don't stare at people.
- Exercise!
- Respect your elders.
- Wear sunscreen.

II. Before you begin writing, zero in on an auditor. To whom are you speaking? You will increase the likelihood of achieving a strong voice if you imagine an auditor and speak directly to that person or persons. This point is valid even if you do not explicitly identify the auditor for your reader.

III. Once you have an auditor in mind, begin drafting your poem. Take a firm stand against the good advice and argue vigorously for your position. Be sure to work some metaphors into your poem.

Variations

I. Take any poem, your own or someone else's, and to the right of each line, write its opposite.

2. Take a lifeless draft of your own. Open up some space after each line in the draft. Then go into each open space and write a negative statement that leaps off the preceding line. Take this line:

>It was an ordinary day, much like any other.

The added line might be:

>The sun did not come out. Songbirds did not sing.

You won't keep all the added lines, perhaps only a few, but those few just might save the poem, giving it new life and perhaps a new direction.

3. Take a piece of poetry advice given to you by a poet or teacher of poetry. Then write a poem in which you disobey the advice typically given to poets:

- Avoid abstractions.
- Don't use clichés.
- Adverbs are not your friends.
- Show, don't tell.

Examples

Y'all Come Back Now, You Hear

>*If a line sounds like it would fit in a country and western song, take it out of your poem.*
>
>~ advice from a well-known poet

Darlin', I was the heartland and you were a train
that somehow moved from coast to coast
without ever once passing through me.
I never cried, though the jukebox said I should.
Beer and whiskey? You bet,
but enough was enough,

though even my old dog mourns
the sound of one less set of boot heels.
Sometimes now we howl together,
two-part harmony instead of three.
Old Blue likes prison songs.
I sing about working my hands to the bone.
On Sundays, we try Gospel,
but I'm too old, rugged and cross to keep up that charade.
Outside there's still a pickup with your name on it.
I sit in it, eyes red in the mirror,
knuckles white on the wheel, Old Blue in the back.
When I see those chrome beauties on the mudflaps,
I think of you, the way you used to shine,
the way you made the rain wish it could be you.
The dog. The truck. The rain.
I know you won't be coming back,
except when I sing the way I always sing
in this circle you left broken by and by.

~ R. G. Evans

Notice that Evans picks up on the cheesy country-western song line and then takes his poem in its own direction. He breaks an old piece of poetry advice: Don't be a cornball. Instead, he lets the corn flow freely. Notice that Evans limits his auditor to a single person, the woman who broke the speaker's heart. Notice also the strategic use of an apt epigraph.

You Should Avoid Young Children

Because they fill their diapers
with reliable ease, sitting on your lap
or spread out on your best mattress.
Guilt is as foreign to them as vichyssoise.

Because they spread sticky fingers
over the piano keys, looking for you
to hoist them onto your lap. They slam
the ivories for the racket they can make.
Re-think your nap.

Because they are blank slates
on which so much waits to be written,
their eyes opened wide to take everything in,
including the lines around your eyes,
the pouches under your chin.

Because they manipulate the controls
on the TV, finger the holes in the electric socket,
stomp the cat's switching tail only to smile
and gaze at you as if you held the keys to joy.

Because you can embrace them but
you can't bind them. Because they have nothing
to give you—and everything. Because
something loosens when they come around.
Something opens you didn't know was shut.

~ *Claire Keyes*

We all know that we're supposed to love children and their company. But Claire Keyes argues that we should avoid children. Her poem presents a catalog of reasons why. I love the irony that emerges at the end of the poem as it becomes clear that the speaker really adores children. I hope that the poet surprised herself with that ending. Notice, too, that Keyes, like Evans, takes some words from my poem and works them into her own poem. She borrows my title—a perfectly legal move—and spins it into her own title. She then grabs my beginning "Because" but goes a step beyond and uses repetition of that word to structure her poem.

Diane Lockward is the author of three poetry books, most recently *Temptation by Water* (Wind Publications, 2010). Her previous books are *What Feeds Us*, which received the 2006 Quentin R. Howard Poetry Prize, and *Eve's Red Dress*. Lockward is also the author of *The Crafty Poet: A Portable Workshop* (Wind Publications, 2013). Her poems have been published in a number of anthologies, including *Poetry Daily: 366 Poems from the World's Most Popular Poetry Website* and Garrison Keillor's *Good Poems for Hard Times*. Her poems have also appeared in journals such as *Harvard Review, Spoon River Poetry Review,* and *Prairie Schooner,* and have been featured on *Poetry Daily, Verse Daily,* and *The Writer's Almanac.*

The World Without Us:
An Exercise in Apocalypse

In 2007, Alan Weisman published *The World Without Us,* an exploration of what might happen to the planet if human beings suddenly disappeared. Weisman interviewed various experts to uncover the science behind how cities and human infrastructure, along with the natural world, would respond to our absence. What, for example, would happen to New York City's subway system? Would cockroaches really survive? Weisman set out to find the likely answers to these unusual questions.

The World Without Us describes the science of a post-human world, but it doesn't get at the poetry of such a world. This exercise asks writers to think large, imagining what the world would be like if humanity suddenly disappeared from the face of the earth.

Procedure

I. Using the format of a list, write a poem that imagines the world without us. What would happen to the world you know? Describe this world using vivid literal and figurative images. What would it look like? Sound like? Smell like? Free association is encouraged. (For more on list poems, see Alfred Nicol's exercise "List Poems & Syllabics: Discovery through Form," page 155.)

II. Experiment with point-of-view. Make the poem personal to your own life or omniscient and objective. The assignment is best left open to the writer's definition. Some writers will make this poem personal and sorrowful, others will be absurd and irreverent, still others rational and tempered.

III. Length: 20 lines. Each line is one complete sentence. Use at least one literal or figurative image in each line. I add a formal constraint of this kind to channel the energy released by such a daunting imaginative task.

Variations

The poet can experiment by writing two drafts: one version where each line is a complete sentence and a second version mixing end-stopped and enjambed lines. **End-stopped lines**, like those in the first draft, come to a stop at the end of a phrase or clause; **enjambed lines** break mid-phrase or mid-clause so that the flow of thought moves from one line to the next without pause.

Note: I teach this exercise early in the term: it gives students permission to take an imaginative leap while working with some fundamental tools of poetry: image and line. (See also Alan Birkelbach's exercise "The World is Ending in Ten Minutes!"—page 3.)

An Example

After Some Time Has Passed, But Not Too Much Time

The cranes in Whitewater Draw would still fly out to gather corn from
   the fields, coming back to the water at night, only the fields
   wouldn't be kept by anyone.

And the man who brought the horses to the wash in the morning, riding
   one, holding the reins of the other, would be like a ghost limb
   to them.

His weight would lead them back for a week or two until they could
   shake it off.

Even the thought of the memory of her would be gone, hood of her
   sweatshirt up, hair blowing out in the evening as you walked
   home.

Warm night of wanting, of not touching her, which is a kind of story—

The stories would become like the image of Apollo in the drawing the
   artist made with ink on vellum.

In the drawing, the struggle between the god and the python is obscured
   by a thousand feathers scattering.

Would the images of her scatter like that?

Light falling across her by the pools of water you'd walked to in the
   Catalinas, yellow leaves on the cottonwoods, blue dragonfly
   landing on her knee.

We could stay here, you said, half-joking, though already you'd gotten up
   to leave.

Smell of lavender, tattoo of a red and green dragon on her back—

And the man you both met at the side of the road near Douglas, black
   clothes, black backpack, who'd been walking through the desert
   for two days since he crossed.

He would have arrived, gotten used to a life of mundane difficulties,
   forgotten how he had to hide in the grass behind the fence.

It's like make believe, you tell your friend, explaining how you'd gone
   back that night.

You'd left water, cans of Vienna sausages, cereal bars, lit a candle for him
   in the mud of the road between the farms.

No, your friend says, *it's like a carefully placed wish.*

And he gets up, goes out into his living room, looking through books to
   find the clues he'd known when he was in the hospital.

I could see it, he says, *I could see how the world was going to change:*

Is it like a door now, you want to ask, *with the smallest amount of light
   coming through the bottom?*

*Is it like your mother, years after she forgot her own name, then remem-
   bered it, when absence slips across her face?*

~ Margaree Little

Keith Ekiss is a Jones Lecturer in Creative Writing at Stanford University and a former Wallace Stegner Fellow. He is the author of *Pima Road Notebook* (New Issues Poetry & Prose, 2010) and translator of *The Fire's Journey* by Costa Rican poet Eunice Odio, a four-volume project, of which the first volume has been released (Tavern Books, 2013). Ekiss is the past recipient of fellowships and residencies from the Bread Loaf Writers' Conference, the Squaw Valley Writers' Conference, the Santa Fe Art Institute, and the Petrified Forest National Park.

Chapter II:
Elements of Poetry

Poetry is the language at its essence. It's the bones
and the skeleton of the language. It teaches you, if
nothing else, how to choose your words.

~ Rita Dove

Repetition & Cadence, or Repetition *for* Cadence

This is a simple exercise, but it works wonders when you feel stuck or when your writing feels stiff, without fluidity or cadence.

Procedure

I. Write a line. It may remain the first line of your poem—but not necessarily.

II. From that line, choose a word—noun, verb, adjective, adverb, or preposition (no articles, no words so short/insignificant as to seem invisible)—that you will repeat in the second line.

III. From the second line, choose *another* word to repeat in the third line.

IV. From the third line, choose another word to repeat in the fourth line— and so forth, a line at a time.

V. Continue doing this choose-and-repeat process for as long as you can keep going.

Variations

Patterns of Repetition: You can choose to repeat two words every other line or weave in another repetition every three lines. You can choose to repeat only nouns, or only verbs. What is important is to keep the repetition going and not write one line without repeating some word from a previous line.

Selective Repetition: You can also choose to start this repetition pattern in the middle of a poem. All sorts of variations are possible.

Revising Your Repetitions: During the revision process, you can eliminate some of these repetitions, but this exercise will free your syntax and fluency, as well as help you propel the poem.

An Example

I used this exercise in the poem that follows. Note that in this early version there were repetitions in each line—boldfaced here so you can easily see them—initially within couplets (e.g., *noon/noon*), and starting with the fifth stanza, between couplets (e.g., *him/him*).

Parentheses An Early Draft

Indiana. A man sits on a motel bed. It's **noon.**
Winds blow in the elm outside his room—**noon**

in the branches, twigs and **leaves,**
in the elm-green shadows of the **leaves.**

On the **walls** of his room, shadows breathe,
wave on his **walls** with the wind.

He sees **waving** arms in those curves,
arms **waving** at **him**—reaching

for **him**? And parentheses too—that open and close
around nothing. A shudder **runs** through him,

runs through his shoulders and lungs,
through his eyes and **thoughts,**

thoughts that make him want to get up
from his bed in the **Indiana** motel,

Indiana, where he's in parentheses
between Chicago and Bloomington

between his last love and the next. . . .

In later versions, for cadence and mostly to accrue tension toward closure, I eliminated some repetitions (some felt a tad forced). I also chose to repeat some words more than twice: the word *between,* for example. I also wove some previously repeated words into the closure. Again, vary this repetition pattern in any way that works for you and the poem!

Parentheses

Indiana. Noon. A man sits on a motel bed.
Wind blows in the tree outside his window
    in the branches, twigs and leaves,
      in the elm-green shadows of the leaves.

On the walls and ceiling of the man's room,
the tree's shadows breathe, wave with the wind.
    He sees arms in those curves,
      waving at him, reaching for something,

and parentheses too—that open and close around
nothing. A shudder runs through him,
    through his shoulders and lungs,
    through his eyes and thoughts,

a shudder that makes him want to get up
from his bed in the Indiana motel (where
    he's in parentheses between
    Chicago and Bloomington,

between his last love and the next,
between selling fence-wire to the last hard-
    ware store and the next, between
    motels, between hopes). Want to get up

from his bed in the Indiana motel and
leave. Or close the curtains at least,
    those parentheses around a window
    he doesn't think of looking through—

and won't. Behind which there's Indiana,
and noon, and an elm, with wind
    blowing through every branch,
    every twig, every single waving leaf.

~ Laure-Anne Bosselaar

Laure-Anne Bosselaar is the author of *The Hour Between Dog and Wolf* (BOA Editions, 1997); *Small Gods of Grief* (BOA Editions, 2001), winner of the Isabella Gardner Prize for Poetry; and *A New Hunger* (Ausuble Press, 2007), selected as a Notable Book by the American Library Association. Bosselaar is the editor of four anthologies. She and her husband, poet Kurt Brown, completed *The Plural of Happiness* (Oberlin College Press, 2006), translations of Flemish poet Herman de Coninck. A Pushcart Prize recipient, Bosselaar teaches at the University of California–Santa Barbara; she is a member of the founding faculty at the Low Residency M.F.A. in Creative Writing Program of Pine Manor College.

Soundscape Poems

This is less a discreet exercise than a set of practices that can be used separately or together and can be integrated into writing practice as a whole. All of these activities are designed to increase awareness of sound and cadence in our poems.

Procedure

The First Strand: Chant

Your chant is the Kundalini mantra—also known as Morning Call—"Ek Ong Kar Sat Nam Siri Wahe Guru."

There are different ways to chant this mantra and the more we practice it, the more we make it our own. For some very precise suggestions on how best to chant this mantra, consult the website of 3HO (Healthy, Happy, Holy Organization).

However you develop your particular chant of this mantra, keep your attention on how and where the vowel sounds of each word resonate in your body.

The Second Strand: Compose by Voice

I. Take yourself on a walk. You might choose paths and environments that help you enter the general mood you want to explore in your piece.

II. Once you're comfortable and your mind has settled some, begin to compose aloud as you continue walking. Remember, no one is expecting polished lines of verse to flow from your mouth. Though you're away from the page or computer, you're just drafting at this stage.

III. As you walk and talk your poem, push yourself to carry as much of the draft in your head—and body—as possible before taking out a pocket notebook to record your draft. At first, you may find you have to write down every two lines; then, after some practice, you may find you can keep entire stanzas (and more) in your head.

A variation on this strand is to remain at your writing desk or other comfortable spot in your home or studio. Once settled, begin composing your poem verbally, line by line, until you can't hold it all in your head anymore and must record in your notebook.

Note: Whether sitting or walking, remember that the notebook is not where the composition happens; it's where the composition is recorded. After you write down each new chunk of your draft, go back to composing by voice.

The Third Strand: Read

I place this strand of the practice before revision because I find it useful to take long breaks between initial composition and revision. As stated above, though, these are less steps to be completed in sequence and more strands to be continually woven into our complete writing practice.

When I teach this strand of the practice, I like to show students Ezra Pound's "The River-Merchant's Wife: A Letter." This translation of a poem by Li Po (known in Japan as Rihaku) works well precisely because it is so familiar to many students. Being asked to consider the sound elements in this poem can be all the more startling against this backdrop of familiarity.

The River-Merchant's Wife: A Letter

While my hair was still cut straight across my forehead
I played about the front gate, pulling flowers.
You came by on bamboo stilts, playing horse,
You walked about my seat, playing with blue plums.
And we went on living in the village of Chōkan:
Two small people, without dislike or suspicion.

At fourteen I married My Lord you.
I never laughed, being bashful.
Lowering my head, I looked at the wall.
Called to, a thousand times, I never looked back.

At fifteen I stopped scowling,
I desired my dust to be mingled with yours
Forever and forever and forever.
Why should I climb the look out?

At sixteen you departed,
You went into far Ku-tō-yen, by the river of swirling eddies,
And you have been gone five months.
The monkeys make sorrowful noise overhead.
You dragged your feet when you went out.

By the gate now, the moss is grown, the different mosses,
Too deep to clear them away!
The leaves fall early this autumn, in wind.
The paired butterflies are already yellow with August
Over the grass in the West garden;
They hurt me. I grow older.
If you are coming down through the narrows of the river Kiang,
Please let me know beforehand,
And I will come out to meet you
As far as Chō-fū-Sa.

By Rihaku

~ Ezra Pound

I. We read the poem aloud several times to get everyone on board with the poem's basic situation, its imagery, its mood.

II. Then we read again and I ask students to circle the prominent vowel sounds. Soon they start to notice the frequency with which short *a* and long *o* sounds appear in the last two full stanzas. Many folks who work in the intersection of poetry and healing arts hold that vowel sounds align to certain emotions, with long *i* and long *e* sounds evoking the lighter emotions and short *a* and long *o* sounds conjuring more melancholy moods.

Notice how Pound, with his prerogative as translator, could have chosen to translate the place name of *Cho-fu-sa* in one of several ways and how instead he chose to leave as the poem's final emotional and semantic gesture that string of mournful sounds.

The Fourth Strand: Revise

Too many discreet qualities go into making your best poems to keep track of all of them at every stage of composition and revision. That being the case, revise a piece you draft by voice as you would any other of your poems. If you continue to practice the mantra and if you continue to read poems with a special focus on the ways sound and emotion reinforce one another, you will eventually be able to privilege sound as one of the many qualities you reconsider in each stage of revision.

One week you might revise the poem with special attention to line breaks and another week you might focus instead on the poem's sounds. When you're ready, for example, you might—like Ezra Pound—choose certain words over others in key places in your poem for the vowel sounds those words offer. You might also assess your draft as a whole and ask if the emotional arc of the poem, the shift in feelings you hope readers experience as they move from line to line in your poem, is reinforced with a sonic arc, a corresponding progression of vowel and consonant sounds.

An Example

Of Mule and Deer

Out of a tin-cold, murmuring black wood
Lightly you lope, pale deer, lifting
A story from pages of snow

Nothing turns in your eye they say

Toward the tin-cold and murmuring black wood
I bear a display case of blue light
Say it was the sky

Say all you want   it was the sky

~ *Farid Matuk*

In this poem I began paying attention to sound only when I hit upon the phrase "lightly you lope" and was taken by the alliteration, which led me to the odd choice of the verb "lifting" as an attempt to visualize how a deer advancing delicately out of the woods might disturb paper which, somehow in this poem, is also snow.

"Lifting" was a key word, though, because I wanted to get across the idea that the mule, burdened by its load and its domesticated relation to humans, might have its heart lifted or buoyed by contact with this wild cousin. More precisely, as this was the first poem in my first book, I wanted to suggest the hopeful idea that attention to the physical world, in all its wildness, its sounds, its mystery, and its chilly indifference, might help lift not just our hearts but also our stories into something magical others might want to read.

A similar gesture happens with the long *i* sounds of "light" and "sky." The third-to-last line underwent several revisions, and though I can't recall all its iterations, I do know that the line began as something like "I bear a case with a soft blue glow." "Light" offered the bright and crisp sound of the long *i*, which I further emphasized with the repetition of "sky."

Farid Matuk is the author of *This Isa Nice Neighborhood* (Letter Machine, 2010), recipient of a 2011 Arab American Book Award, and a finalist for the Norma Farber First Book Award. He was chosen by Geoffrey G. O'Brien for the Poetry Society of America's New American Poets series. Matuk is also the author of several chapbooks, including *My Daughter La Chola* (Ahsahta, 2013). New poems appear in *Critical Quarterly, Third Coast, Iowa Review, Poets.org, The Baffler,* and *Denver Quarterly,* among others. Matuk serves as contributing editor for *The Volta* and poetry editor for *Fence.* He lives in Tucson and teaches in the M.F.A. program at the University of Arizona.

Where the Line Breaks

We are so accustomed to seeing poems in lines that we tend to take the line for granted. We forget that without end rhyme and/or meter, there are many ways a poem might be arranged on a page, many ways in which lines can be broken. This exercise encourages awareness of lines and the art of line breaking; I have used it with community college students in poetry and general creative writing courses.

Procedure

I. I read aloud "Nantucket" by William Carlos Williams and then hand out the poem with all line breaks removed so that it looks like a prose paragraph:

Nantucket

Flowers through the window lavender and yellow changed by white curtains— Smell of cleanliness— Sunshine of late afternoon— On the glass tray a glass pitcher, the tumbler turned down, by which a key is lying— And the immaculate white bed

Note: In a standard block of prose, these phrases would probably be punctuated by periods (full stops), and they would be considered sentence fragments, each ending with a period, instead of dashes. To increase the challenge of this exercise, you could remove the dashes. For an even greater challenge, you could set the entire poem in lower case letters and with no punctuation.

II. We discuss the choices poets make with line breaks and why they might have made them, how line breaks can make a poem more powerful or weaker.

- Line breaks can serve to determine the pace or the music of a poem through short and choppy lines, versus long, sweeping lines.

- Some poets use syllable counts to determine line breaks, while others use a normal breath count (i.e., where one pauses to catch a breath).

- Line breaks can highlight internal rhymes or particular words for special effect, such as the first and last words of a line.

- No two poets are likely to break the same poem's lines in the same way, and it's important for students to realize that there is no right or wrong way—but there should be a reason they break a line where they do.

This is also a good time to discuss end-stopped lines and enjambment.

- An **end-stopped line** closes with a complete phrase or clause; the reader pauses or stops at the end of the line, where the phrase or clause comes to an end, often with punctuation.

- By contrast, an **enjambed line** breaks a phrase or clause into two parts; the reader doesn't pause or stop at the end of the line but continues, following the broken phrase or clause to the next line, as in these enjambed lines from "old age sticks" by e. e. cummings:

> scolds Forbid
> den Stop
> Must
> n't Don't

The first enjambment creates two readings: "scolds Forbid" and "scolds Forbidden." The second enjambment creates contradictory readings: "Must" versus "Mustn't." The line breaks add complication and depth to the poem.

III. Students next arrange "Nantucket" on their own, breaking the lines where they think appropriate, using any of the reasons cited above.

IV. Finally, I show students the poem as Williams published it and we comment on his line breaks, as well as his arrangement of the poem into couplets.

Nantucket

> Flowers through the window
> lavender and yellow
>
> changed by white curtains—
> Smell of cleanliness—
>
> Sunshine of late afternoon—
> On the glass tray
>
> a glass pitcher, the tumbler
> turned down, by which
>
> a key is lying—And the
> immaculate white bed

> *~ William Carlos Williams*

Discussion can include the double use Williams achieves with "On the glass tray." Grammatically, "a glass pitcher" is "on the glass tray." But by breaking "On the glass tray" into a line of its own and pairing it with "Sunshine of late afternoon—" Williams has it both ways. Readers see late afternoon sun on the glass tray and then a glass pitcher on the same tray.

Here are some poems I like to use to demonstrate line breaks:

- "Flow-Chart" by John Ashbery
- "I Know a Man" by Robert Creeley
- "Adultery" by James Dickey
- almost anything by Emily Dickinson
- "The Waste Land" by T. S. Eliot
- "Fly" by W. S. Merwin
- "The Red Wheelbarrow" by William Carlos Williams

Examples

A block version of "Dog Days" by Houston poet Stan Crawford appears below. Wade Martin and Kathi Stafford arranged the poem into lines of their own and offered a brief commentary as to their very different approaches. Stan Crawford also sent a rationale for the poem as he arranged it, which follows the two line break experiments. No two are exactly alike, though all have some line breaks in common.

Dog Days

Just when we think we have escaped, drought tightens its parching grip again. Our own carbon footprints stalk us while outside our sweating bedroom window mourning doves express soft laments until heat stifles their cries. Rain braises only the narrow coast, where fringes of kudzu swarm, fecund as maniacs' dreams. Trees near water explode in burnt green, stop-action Hiroshimas. Shuddering, my wife tells how a dreamed killer, faceless as the heat, trapped her in a limousine blacker than a hearse. From a brown gunnysack, he produced rope, sharp knives, duct tape, and one patent pump still warm from the foot of a previous victim. My wife couldn't breathe, couldn't scream. Then the wail of approaching sirens saved her. No. Not sirens. The hungry whining of our skewbald, wall-eyed Shih Tzu awakened her. The pet she saved from death in a Houston pound, returning the favor.

Experiment I:

Dog Days

Just when we think we have escaped,
drought tightens its parching grip again.
Our own carbon footprints stalk us
while outside our sweating bedroom window
mourning doves express soft laments
until heat stifles their cries.
Rain braises only the narrow coast,
where fringes of kudzu swarm,
fecund as maniacs' dreams.

Trees near water explode in burnt green,
stop-action Hiroshimas.
Shuddering, my wife tells how a dreamed killer,
faceless as the heat,
trapped her in a limousine blacker than a hearse.
From a brown gunnysack,
he produced rope, sharp knives, duct tape,
and one patent pump
still warm from the foot of a previous victim.
My wife couldn't breathe, couldn't scream.

Then the wail of approaching sirens saved her.
No. Not sirens.
The hungry whining of our skewbald,
wall-eyed Shih Tzu awakened her.
The pet she saved from death in a Houston pound,
returning the favor.

~ Line breaks by Wade Martin

Note from Wade Martin: I've broken the poem into its separate images
and/or descriptors, due to the narrative and lyric tones of the poem, and then
used those tones as a way to bridge the stanzas. Rather than separate the story
of the dream from the opening imagery and closing reality, I've chosen im-
ages that pull the separate sections together. For example, the images "kudzu

swarm, / fecund as maniacs' dreams" and "Trees near water explode in burnt green, / stop-action Hiroshimas" create two facets of the same picture. Calling attention to each detail with line breaks, while using stanza breaks to thread the separate tones or modes of the story together, lends the poem's form the same uneasy shifting of tension and relief already present in the story itself.

Experiment II:

Dog Days

Just when we think we have escaped,
drought tightens its parching grip again.
Our own carbon footprints stalk us while outside
our sweating bedroom window mourning doves
express soft laments until heat stifles their cries. Rain braises
only the narrow coast, where fringes of kudzu swarm,
fecund as maniacs' dreams. Trees near water

Explode in burnt green, stop-action Hiroshimas.
Shuddering, my wife tells how a dreamed killer,

Faceless as the heat, trapped her in a limousine
blacker than a hearse. From a brown gunnysack,
he produced rope, sharp knives, duct tape, and one
patent pump still warm
from the foot of a previous victim.
My wife couldn't breathe, couldn't scream.

Then the wail of approaching sirens
saved her. No. Not sirens. The hungry whining
of our skewbald, wall-eyed Shih Tzu awakened
her. The pet she saved from death
in a Houston pound,
returning the favor.

~ *Line breaks by Kathi Stafford*

Note from Kathi Stafford: I inserted line breaks to allow maximum emphasis on closing and ending images. The vivid scenes of Hiroshima, kidnapping, and the saved pet I split to put the spotlight on themes arising in sequence as the poem develops. The lyricism of the lines contrasts beautifully with the imagery, requiring the phrases to be organized so that the specific details are pulled to the end of the line—"gunnysack," "victim," and "sirens," for example—in order to place greater emphasis on these evocative words.

The Original Poem:

Dog Days

Just when we think we have escaped,
drought tightens its parching grip again.

Our own carbon footprints stalk us while
outside our sweating bedroom window

mourning doves express soft laments
until heat stifles their cries. Rain braises

only the narrow coast, where fringes
of kudzu swarm, fecund as maniacs' dreams.

Trees near water explode in burnt green,
stop-action Hiroshimas. Shuddering,

my wife tells how a dreamed killer, faceless
as the heat, trapped her in a limousine

blacker than a hearse. From a brown
gunnysack, he produced rope, sharp knives,

duct tape, and one patent pump still warm
from the foot of a previous victim. My wife

couldn't breathe, couldn't scream. Then
the wail of approaching sirens saved her.

No. Not sirens. The hungry whining
of our skewbald, wall-eyed Shih Tzu

awakened her. The pet she saved from death
in a Houston pound, returning the favor.

~ *Stan Crawford*

Note from Stan Crawford: When I was revising "Dog Days," I wanted to keep the lines in couplets to give the images more space to unfold on the page, and since I intended to submit the poem to the *Texas Poetry Calendar*, I needed to keep all of the lines roughly equal in length, to stay within the line limits of that publication.

Four of the first five lines of the poem are either end-stopped or break between complete clauses. I felt this provided a balanced, logical pacing that worked well as an introduction to the setting and subject of the poem. Four of the next five lines are enjambed to increase the tension in the poem's diction and to highlight the echoes between the words ending each line: *braises, fringes, dreams, green* and *shuddering.*

From line 10, at *shuddering*, through line 18, I broke the lines abruptly to jerk the reader back and forth, like a bad carnival ride. Then line 18 is end-stopped once again, to slow the poem as the nightmare ends. The last four lines break as they do to focus the reader on our pet and his actions, as a way of earning the poem's title.

Millicent Borges Accardi, a Portuguese-American poet, is author of three books: *Only More So* (Salmon Press, forthcoming), *Injuring Eternity* (World Nouveau, 2010), and *Woman on a Shaky Bridge* (Finishing Line Press, 2010). A CantoMundo fellow from Topanga, California, Accardi has received awards from the National Endowment for the Arts, The Luso Foundation, the Barbara Deming Memorial Fund ("Money for Women"), and the California Arts Council. Recently, she has been visiting faculty at Nimrod Writers Conference, the University of Tulsa, and the University of Texas–Austin. She also organizes the Kale Soup for the Soul reading series.

Energy of Three:
Unity & Imbalance in the Tercet

torytelling comes as naturally to me as breathing. Small surprise that some thirty years ago, when I started writing poetry, I turned to narrative. I don't know why, but I didn't actually *think* about form. I wrote reflexively in free verse. Eventually, though, I tired of my poems, of their shape on the page—an irregular column of lines, propelled forward by story logic, rarely interrupted by white space, and never broken into stanzas of equal length.

I started to experiment, arranging a draft in spaced couplets or tercets, sometimes in quatrains or five-line stanzas. Quickly, I found myself drawn to couplets and tercets. But tercets are a special challenge—the energy, the imbalance that resides in the number three.

Background

I was raised in the Roman Catholic church. Three is at the center of church teaching: the Trinity—three Gods in one, Father, Son, and Holy Ghost—often represented by an equilateral triangle or three interlocking ellipses connecting the points of an equilateral triangle in a three-pointed loop that never ends. The three of theology, of geometry, resonates with a special kind of energy. Consider, then, the three of literature, of story—the love triangle. Think classical epics (Helen–Menelaus–Paris), opera (Carmen–Don José–Escamillo), the novel (Anna–Karenin–Vronsky), or movies (*Casablanca*, anyone?).

The triangle—its siren call, its ultimate imbalance—is everywhere in stories as old as language. And not just love triangles. Consider Hester Prynne and Arthur Dimmesdale—ill-fated lovers of *The Scarlet Letter.* Hester's estranged husband Roger Chillingworth is not a candidate for her affections, but put him near the doomed pair and he tips the balance toward certain ruin. Or Hester's daughter Pearl, upsetting balances, too—between Hester and Dimmesdale, Hester and Chillingworth, Hester and the citizens of Boston.

To sum up: The number three encompasses the unity, the perfection, of the equilateral triangle—and the perfect impossibility, the imbalance, of relationship triangles. In poetry, the tercet can express the energy of both.

Phase I: Material before Form, Lines before Stanzas

I. With free verse, I find that form rarely works at the outset. I recommend setting formal concerns aside and just getting words on the page. Write first—spills of words and associative leaps.

A decade ago, for example, in a Barbara Ras workshop, I tried to write about the sound of my grandmother's voice: Grandma died in 1979, and during her lifetime no recording was made of her voice. Here are parts of what I scribbled during the workshop:

> Poetry lives inside my grandmother's voice which no one has heard spoken in 24 years, the lilting cadences of German . . . in her farmer's English — up & down with gestures — conducting a music of her own — can never be heard again — at the edge of a dream, on the tip of my tongue — like telling my nerve endings to imagine an experience I've never had | Helen Keller's fingertips gentle at Annie Sullivan's throat | She slips away from me — our hands holding in a crowd & we don't know we are separating & will never see one another again — but the dreamer knows — says listen, remember, record — you will not see this face hear this voice again . . . Awake today you want that — yearn dreamward . . . Something you can't have — waking won't let it, sleep perversely won't bring it | ashes, silence, graveled grave site — chiseled stone — a name & dates | erratic as the trail cows make wandering home from pasture — around trees, prickly pear, agarita . . . the same path thereafter — whimsy transformed into pattern/habit — I walk the trail — Grandma walked this trail before me . . . a path that ambles circuitously but predictably — to tread the well-worn path again — to experience it as we did the first time not knowing the twists & turns ahead — no trail yet, just trees, brush, cacti, shadows — & something beckoning — yearning to step into the unknown — to hear Grandma's voice with a child's wonder — like the voices of old friends in Texas after a 10-year hiatus — I could *hear* Texas — & then it faded — nothing left but words, information — like hearing silence as a palpable presence . . . the alphabet for birdcalls — scissortails, fieldlarks, sparrows . . . the words are inept, inadequate — like trying to hear her voice — it is an empty space in the silence along the trail this afternoon

Looking back over these fragments, I set aside my embarrassment to reiterate perhaps the most important lesson I've learned about writing: When you're in search of a poem—or a story, an essay, a novel—*banish the editorial voice and let yourself write badly. Welcome whatever comes.*

I wasn't trying to write a poem here. Rather, I was jotting ideas that might lead to a poem, or at least the impetus. Two things here moved me to sit down and start working in lines:

1. The phrase "the alphabet for birdcalls." I liked that phrase, liked the way it evoked for me the impossibility of capturing the voice my grandmother took with her when she left this earth.

2. Impossibilities. Poetry is where we go to say what can't be said. I didn't see it yet, but this material was ripe for tercets.

II. Shape the shapeless until you have a draft.

This is not a linear process, not simply a matter of turning jottings into syntactical English or of weeding out the dreck along the way. It's a hybrid process, using the editorial eye but not banishing the intuitive. Lift pieces that strike you. Arrange. Embellish. Arrange again. Order. Re-order.

You might see tercets at this stage, might not. I didn't.

III. Read your draft with an editor's eye.

- Look for extraneous material—words, phrases, ideas that belong in some other poem.

- Look for language that over-explains—or that explains at all. A poem's job is not to explain itself but to make itself breathe.

- Ask where the poem needs less, where it needs more.

- Look at the poem's movement, the way it orders itself. Is it predictable, linear, chronological? Does it work in chunks, like a five-paragraph essay? There's nothing wrong with orderly movement, per se, but if a poem plods along, I say shake it up.

Here's the draft I developed from the jottings cited earlier in this exercise, with editorial notes (boxed) to explain material I crossed out:

An Alphabet for Mockingbirds   An Early Draft

Lillie Bruns Meischen
6 April 1896 – 12 June 1979

~~I can feel Helen Keller's fingertips~~
~~tremble touching Annie Sullivan's throat,~~
~~feel at the tip of my tongue the one word~~
~~that will unlock what I want to hear.~~ At
the moment of waking, it slips away from me,
this voice, this dream inside a dream,

leaves me alone, trailing cows
home, following the trail they made wandering
out to pasture and back, ambling

> *When I wrote the opening lines about Helen Keller and Annie Sullivan, I loved them. But almost before I had a draft, I could see that they did not belong in this poem.*

around oaks and hackberries, cactus spines
and agarita, the dust of the trail bed
fine as sifted flour, cool
and light between bare toes.

*The first deletion on this
page is unnecessary infor-
mation. I added phrases
to the right, trying to ex-
tend images of the voice I
was trying to evoke here.*

*The second deletion is as-
sertion at the expense of
mystery. It needs to go.*

The lead cow found her way through
this untrailed patch of trees and brush
fifty years ago, the other cows
in the small herd following her and
then the way was set. I want to walk here
as if for the first time, not knowing
the twists and turns ahead, just
trees, brush, prickly pear, the play
of shadow and light, the stir of something

not quite audible, like an alphabet
for mockingbirds, like the voice
of my grandmother, ~~lost~~
~~with her last breath~~
~~twenty-four years ago,~~

subtle colorations,
the richness of vowels
the ease of the glide on vowels
shapes of sounds

the cadences of German imprinted
on Texas English, ~~her breath, her voice, her life~~
~~alive inside the words~~. I want
to hear Grandma again
the way I once heard Texas
in voices everywhere around me
returning home
after a decade elsewhere.

        ~~I lost it~~
~~a few minutes at a time, felt it slip away,~~
~~turned tonedeaf again within months, heard only words~~
~~when people spoke to me.~~

        Grandma's voice
was like a fingerprint impressed
into the vapor of a single breath
against a windowpane,
the imprint of her breath vibrating
the reedy instrument of her vocal chords—
gone when she stopped breathing,
except sometimes in dreams
~~like this~~ that yield to waking silence,

*The little aside about
returning to Texas after a
decade elsewhere: it ex-
plains. It is dull, dull, dull.*

a graveled gravesite, a chiseled headstone,
a name and dates.

Note: This draft orders itself in narrative/expository chunks. I didn't want that. I wanted surprise—as in the one place where I enjambed between stanzas—so that one stanza breaks on "the stir of something," allowing that unknown something to arrest itself in motion at the poem's right edge, letting the succeeding stanza open mid-breath, on "not quite audible" and lead into the poem's title phrase.

Phase II: Matching Material and Form

Now comes the hard part: revising, seeing the poem in tercets, shaping—and re-shaping—until the number three sings its little song of unity and imbalance in each and every stanza.

Guidelines:

- Banish explaining.
- Work with movement, with associative leaps, with enjambment—so that each tercet tips into the next, moving the poem smoothly forward.
- Work in lines of three until each tercet is a little world of its own, comprehensible at a glance.
- Look for surprise in the first and last word of a line, a tercet.
- Edit for first lines and last lines that resonate, that linger in your inner eye when you step back and read the poem as a stranger, as your first reader.
- Look at your poem on the page, the pleasing sequence of three-line segments, the white space above and below each tercet. Tweak, as needed, until the lines earn their arrangement.

An Example

An Alphabet for Mockingbirds

Lillie Bruns Meischen
6 April 1896 – 12 June 1979

Hackberries bend the light, the brush
    beneath prodigal with edge and thorn,
        dust sifting cool and fine between bare toes.

The lead cow found her way here
    fifty years ago, the others plodding
        after. You want to follow

as on the first day, not knowing
    the twists and turns beyond, just
        agarita, huisache, mesquite, the dapple

of shadow and sun, ahead the stir
    of something not quite audible—
        like an alphabet for mockingbirds,

their vibrant singing silenced—
    a voice not quite remembered,
        the lilt of German rippling easy

Texas vowels, bright chorus
    of her and her widow friends
        at home over coffee and cake:

Breathe once against a windowpane,
    touch the vapor warm against the cool
        glass. Step back and watch your fingerprint

for the moment that it lasts, the imprint
    of breath against the reedy
        instrument humming in her throat.

Fading. Except in dreams that yield
    to waking silence, to mossy branches
        sifting ambered light, pools of paleness

lapping the shadows here, a trail
    unfurling homeward through
        bottomland silt of the Agua Dulce.

       ~ *David Meischen*

Note: Because cows and their trails meander, I didn't want a straight left margin, hence the stair-step arrangement of each tercet.

Variations

- Pull out a stalled poem—or any draft awaiting further work—and try shaping it with tercets.

- Try a poem in terza rima, a form pioneered by Dante in the Italian Renaissance. **Terza rima** is a form of linking tercets through rhyme. The first and third lines rhyme. The middle line in each succeeding couplet rhymes with the first and third lines of the preceding tercet: *aba, bcb, cdc.* . . .

- Create a form of your own, as Frost did, when he wrote "Acquainted with the Night," a sonnet that uses terza rima (four tercets and a couplet) instead of three quatrains and a couplet, as in the traditional English sonnet.

- Read up on numerology. Let numbers help you shape your poems.

David Meischen has been writing poetry and teaching the writing of poetry for thirty years. He has had poems in *The Southern Review, Southern Poetry Review, Borderlands, Cider Press Review,* and other journals, as well as *Two Southwests* (Virtual Artists Collective, 2008), which features poets from the Southwest of China and the United States. Meischen has participated in four collaborative poetry and art shows, most recently *Ekphrasis: Sacred Stories of the Southwest* (Phoenix, AZ, Obliq Art, 2014). Also a fiction writer, Meischen has recent stories in *The Gettysburg Review, Bellingham Review,* and elsewhere. He won the 2012 Talking Writing Prize for Short Fiction. Co-founder of Dos Gatos Press and co-editor of the first *Wingbeats,* Meischen lives in Austin, TX, with his husband—also his co-publisher and co-editor—Scott Wiggerman.

Rhina P. Espaillat

Getting the Beat:
Methods for Teaching Rhythm

The first time I set up a poetry unit, I tried approaching the task from the perspective of the reader, that is, beginning with content and then going on to discuss those poetic devices used by poets to convey content. Class discussions were enjoyable and stimulating, but the student writing that sprang from this approach was worse than disappointing. Most of it was tuneless chopped prose, some was jingly doggerel, and almost all of it attempted to make pious, grand statements about abstract themes.

I backtracked, dug into memory to discover what it was about poetry that had drawn me irresistibly as a very young child, and came up with the notion that poetry is fundamentally song. We hear and respond to song physically, as an amalgam of rhythm, melody, and meaning. We don't listen for the message of the lyrics first and then examine dispassionately those musical devices the composer used to convey that message. Such a division would be artificial, since the meaning is inherent in the whole song, including such nonverbal elements as the beat that causes our bodies to move involuntarily. The beat in verse is, in fact, what hooked me for life.

Rationale

My second attempt at a poetry unit began from the inside, that is, from the poet's view, with the making of the poem, not the examination of finished work. I tried to keep as unbroken as possible the connection between poetry and music. I put content aside and began with rhythm as the most basic, visceral aspect of the art, and introduced meter as a series of verbal games. I taught my students the essentials of traditional versification first—and only later encouraged them to try free verse, which is difficult to write well precisely because it looks so easy. Ideas emerged by themselves, as they do wherever there are human beings. Gradually the games, the little empty exercises that my students had come to enjoy doing and sharing, began to fill with content drawn from their own lives and observations. The craft itself acted as a kind of magnet for whatever in their experience needed to be put into words.

This second approach is the one I kept and developed, and is the chief source of the suggestions in this exercise.

Note: Students accustomed to nothing but free verse sometimes balk at the notion of attempting traditional form. They ask if poetry should not be simply put down "just the way it comes out," and suggest that it's unnatural to create anything mathematically. A good response is a display of seashells, pinecones and other highly ordered objects from nature. Point out, in simple terms, that symmetry is older than life, and that the beauty of nature is not diminished by order, any more than the beauty of music is diminished by the fact that composers arrange the notes in some sort of sequence, not at random.

Procedure

Accentual Verse

Read aloud some strongly rhythmical nursery rhyme. "Pease Porridge Hot" is a good choice because it's fun and easy:

> Pease porridge hot, pease porridge cold,
> Pease porridge in the pot, nine days old;
> Some like it hot, some like it cold,
> Some like it in the pot, nine days old.

Clap your hands at the accented syllables to show that their number is constant, but the number of unaccented syllables varies from line to line. In "Pease Porridge Hot," for example, each line has six accented syllables. This is a good way to introduce **accentual verse**, verse in which only the number of accented syllables per line is counted.

Syllabic Verse

I. Distribute a sheet of cinquains, haiku, or tanka poems, to serve as introductions to syllabic verse. This is an easy meter, because the student has only to count so many syllables per line, regardless of whether they are accented or not. The requirements of these forms have more to do with imagery and selection of detail than rhythm; they are good for encouraging restraint and the careful choice of just a few words.

The **cinquain** has five lines: two syllables in the first, four in the second, six in the third, eight in the fourth, and two in the last. The traditional **haiku** has three lines: five syllables in the first, seven in the second, and five in the last. The **tanka** has five lines: it is like a haiku with two seven-syllable lines added to it. The haiku usually deals with some aspect of nature, and works by suggesting more than it says. The language is simple, with few, if any, figures of speech. Typically, the reader is asked to observe something and arrive at some unspoken insight of his own.

II. After your students have tried writing cinquains, haiku, and tanka, ask them to invent a syllabic pattern of their own. Put up on the board as many samples as possible, and read them aloud. Invite students to name their invented forms. Encourage them to experiment with each other's new forms. Tell them that famous poetic forms we have today, such as the sonnet and the limerick, were also invented by individual poets. If possible, tape your students reading their work aloud, and invite them to self-criticism based on the playback. Reading aloud is one of the best ways to get inside a poem, as the subtleties of stress and tone of voice are dependent on meaning, and the reader must understand the poem on a gut level to read it well.

Accentual-Syllabic Verse

I. Teach rhythm first and directly by doing with syllables what music teachers do with notes. Start with your students' names. Put several two-syllable and three-syllable names on the board, and scan them to show where the accent falls in each, as below:

Annette	∪ /	iamb
Andy	/ ∪	trochee
Marguerite	∪ ∪ /	anapest
Dominick	/ ∪ ∪	dactyl
Deedee	/ /	spondee
Belinda	∪ / ∪	amphibrach

There's nothing wrong with teaching the real names of metric feet: any child who is taking music lessons has already learned about two-four time, three-quarter time, half notes, and so forth. The vocabulary of verse-making is not really any harder or more complex than that of music, and your students won't be afraid of it if you're not.

As for students with monosyllabic names, let them use last names too:

Greg Brown	/ /	spondee
Jill McCarthy	/ ∪ / ∪	two trochees

There are many more feet, but you could easily dispense with all but the first four—iamb, trochee, anapest, and dactyl. They are the most commonly used.

The advantage of starting with students' names is that it makes them feel personally involved in a kind of word play at the hand-clapping, foot-tapping level that still doesn't demand much from them emotionally or intellectually. Let those demands come later, just as the music teacher begins with finger exercises, not symphonies. Tap out the meter with a pencil or your knuckles or some percussion instrument: it's the ear you're trying to train, not the eye.

II. Break up the class into groups of students whose names scan the same way, and ask them to list words and phrases they can think of that scan like their names. Have each group put up on the board and tap out several items from their list, and have the rest of the class make corrections, as necessary. This is a good introduction to **accentual syllabic meter**, which takes into account both the number of syllables per line *and* the pattern of accents.

Be sure the examples include whole phrases as well as single words, and work toward the use of whole lines of similar feet, containing two feet (dimeter), three feet (trimeter), four feet (tetrameter) and five feet (pentameter).

Tell students that a line of verse is described by the kind of foot most of it consists of *and* the number of feet per line: for example, trochaic trimeter (three feet of trochaic meter) and iambic tetrameter (four feet of iambic meter). If they want to forget those phrases as soon as they've heard them, that's all right: future learning will reinforce them. The important thing is that they hear what such lines sound like, and know that regular rhythm—meter—is one of the most valuable tools of the poet.

III. Ask students to begin poems with the names of people they know and then go on to describe those people in lines that scan like the names.

IV. Give your students opening lines and let them add three or four more in exactly the same meter. Again, you can easily use nursery rhymes:

iambic	a pocket full of rye
trochaic	Jack and Jill went up the hill
anapestic	and the dish ran away with the spoon
dactylic	Hickory, dickory dock

Don't bother with rhyming, or with serious meaning: nonsense verse is fine, so long as they enjoy it and practice shifting syllables around to achieve different sound patterns. To make for variety and add a little healthy competition, offer each row a different opening line, or offer the whole class several and let each student decide for himself which one to try. Vary your openings, so they'll get to practice as many different metrical patterns as possible. Make clear to them that you're not looking for deep thoughts or admirable sentiments, but simply exploring with them the many ways in which common language can make music and give pleasure.

V. Have students copy newspaper headlines and scan them at the board. Put up a few lines of traditional verse or some strongly rhythmical free verse, and point out that both are more patterned, and more likely to use repetitions of patterns, than the headlines. The same may be done with traffic signs, grocery lists or any other bits of non-literary prose.

VI. Introduce the notion of variation—also called **metrical substitution**—by asking students to imagine forty or fifty lines of perfectly regular meter. Tap it out for them to emphasize the monotony. Point out that poets like to set up a regular meter for their readers to expect, then surprise them by moving away from it, and then please them by returning to it.

I show them how in a poem such as "Bilingual/Bilingüe," I substitute a different kind of foot somewhere in a line of iambic pentameter, even adding a syllable or taking one away, to break the monotony of perfect meter. "Fix" several lines of this poem by making them perfectly regular to show how the poem loses some of its excitement. Have them practice substitution in a few lines of their own work, and discuss the results.

An Example

Bilingual/Bilingüe

My father liked them separate, one there,
one here (allá y aquí), as if aware

that words might cut in two his daughter's heart
(el corazón) and lock the alien part

to what he was—his memory, his name
(su nombre)—with a key he could not claim.

"English outside this door, Spanish inside,"
he said, "y basta." But who can divide

the world, the word (mundo y palabra) from
any child? I knew how to be dumb

and stubborn (testaruda); late, in bed,
I hoarded secret syllables I read

until my tongue (mi lengua) learned to run
where his stumbled. And still the heart was one.

I like to think he knew that, even when,
proud (orgulloso) of his daughter's pen,

he stood outside mis versos, half in fear
of words he loved but wanted not to hear.

~ *Rhina P. Espaillat*

Free Verse

Bring in several examples of free verse to show how a poet makes up for the absence of regular meter by giving the reader other kinds of repetition to create a pattern. Point out repeated phrases or word patterns, repeated cadences, sections of regular rhythm in an otherwise irregular line, lines of roughly similar length, images that recur, comparisons that carry through a whole poem and therefore unify it, and so forth. (For an excellent exercise on repeated phrases, word patterns, and cadences, see Laure-Anne Bosselaar's "Repetition & Cadence, or Repetition *for* Cadence," page 61.)

Tips

Use imagination and draw on your own resources. Don't be afraid to do surprising, even weird things, or to make students laugh. In fact, we all tend to notice and remember the unexpected, the incongruous, and the funny. Teaching, by example, that poetry is a source of joy may turn out to be one of the most valuable things you'll do for your students.

Rhina P. Espaillat has published poems, essays, short stories and translations in numerous magazines and in over sixty anthologies, in both English and her native Spanish, as well as three chapbooks and nine full-length books, including four in bilingual format. Her most recent publications are a poetry collection in English, *Her Place in These Designs* (Truman State University Press, 2008), and a book of her Spanish translations of poems by Richard Wilbur, in bilingual format, *Oscura fruta: cuarenta y dos poemas / Dark Berries: Forty-two Poems* (Ediciónes El Tucán de Virginia, Colección Bífidos, 2013).

Tell It Slant:
The Extended Metaphor

The main point of all creative writing, I think, is to make the reader feel something—move him or her to laugh, shudder, cringe, cry, shout. The job of the writer is not to tell about experience, but to recreate it so the reader feels the experience as if it's happening to her or him.

In this exercise, we'll explore the power of the extended metaphor to come at a truth sideways and create poems that express the otherwise inexpressible. As Emily Dickinson said, "Tell all the truth, but tell it slant."

Poems in this mode speak about an extremely difficult experience in a wide-reaching way. I say *difficult* in that the subject is hard to hit head-on; the poem provides a vehicle to write about something without actually writing about it. I'm talking about poems that express our feelings—about an important subject, a life-changing experience, a horrific or awkward/embarrassing experience, a funny sexual experience, or maybe some type of awakening—by comparing it with something else entirely. The actual subject is never mentioned explicitly except in the title. The poem is entirely metaphor. It presents the opportunity for a new perspective and a surprising kind of honesty.

Preparation

I. Abstract vs. Concrete Language

I begin by talking briefly or at length—depending on the age/experience of the participants—about abstract versus concrete words. Poems by young or inexperienced writers are often filled with abstractions (love, beauty, angry, ugly, fun, sad). I point out that I can't imagine what their idea of beauty is.

I ask for examples of beauty, asking students to be as specific as possible. If they mention a sunset, for example, I ask them to say where they are witnessing the sunset. Is it over water? Are there mountains in the foreground? What time of year is it? Is there snow? Is the air hot? Is the landscape green, brown, white? What colors does the sky turn? Can they hear birds? What kinds of birds? What do their calls sound like?

I go through this process with one or more abstract words. This practice gets students speaking in concrete terms, and they begin to understand how **concrete language** engages the senses and enables them to see, taste, touch, hear, and smell what began as an abstract word or phrase.

II. The Poem as Extended Metaphor

Published poems demonstrate how an extended metaphor works, how an extended metaphor can transform the abstract into the concrete.

Important: If copies of the poems are to be provided, do not hand them out until it's time to reveal the titles!

The First Example: Read David Kirby's "Broken Promises" without revealing its title. This kind of reading provides a great opportunity for students to practice focused listening.

Broken Promises

I have met them in dark alleys, limping and one-armed;
I have seen them playing cards under a single light-bulb
and tried to join in, but they refused me rudely,
knowing I would only let them win.
I have seen them in the foyers of theaters,
coming back late from the interval

long after the others have taken their seats,
and in deserted shopping malls late at night,
peering at things they can never buy,
and I have found them wandering
in a wood where I too have wandered.

This morning I caught one;
small and stupid, too slow to get away,
it was only a promise I had made to myself once
and then forgot, but it screamed and kicked at me
and ran to join the others, who looked at me with reproach
in their long, sad faces.
When I drew near them, they scurried away,
even though they will sleep in my yard tonight.
I hate them for their ingratitude,
I who have kept countless promises,
as dead now as Shakespeare's children.
"You bastards," I scream,
"you have to love me—I gave you life!"

~ *David Kirby*

Ask students to tell you what they remember from the poem: What is its first line? What are some of the words and phrases they remember? What is the last line? Finally—this is getting to the heart of the matter—what is the tone of the poem? How does it make them feel? If they could give the poem a title, what would it be? Note—and point out to students—that their language turns abstract as they come up with expressions of feelings and tone as well as a possible title.

Chances are, students will come close to nailing the tone of the poem and to imagining titles that could fit quite well. Now, tell them the title of the poem and read the poem again.

The Second Example: Repeat the process, but this time use my poem "First Blow Job." Again, don't tell students the title when you read the poem!

First Blow-Job

Suddenly I knew what it was to be my uncle's Labrador retriever,
young pup paddling furiously back across the pond with the prized
duck in her mouth, doing the best she could to keep her nose in the air

so she could breathe. She was learning not to bite, to hold the duck
just firmly enough, to control its slick length without leaving marks.
She was about to discover that if she reached the shore, delivered this

duck just the way she'd been trained, then Master would pet her
head and make those cooing sounds, maybe later he'd let her ride
in the cab of the truck. She would rest her chin on his thigh all the way

home, and if she had been good enough, she might get to wear
the rhinestone-studded collar, he might give her a cookie, he might
not shove her off the bed when he was tired and it was time for sleep.

~ *Meg Kearney*

Additional Examples: Repeat the process with at least one more poem. Here are some possibilities, including one of my own:

- "Happiness" by Stephen Dunn
- "Success" by Cornelius Eady
- "Michiko Dead" by Jack Gilbert
- "Loneliness" by Meg Kearney

- "Happiness" by Jane Kenyon
- "Despair" by Maxine Kumin

If using the Gilbert poem "Michiko Dead," for example, note that not once does the narrator say anything about grief or mourning; he mentions death only in the title. The poem is an extended metaphor of a grief that won't let go—by talking about something else entirely. The poem says, *It's like this,* and by the end the reader can feel what the poet feels because the poem is grounded in something concrete.

Procedure

I. Let students know that you'd like them to write a poem. They should give it an abstract title—emotions work well—but the poem itself has to express that abstract concept by talking about something else entirely, saying what it's like.

It helps if students choose a subject that feels important to them; they should think about some emotion or experience they have a difficult time explaining/sharing. Ask them to use at least three of the five senses in the poem, along with other strategies they may want to employ—rhythm, line length, and so on. Imagery should come naturally with this exercise.

Read one more poem to them out loud, letting them know that when you finish you're going to be quiet and they should begin. Give students at least twenty minutes to draft something.

II. Have students share their poems with the class, first pointing out that these are rough drafts. None of them will be finished, and the quality might be iffy, but they will have great potential if students continue to work on them. Praise what's strong in the writing, but do point out any abstractions or clichés, and challenge students to come up with language that is fresh and surprising.

Variations

I. You might have all students write a poem about the same emotion or abstraction. The results would demonstrate the many directions concrete language can take in transforming an abstraction.

II. In addition to writing a poem with an abstract title, I often give students the option of writing a poem titled "What It's Like to Be Me" (which they can later title anything they want). Again, develop the poem through metaphor and the senses. No abstractions or clichés allowed!

An Example

What It's Like

I'll try to tell you only because of that song you wrote;
because of your lost son; because you noticed me searching
your face and stroking my chin, and you said, Do that again,
it's okay. That's part of what it's like. I search faces
on the street, at the supermarket, laundromat; I try
not to be rude; I stroke my chin—Do I have your nose?
Would you turn your head? Do you have this little point
on your right ear? Do you like milk in your coffee, but
only in the afternoon? Do you know Yeats by heart? Does
Whitman make you do a little dance? Do you like music?

Chopin calms me; the piano tastes like Cabernet; it smells
like buttered popcorn, then it smells like bread; it makes
the knots in my shoulders relax a little. Sometimes the music
feels so safe I lie down on the floor, belly up like a cat
who trusts her world completely. Jazz makes me tremble—all
that freedom, all those risks, those loose threads threatening
to pull and never stop unraveling—if I listen too long I
begin to fall. I weep so easily. It's hard enough clinging
to this floor, not tumbling into that hole in the ceiling
where there's not even a night sky to catch me.

Candlelight quiets the chatter in my head, all those monkeys
gabbling at once telling me *Be good! Be good! Don't
tell; don't don't.* In a candlelit room there's a possibility
of starting all over again; it's what it must feel like to be
born—all that watery light, and there, on the wall,
a woman who could be my mother. As long as I stay here
with the candles, she won't disappear. There's a possibility
you might see me here, I mean really *see* me—though please
don't ask me where I'm from. It's an unreachable place
where wind has worn everyone's face away; it's a child's
tea party where you just pretend to eat the cookies.

Are you beginning to feel what I feel? I practice and I
practice, but my prayers are not grateful enough; they're
mustard seeds though they should be forest fires, so
hot, so smoky all the monkeys stampede and there's
nothing left at the end when it all clears but a place
where the earth is rich and humming like a saxophone's
throat, where I can let that music fly because I'm up
to my knees in it, where there are people beside me
tapping their feet and no one's threatening to leave;
where I can turn to you and say After this tune maybe you
will play that song again, and It's okay if my eyes don't
look like yours because I've never felt so much at home.

~ *Meg Kearney*

Meg Kearney is author of two books of poems for adults, *An Unkindness of Ra-vens* (BOA Editions, 2001) and *Home By Now* (Four Way Books, 2009), winner of the 2010 PEN New England/L. L. Winship Award; she has two novels in verse for teens: *The Secret of Me,* and its sequel, *The Girl in the Mirror.* Her short story "Chalk" appears in *Fresh Flash: Short Short Stories About Youth.* Kearney's picture book *Trouper* (Scholastic, 2013) was illustrated by E. B. Lewis. Her po-etry has been featured on *Poetry Daily* and Garrison Keillor's *The Writer's Al-manac,* and has been published in myriad literary magazines and anthologies. Formerly Associate Director of the National Book Foundation (sponsor of the National Book Awards) in New York, Kearney now lives in New Hampshire and directs the Solstice M.F.A. in Creative Writing Program of Pine Manor College in Chestnut Hill, Massachusetts.

Nickole Brown

Defamiliarizing the Apple: Ostranenie & Awareness

How do you teach writers to use imagery? How do you hound them out of cliché? How do you convince them that the body—with its imperfect clash of all the senses—is the way into language? The trick, to me, has not been to shame writers away from the emotions and abstractions that likely brought them to the page in the first place. Instead, I teach awareness: attention as a form of devotion, a raw, muscular kind of seeking, an unflinching dedication to scrub away one's preconceived notions of a thing in order to see it for what it really is. This is attention as discipline—the core discipline—of writing.

Awareness—as it's taught to visual artists in the drawing studio or to practitioners of meditation who sit silently for hours on end—isn't a passive reception of information. No, it is focus, a striving, something beginners will fail at time and again. But its worth? Invaluable. Those who achieve true awareness are changed by it. This exercise is the most succinct way I know to demonstrate this transformative power and to have students begin that practice.

Materials

- Apples. One for each student. Preferably a variety of apples, so that each has a slightly different shade and size. (It's a thoughtful gesture to wash them beforehand, but don't remove the grocer's sticker.)
- Some napkins or paper towels.
- Sample poems about apples.

Procedure

I. Ostranenie (or Defamiliarization): Start with a discussion. In "Art as Technique," Russian critic Viktor Shkovsky, developed the concept of ostranenie as a means "to make objects 'unfamiliar,' to make forms difficult, to increase the difficulty and length of perception because the process of perception is an aesthetic end in itself and must be prolonged."

Ask: if we are all telling the same stories of love and sex and death, how can we write something new? How can we sidestep the spiritual nausea of cliché? The answer doesn't lie in writing about something completely different (if that's possible) or in shocking your readers awake, but rather in writing well about those things you know intimately, so much so that perhaps you don't even notice them yourself anymore.

Note: If you meet the class regularly, it's a good idea to incorporate as homework the night before Charles Baxter's wonderful essay, "On Defamiliarization," from *Burning Down the House;* he makes his argument eloquently.

II. Drawing the Familiar: As a quick exercise, students take out their notebooks and draw a picture of a tree. Most likely, each participant will draw something that looks like a cloud on a stick. Does this really look like a tree? What are those odd, ticking sticks in the breeze? And how is it that each student has drawn a tree without first asking what kind? Does a palm look remotely like a ginkgo? Or how about a river birch or an oak (crepe myrtle, holly, white pine—the list goes on)? How is it that we've simplified the world, that we've wired ourselves for simplicity and efficiency so much that we've washed out the strangeness, the true complexity of the world?

III. Word and Thing: If there's time, take a quick dip into linguistics. Discuss the difference between the **signifier** (the word itself, spelled out in four letters—T-R-E-E) and the **signified** (the thing itself, whatever particular tree it is, which is far more complex than the word can even begin to address). This distinction points to the essential lack in language itself and—most important—how hard one must work to try to carve out reality on the page.

IV. The Apple: An easy segue at this point is to talk about the apple. What fruit is more commonplace and thus more overlooked? Humans have enjoyed apples since about 6500 BC, and no other fruit is rife with more clichés. From Eve's temptation to a doctor's prescription, we've been inundated with the apple since we put a shiny red apple on the grade school teacher's desk. In turn, she taught us, flash-card icon of an apple in hand: "A is for apple." There's likely no food that we take more for granted than the lowly apple—and thus, no fruit more difficult to write about in a fresh way.

At this time, tell students exactly what they're going to do: Write about an apple—one particular apple, that is. Then take out the bag of apples and ask them each to choose one carefully, as they'll be with it for quite a while.

V. The Senses: Take ten minutes with each of the senses. With each sense, give students time to jot the particulars for the apple they have chosen. I usually start with sight, stressing the importance of seeing something new, as if you've never seen it before in all your life. Attention to color is important (most will assume, quite wrongly, that apples are uniformly red), as is shape (which is never, as assumed, symmetrical).

I move on to touch, asking students to ascertain the exact texture and form of the apple in their hands. Does it feel like anything else? What about the temperature? Or the ridges one can feel around the horizontal circumference of an apple? Move on to taste, smell, and sound. Have students reach for metaphors whenever possible, especially if the comparison is completely unexpected, making the description new.

- As I prompt students to observe, I advise them *not* to write a poem. Reaching for something profound and writerly can get in the way of true observation. This exercise is more like sketching, taking down details, discovering metaphors, not necessarily imposing cohesion or meaning yet.

- As students write through the senses, I remind them of kinesthetic—tactile—learning. I encourage them to apply force, to puncture and roll and toss their apples. Descriptions can feel as if they're frozen behind museum glass; this kind of play can do a lot to move the exercise along.

- I recommend having students bite into their apples at one time, perhaps on the count of three—even better if you can turn off the lights and have them take that first bite in the dark!

VI. Shared Observations: Haves students share their perceptions, without necessarily reading from the page. The point is not performance—or the production of a written piece—but observation. Awareness in itself is enough.

Ask: Did anyone notice something completely unexpected about your apple? How can you see it new, make it strange? Later, these observations can go into a poem about an apple or about something completely different that employs apple imagery. It's all about filling up one's warehouse: a simple observation made today, during a concentrated time, with something commonplace, could provide the exact line you need to use in a poem, perhaps years down the road.

VII. Apple Poems: To wrap up the class, I like to share a variety of poems that talk about apples in completely different ways, including:

- "White Apples" by Donald Hall
- "Fallen Apples" by Tom Hansen
- "A Short History of the Apple" by Dorianne Laux
- "Apples" by Grace Schulman

As homework, I often assign a poem developed out of this exercise. If possible, I try to give the group a few weeks to find their own lines.

Variations

This exercise can be done again and again with numerous variations on things we take for granted. A trip outside to examine trees can have fantastic results, but you could use most anything we think we "see" but no longer see at all.

Examples

Here are two poems—one that describes the apple directly and another that uses the apple as metaphor to flesh out a range of complex emotions.

Morning Snack

Stomach growling by ten,
I reach for it in my purse.
As green as celery leaves with
scratches like week-old paper cuts and
a dirty baby belly button on both ends.
It fits perfectly in my palm the way
a cold heel fits into a fuzzy sock or
a bald scalp into a hat. The weight
of a coin purse full of pennies.
When I bite into it, it sounds like
sticks splitting and tastes of
coarse, sweet water.
Apples, hold me over.

~ *Kiley Williams*

Bloodswoll

You claim you are numb. Still
I watch you finger your
stomach and press
the twist of navel.
I want to ask:
Do you miss your mother?
How she held you
kinked in her arms? Or
when she let you go—
was that too much?

Your skin isn't different from mine.
You tell me you are softer
but know it's only your young age.
I point to each scar, and you
recite their stories with the same fervor
as Bradbury and his tigers. I have
a favorite—in your roundness
I found a globe's mountain
range raised from a paring knife.
It matches my mother's on her right
hand; a bottle scar, a memory:
a mad sister, her heroin
flushed. Neck bloodswoll, crying out,
thin-boned.

There are days when I bite into you,
and you only taste of pink and water.
Like I'm tasting the last of all
you have to offer.
I leave my mark in you
with my whole mouth, and you rest.
This is how
you want to be used.

~ *Seth Pennington*

Nickole Brown is the author of two poetry volumes—*Fanny Says* (BOA Editions, forthcoming) and *Sister,* a novel in poems (Red Hen Press, 2007) . A graduate of The Vermont College of Fine Arts, Brown was the editorial assistant for the late Hunter S. Thompson. She has received grants from the National Endowment for the Arts, the Kentucky Foundation for Women, and the Kentucky Arts Council. She worked at Sarabande Books for ten years and was the National Publicity Consultant for Arktoi Books. She has taught creative writing at the low-residency M.F.A. Program in Creative Writing at Murray State University. Her work has appeared in *Bloom Magazine, The Los Angeles Review, Post Road, Diagram Magazine, The Oxford American,* and *storySouth.* Currently the Editor for the Marie Alexander Series in Prose Poetry, Brown is an Assistant Professor of poetry at the University of Arkansas at Little Rock.

Becoming Another:
The Persona Poem

I have been thinking a good while about the uses of the persona poem for both poets and prose writers. It is such an interesting form—how one becomes another, retaining the sense of self, poetic or prose self, while at the same time enacting inside the other. Persona poems are an invitation to speak in the voice of the imagined. As with acting, you enter the character, but it is the *you,* the poet/actor who enters, and takes on or adds the persona. It is a possession of sorts.

Background

The persona was the mask worn by an actor in Greek drama. The actor is the god—and conscribed by the story—but through the mask may reveal a deeper view. Masquerades and carnivals employ a similar masking—a place where one can be free to be one's self—without the use of the *I.*

The use of the term **persona**, as distinct from *author,* stresses that the speaker is part of a fictional creation, invented for the author's particular purposes in a given literary work. Teaching the persona poem to fiction writers as well as to poets would do service to both in developing character—a character in a story, as well as our own character—giving us an exercise in empathy and analysis, in psychological complexity, wit, and endurance.

Another reason a writer might choose to use a mask or persona in her poetry is the issue of power and politics. A writer might choose to use a persona for the subversive remaking of narratives. A mask might help the writer assume power that he or she does not have.

In my first book, *A Bell Buried Deep*, the original framework was the Biblical story of Sarah and Hagar, brought through American slavery as Sara and Harriet, following the framework of the slave narrative by Harriet Jacobs. In the Coda I place the two women in the mythic present in Coney Island, New York, as Sadie and Hattie. Using a **frame**—an already-told or known story—gave me license, paradoxically, to enter more deeply into the characters, my imaging of them.

The frame also gives the writer a chance to contradict or deepen the story that everyone thinks he or she knows—telling the story from a different slant, upending people's assumptions (and our own).

Persona Poems in Published Poetry

Here are a number of recent poetry books that make impressive use of personae:

- *Tongue of War: From Pearl Harbor to Nagasaki* by Tony Barnstone: voices of individuals from both sides of the Pacific theater of World War II
- *Brutal Imagination* by Cornelius Eady: the voice of the Black kidnapper invented by Susan Smith to cover up the killing of her two small sons
- *The Wild Iris* by Louise Glück: the voice of Eden's flowers
- *M-A-C-N-O-L-I-A* by A. Van Jordan: the voices of MacNolia Cox, the first African-American student to reach the final round of the National Spelling Bee, and her husband John Montiere
- *What to Tip the Boatman?* by Cleopatra Mathis: the voices of Demeter and Persephone
- *Slave Moth* by Thylias Moss: the voice of an enslaved Black woman
- *Orpheus & Eurydice: A Lyric Sequence* by Gregory Orr: the voices of doomed lovers Orpheus and Eurydice
- *What the Water Gave Me: Poems After Frida Kahlo* by Pascale Petit: Kahlo's voice
- *The Wanton Sublime* by Anna Rabinowitz: narrative of the Virgin Mary and the Annunciation from numerous angles
- *Blood Dazzler* by Patricia Smith: voices of the men and women upended by Hurricane Katrina—and of the hurricane itself
- *One Big Self* by C.D. Wright: the voices of Louisiana prisoners
- *Eating in the Underworld* by Rachel Zucker: a reimagining of the Persephone and Demeter story

Procedure

Choose one or more of the following options for a persona poem:

- Take a Biblical character and re-imagine him or her as a modern person.
- Take a fairy tale, one that seems familiar to you, and take the part of the villain. I find that this approach is very, very helpful. It can enhance psychological nuance in poems.
- Be a fly on the wall watching President Bush or President Obama or President Lincoln. Imagine him alone, or in an intimate moment.

- Take a historical figure, and research—research is crucial in persona poems—the life of the person, his or her letters, lectures, famous sayings. Write a poem about his or her last night living.
- Take a painting and develop a figure in the painting speaking to the painter.
- Take someone who has died, and write a letter from him or her to someone in the person's life.

(See also Robin Chapman's exercise "One More Mask: Exploring the Theater of Poetry," page 28.)

An Example

Here is a poem in the voice of the Biblical Sarah:

The Sacrifice of Sarah

What did he hope for,
when he dove into the damp

cavern of her body? A son, he said.
I swear, I thought he would refuse. But he took

his pleasure, opened himself into her.
And, after, he wiped her lush color from his palms,

lifted his hands to his face, as if to smell what had been crushed.
Even so, her scent, ripe as desert jasmine, drifted toward me.

Tell me: What God bled him, till in his eyes, I saw a whole generation
crumbled into soot? The shale of a million lives burning

inside the oven of his gray, gray eyes? Or was it I
who set it all in motion, obedient to the last,

when he cast away all I loved, or laid his son upon the altar stone?
I lay out my questions like a shroud. What is sacrifice

if not that all is taken from you? Each part you love,
revere, whatever you count on, or hold close,

loosened, till the hollow of your chest becomes a ringing bell,
and you are nothing but the air in which the clapper tolls.

~Veronica Golos

Veronica Golos is the author of *Vocabulary of Silence* (Red Hen Press, 2011), winner of the New Mexico Book Award, poems from which have been translated into Arabic by poet Nizar Sartawi. She was the co-winner of the 16th Annual Nicholas Roerich Poetry Prize for *A Bell Buried Deep* (Story Line Press, 2003), to be re-issued by Tupelo Press. Golos's poems are included in *A Poet's Craft, Collecting Life: Poets on Objects Known and Imagined, Spillway, Drunken Boat, Cimarron, Contemporary World Literature, Verso* (Paris), *Poetry* (London), *Rattle, World Literature Magazine Spring's Forum* (Syria), *Maqal* (Kuwait), and other publications. Golos is Poetry Editor for the *Journal of Feminist Studies in Religion* (Harvard Divinity School) and co-editor of the *Taos Journal of International Poetry & Art.*

Poetry Superpowers
vs. Poetry Kryptonite

I've come to actively dislike the advice repeatedly given younger/emerging poets to "find their voice"—as if this is the magical formula one needs to "master" in order to learn to write "successful" poems. There's an underlying assumption here that all poems are—or should be—personal/representative/ coherent/stable/univocal, that once poets discover how to write a "successful" poem (whatever that means), they've discovered their "voice" and should continue to (re)produce the same type of poem in said "voice" for the duration of their poetic careers.

This way of thinking strikes me as depressing and deathly boring—a Starbuck's mentality to writing (or should I say "producing"?) poetry that privileges consistency of product over individual artistic exploration or experimentation. This type of static fixity, predictable accessibility, implied "mastery," and pin-downability all connote desirable attributes of consumer commodity fetish culture—rewarding the performance of a reliably branded Author Function, as opposed to poets exploring the possibilities of, well . . . poetry.

Rationale

Maybe instead of being so concerned with discovering and "perfecting" our "voices," we might be better served by learning to avoid entrapment within the complacent amber of our own stylistic and linguistic tics, thematic obsessions, formative aesthetic preferences, and ritualized writing processes. Perhaps, as poets, we should resist the impulses of mechanical reproduction, the de facto self-commodification of enacting our own Author Functions within our poems. I've always believed in rigorously questioning myself as a poet— painful as that can sometimes be—and conscientiously cultivating an ongoing state of Beginner's Mind. Not that one should attempt to efface oneself as a poet; in fact, I think it's also important to resist the peer pressure of aesthetically successful formulas and/or aesthetic trendiness.

The elements of who we are as people/poets are deeply ingrained in us— so much so that I don't think it's possible to simply shake off these ways of being/writing. So instead of "finding our voice," isn't it a much more appealing and interesting challenge to figure out new ways of being/writing as a poet?

In other words, perhaps we can all stop trying to find our voices, which were never lost to begin with, and instead imagine ourselves writing our way into those mysterious and serendipitous zones where we find ourselves working as our strongest and most invincible Superpoet selves at a particular moment in time—that harmonious confluence of creative and formal elements that balance surprise/discovery/freshness with expertise/experience/confidence.

This exercise is meant to address what happens when these zones become static and harden into mere (re)production, the repetitive performance of an established Author Function—a complex nexus of elements that has been commonly and somewhat reductively referred to as Writer's Block. Can we attempt to face our Kryptonite and learn new/different superpowers so that we can discover ways of writing ourselves into a new—and different—zone?

Phase I. Own Your Superpower/ Acknowledge Your Kryptonite

Although initially playful in its approach, these questions can yield serious reflections/insights on your origins, strengths, proclivities, biases, and habits as a poet. Begin by thinking about each of these questions and writing down your responses:

1. What is your Poetry Superpower? Has this always been your Poetry Superpower or has it changed over time? This superpower can, of course, be an element of craft and technique, but it might also revolve around certain aesthetic approaches, or it might have something to do with your choices in thematic content, or it might be tied in with your writerly processes.

2. How did you acquire this Poetry Superpower, or when did you initially become aware of it? Was it purely instinctual, in that you were genetically hard-wired or predisposed to exercise this superpower, or was it perhaps mystically gifted to you?

3. At any point were you shown how to use or develop this superpower by a mentor or by being introduced to the works of a writer you particularly admire? Did you consciously acquire this superpower through deliberate practice, training, and hard work, or did you discover it accidentally in a dangerous experiment involving radioactivity?

4. Are there ways in which you actively nurture, develop, or hone your Poetry Superpower? If so, how? If not, how might you actively nurture, develop, or hone your Poetry Superpower?

5. Do you ever use your superpower as a crutch? Or use it when you don't really need to? When, how, and why?

6. Do you have a Poetry Superpower that you have been either consciously or unconsciously avoiding or hiding from? What is it? And why do you think you have been avoiding/hiding from it?

7. What is your place of Poetry Kryptonite? In other words, in what places/ways do you feel helpless, stymied, powerless, vulnerable, or weak as a poet? Once again, this place of Poetry Kryptonite can simply be an element of craft and technique, but it might also revolve around certain aesthetic approaches, or it might have something to do with your choices in thematic content, or it might be tied in with your writerly processes.

8. Why do you feel this is your place of Kryptonite?

9. If you had to write a poem out of your place of Poetry Kryptonite, what might this poem look like, or how might it manifest?

Phase II. Developing an Immunity to Kryptonite

As a poet, how can you go about actively developing resistance or building up immunity to your Poetry Kryptonite? Make a concrete list of potential strategies. For example, your list might include, but would certainly not be limited to, some or more of the following:

1. Write a poem in which, like Wonder Woman, you're being held hostage in bondage (as seems to happen with startling frequency for Wonder Woman)—your Writerly Superpowers neutralized, and your Lasso of Truth, your Bracelets of Victory, your Royal Tiara, and Magical Sword confiscated. In other words, write a poem in which you consciously eschew your own particular set(s) of Writerly Superpowers and are forced to rely upon and actively cultivate an alternate array of skill sets.

2. Write a poem in which you are forced to don a disguise and enter a foreign aesthetic enclave toward which you feel, at minimum, highly ambivalent, if not downright antagonistic, as a secret double agent. Imagine, for example, that you are the Phoenix Force masquerading as Jean Gray, among the X-Men. Your success at this mission—and your ability to gather quality information—relies upon your ability to identify, learn, understand, and internalize the admired practitioners, artistic values, formal structures, and cultural capital of this alternate aesthetic universe.

3. Write a poem in which you abandon your typical palette of themes, tropes, obsessions, etc. and instead allow your evil doppelgänger (think Jean Gray's Phoenix, or Whedonverse's Dark Willow) to rise and topple your poetic universe. I'd like to suggest avoiding the sim-

ple binaries of "good" vs. "evil" (although, depending on what sort of poet you are, that could potentially yield interesting developments as well). Instead, focus more on the complexities of exploring your inverse poetic self—i.e., writing as the poetic doppelgänger who is a photonegative image of your "default" writing self.

4. Along similar lines, imagine that you have slipped through a wormhole into an alternate Bizarro universe in which your usual/typical writing practices, your relied-upon creative processes, no longer hold true and have been rendered completely ineffective, so that you're forced to cultivate a different set of writing habits/processes.

For example, do you, like Sylvia Plath, write "dawn poems in blood" while the children are still asleep? What happens if, instead, you write a midnight poem in hot milk and honey? Alternately, do you, like Elizabeth Bishop, write in the middle of the night in the grip of an asthma attack? What would happen if you were to write in the middle of the afternoon without the bronchodilator? Do you word-process your poems? What would happen if you drafted a poem in a typewriter store, as did Frank O'Hara? Do you religiously write on yellow legal pads with a #2 pencil? Try text messaging a poem to yourself from your smartphone into your Twitter account.

Procedure

I. Select strategies—from either of the preceding lists—that either jump out at you as particularly intriguing/engaging challenges, or that make you feel particularly uncomfortable.

II. Write your way through these strategies and see what happens. Do you find you have new superpowers—or potential superpowers—that you're interested in cultivating/exploring further? Or perhaps you've discovered new ways of employing your existing superpowers? Or having temporarily removed your existing superpowers, do you understand them differently/better, such that you're not going to take your existing superpowers for granted any longer?

An Example

I remember being taken aback a number of years ago, when the editor of a well-respected literary journal turned down some of my new poems from what eventually became my third book—vehemently urging me to go back to writing the types of poems which had made up a substantial portion of my second book. I was okay with the fact that he didn't care for the new poems, but what really bothered me was the authoritative and heavy-handed suggestion that I needed to replicate the same poem/concept/approach/theme from a prior (and very different) book project—a poem/concept/approach/theme that I'd thoroughly played out by that time and from which I had nothing more to learn. It was the notion of *should* that I really took umbrage to. And I realized that I didn't want to waste my life as a poet writing the poems that someone else thought I should be writing. And I think that's when I started to seriously consider some of the issues/concerns framed here in this discussion of Poetry Superpowers vs. Poetry Kryptonite.

Lately, I've also been thinking a lot about vulnerability, which is both caused by Kryptonite and also a form of Kryptonite. But vulnerability can be a superpower, too, I think. As a person—but also as a poet—I find it very difficult to be vulnerable. It feels crippling; it triggers an entire host of ornate defense mechanisms. It has occurred to me that I avoid feeling vulnerable within a poem—even while creating the illusion of invulnerability/openness—through the ornate defense mechanisms of virtuoso imagery and tour-de-force metaphor. "Look at this shiny thing, or become mesmerized by the hypnotic veronica of this gorgeous spiral," my poems sometimes say, while I quietly and sneakily try to slip in the vulnerable bits under the radar. Poem as painstakingly decorated mask. Poem as ornately wrought shield.

In developing an immunity toward this particular form of Kryptonite, I've been exploring poems about the Fukushima disaster (also a vulnerability, a wound), through the trope of a comics-inspired supervillainess and alter ego, Tsunamigeddon. Like Magneto, Tsunamigeddon (yes, still a mask of sorts, a shield) is a super-villainess created through trauma, much in the way that the tsunami is created through fault-lines and their subsequent earthquakes in the ocean floor. These poems explore aspects of personal and cultural trauma, aspects of the radioactive and the monstrous, as well as the taboo nature of female rage. These poems were written quickly (not my usual modus operandi); they are much more jagged/fractured in their execution, and much less reliant on imagery than some of my other work.

At the moment of this writing, these are my poems of Kryptonite.

origin of tsunami

a cracked moon smithereened
on the porch room floor

broken mayonnaise jar's vinegary
infection fault-lining the basement

fractals of shattered wood
striking her into subjectivity

mothballed kimono's too-tight obi
binding her into compliance

picture frame that frames her
guilty accomplice in disguise / face
effaced behind a ko-omote mask

doll she shames / tortures in the attic
(hates its cracked helplessness)
(hates its broken imperfection)

afterwards she feels sick
hides in the closet and cries

barbed wire that interns her

the shoes that pinch
the jeans that ride
the bra that chafes

gunpoint that coolly splays
and pins her into place

chloroformed lepidoptera / dangly carrot on a stick

the silver bar behind which lies
the perpetually withheld pellet

a hoop of flame licked / by a flickering whip

boy in a drunken rage
who smashes her face:
pulped lips / black eyes
her hair in his fist
head slammed hard
on the hardwood floor

(afterwards he sets her best dress
on fire with his cigarette lighter)

vise clench of the hole / she's supposed to fill

the tiny hostage crawlspace
into which she must try
to contain her shrilled edges
those monstrous feelings
her needy needs / shut the fuck up
sandbag them back
keep it all from vomiting out

landslide of gag rules shoved down her throat:

don't tell don't tell
don't rock the boat
shhhh / shhhh
don't make any waves

~ *Lee Ann Roripaugh*

Lee Ann Roripaugh is the author of four poetry collections: *Dandarians* (Milkweed Editions, 2014), *On the Cusp of a Dangerous Year* (Southern Illinois University Press, 2009), *Year of the Snake* (Southern Illinois University Press, 2004), and *Beyond Heart Mountain* (Penguin, 1999). Roripaugh is currently a Professor of English at the University of South Dakota, where she serves as Director of Creative Writing and Editor-in-Chief of *South Dakota Review.*

Chapter III:
The Role of Repurposing

Immature poets imitate; mature poets steal;
bad poets deface what they take, and good
poets make it into something better, or at
least something different.

~ *T. S. Eliot*

Inside/Outside

When I started teaching poetry, I was surprised that I was supposed to give my students exercises. I had expected to give them a reading list for discussion, not help them generate poems. My own pedagogical commitment was to help my students realize the vision they had for their work; I quickly realized they needed help developing that vision before they would be able to work toward it. Still, my students mostly needed to read more poems. Their work revealed a limited sense of what a poem could do. I wanted them to be immersed in the poetic tradition, and they wanted to be writing poems. I find that this exercise satisfies my concern for students' literary education as well as my students' desire to be practicing poets.

Note: I initially developed this exercise in conversation with Ada Limón when she was teaching at Columbia University. (See Limón's exercise "The Echo: Same-Language Translation," page 121.)

Rationale

This exercise has a number of positive outcomes.

- Students encounter a broad range of poetic styles, approaches, and forms.
- Students begin to think in terms of structure, style and form, rather than just content.
- Students develop a shared archive and a sense of community.
- Students see how reading can inform their writing practice.
- Students see the importance of understanding literary history.

Materials

You will need a set of 10–15 poems drawn from a variety of sources. The American Academy of Poets has a wonderful PDF set online for Poem in Your Pocket Day, each poem on a half page. I include a diversity of styles, forms, time periods, and authors. I also include poems that I adore as well as poems that I don't really like (though I concede their historical importance). My own archive is a little light on the avant-garde, so I draw heavily from Jerome Rothenberg and Pierre Joris's *Poems for the Millennium*.

It is important that you develop your own arsenal of poems based on your own aesthetics and the particular needs of your students; however, here are a few poems I find particularly useful:

- Amiri Baraka's "Wise 1" from "Why's/Wise" (in *Poems for the Millennium*). This poem addresses the legacy of slavery with a cleverness that borders on flippancy, and we can talk about how the poem forcefully makes a complex argument in a compressed space through sound play and by capturing the sounds of speech.

- Anthony Hecht's "The Book of Yolek" (from *The Transparent Man*). This poem about a boy murdered by the Nazis often intrigues students, particularly those who are Jewish or have recently had a modern history class. The students rarely notice that it is a sestina, and it gives me an opening to discuss the formal constraints at work. You can also discuss the way the story is told and how the process of remembering can be used in a poem.

- Stephen Dobyns's "Tomatoes" (From Myers and Weingarten's *New American Poets of the '90s*). This poem intrigues students with its swerving storytelling and its absurdist approach to violence and love. The students find it both horrifying and hysterical, and we talk about the element of tonal juxtapositions at work. Also, the method of storytelling is quite surprising; we can examine the method itself—and how a poet might approach a narrative from an unexpected point of entry.

- Anything by Gertrude Stein. I like passages from "Lifting Belly." We usually focus on the playful approach to syntax and language, although the class is often split between those who see it as playful and those who see it as annoying and garbled. I might mention the coded eroticism depending on the class dynamics, and it can be interesting when that coded eroticism becomes a requirement in a student poem.

Procedure

I. Give the students the packets of poems, and have them start reading.

II. As the fastest readers reach the midway point of their packets, tell the students, "I want you to select one poem that makes you feel like an insider, and one poem that makes you feel like an outsider." You can explain this request further, although I find that the insider/outsider labels usually make sense to students.

Each student identifies an inside poem and an outside poem.

III. Instruct students to list three elements of the poem that give them this sense of being inside or outside. Only one of these elements may be content; if a poem is about cancer or slavery or the Holocaust, for example, the subject itself accounts for no more than one item on the list. Students usually need some help in thinking beyond content. Here, I often suggest elements such as "tone of voice," "humorous approach to serious topic," "very short sentences," "line breaks that cut across expected syntax," "a story that suddenly turns dark in its telling," or "very simple words to convey a very complex idea." The idea is to help them focus on structure and voice.

IV. Go around the room and have each student share which poems she or he chose, and what elements they listed. It's great to compare as you go, showing how the same poem may have made one student feel like an insider, and another student feel like an outsider. It is particularly useful when two students choose the same poem, but have completely different elements.

V. Have the students write a poem that incorporates the elements they listed for their insider poem—in class or as homework.

VI. Have the students write a poem that incorporates the elements they listed for their outsider poem—also in class or as homework.

VII. When you discuss or workshop these poems, be sure to have students focus on what it was like to incorporate the elements they chose, especially the elements from the outside poems.

Variations

This is a time-consuming exercise, and I find it especially useful for students who will be together for a while. It works well on the first day of a writing workshop, when you have three hours and no student work to discuss yet. It sets in motion the first set of poems to workshop, while building a shared vocabulary and helping students focus on aesthetics rather than content.

To reduce the amount of time the exercise takes, you can:

- Use a smaller packet of poems, or only give two poems.
- Have half of the students choose an inside poem and have the other half choose an outside poem.
- Let the students choose either the inside or outside poem, but not both.
- Ask the students to find an inside and outside poem on their own as homework, and start the exercise with step III.
- Have students work in groups. You will have fewer poems to discuss, and group writing can be an enjoyable way to build community. According to current research, students work well in pairs or in groups of five.

- Focus on a particular aesthetic. Or use poems from a single writer—a useful approach if a writer will be giving a reading to your students—displaying the variations in a writer's work. You might also wish to use poems from one movement or time period.

Tips

Include poems that will confuse or frustrate students; resist your urge to defend or explain the poems when complaints arise. Depending on the level of students, I recommend Tristan Tzara, John Ashbery, or Stéphane Mallarmé as a way to ensure howls of complaint. Still, once students make a list of elements, they have to write poems using traits such as "looks like it makes sense at first, but really doesn't" or "crosses out words." In the process, they'll discover that these poems offer a set of tools that can be quite exciting.

Students often write parodies of the poems they dislike; these can have their classmates howling with laughter. They adore parodies and congratulate each other on their wit and sophistication. I usually ask, "If someone had joined the class today, would they get the joke?" When they say no, I ask if the poem they disliked in the first place might also have been a response to something else. I show them how they have developed a sense of literary history, and by engaging it, they have created a community with new values they could not have anticipated. One of the things I particularly like about this exercise is that students engage and inhabit styles that they initially find idiotic.

An Example

For the poem that follows, Veronica Castrillón worked from these three elements she identified in Emily Dickinson's "I measure every Grief I meet" (561).

1. Sound-scaffolding.
2. The dash as rhetorical device; the way it enacts the process of thinking, what Pinsky called "the mind's steps"; the turning, screwing, and tightening of a thought.
3. Setting.

Hard Bright Strung

And this godlessness is not—

By my own admission, more than anything,
I am a condition of un-.
And I want, like you,

to throttle my own throat, to strangle
its lawlessness.
But I know it is not just,
not only a lawlessness. If I asked you for forgiveness,
if I asked you—no.
That would be, somehow, the launch of a lie.
So I'll ask for nothing,
and trust that a truer asking
might be heard in the repetition of
the imperative; how that very repetition will illume the glorious
   dark hues
of need underneath:
Forgive me. Forgive me. Forgive me.
Like anyone else, my un- comes
with strings, but on those strings I myself
have strummed,
and from that music I learned the lush, hushed timbre
of *please*.
And yes,
maybe I have rhapsodized only to then blaspheme,
but because, as with anyone else, loss
has had its way with me.
So whether or not my godless a kind of Godful,
my *mine*—full of for,
with and in.
Not less this hard bright beautiful thing.

~ *Veronica Castrillón*

Jason Schneiderman is the author of *Striking Surface,* winner of the 2009 Rich-
ard Snyder Prize from Ashland Poetry Press, and *Sublimation Point* (Four Way
Books, 2004), a Stahlecker Selection. His poetry and essays have appeared in
numerous journals and anthologies, including *American Poetry Review, The Best
American Poetry, The Penguin Book of the Sonnet, Story Quarterly,* and *Tin House.*
Schneiderman has received fellowships from Yaddo, The Fine Arts Work Center,
and The Bread Loaf Writers' Conference. The 2004 recipient of the Emily Dick-
inson Award from the Poetry Society of America, he is an Assistant Professor
at the Borough of Manhattan Community College, City University of New York.

Pablo Miguel Martínez

Jump-Start that Poem-Making Project: A Repurposing & Caulking Exercise

In her collection of essays, *Proofs & Theories*, poet Louise Glück reminds us that the collaboration of poetry—a beautiful, dynamic division of labor shared by poet and reader—is often prompted by the left-open spaces. Just as the eye fills in what is missing in works of art such as the Venus de Milo and the Nike of Samothrace, so too the reader's mind fills in the spaces where things are left unsaid by the poet, Glück argues.

This exercise was inspired by an unlikely pairing: the Louise Glück essays mentioned above and several HGTV programs that encourage viewers to repurpose found or soon-to-be-discarded household items and refashion them into repurposed things of beauty. The secret to success with these projects, HGTV designers tell us, is to identify articles that have "good bones," things we are eager to preserve through this reworking.

Procedure

I. Take a line from a "good bones" poem, ideally, one by a poet whose work you cherish. Select a line that bristles with vitality, e.g., one driven by a vivid image or wondrous music, one with a hard-working verb.

II. Re-imagine the key word(s) in the line so that a verb in the original line—e.g., *shield, veil, screen*—is transformed into a noun (*shield, veil, screen*) in your repurposed line. Or vice versa.

III. Use the repurposed line to jump-start your own poem.

Examples

I. I chose the opening line of Kimiko Hahn's "On Fidelity" from her collection *Toxic Flora:*

> Australian magpie-larks that couple and clasp

Repurposed, the verb *clasp* becomes part of the compound noun *clasp-pin*, and the line serves as the beginning of a narrative memory poem:

> The Australian topaz clasp-pin, a lark—
> extravagantly-throated souvenir:

when she was young, Abuela sailed
to an island where yellow brilliance
was abundant and cut and clear.

II. Similarly, by transforming *blades* from a noun to a verb, I honor and repurpose Lisa Russ Spaar's line from "Mourning" (*Blue Venus*):

this window where green blades

I use the transformed line to create a new vision:

Green blades through the gray
of insomnia, just as Spring
scythes unsparingly, leveling
the dull of winter dreams,
leaving fields of budding news.

III. Or take the first line of Lynda Hull's "Love Song during Riot with Many Voices" (*Star Ledger*):

The bridge's iron mesh chases pockets of shadow

After some initial repurposing, changing *pockets* from a noun to a verb, my version reads:

The shadows I pocket
seep through shirt and jacket.
Even folded memories stain. Dad
chases me long past
his earthly commission,
cables from a sad frequency:
"Take care with those
bridges you're building."

Summing Up

As you draft your poem, continue reading, especially those poems that insist we fill in where things are left unsaid by the poet.

I. Here is the trochaic opening line of Clarence Major's "Heartland Music" (*Configurations*, 1998):

Crickets cranking shifting gears

Now let those cranky crickets provide the music for your own poem.

II. If you find your poetry gears are still sticking, here's a sampling of lines:

"the scar on her knee winking / with the evening chill"
   from "Summit Beach 1921" by Rita Dove (*Grace Notes*)

"Three vultures walk the ground clumsily / and hunch their wings"
   from "The Intelligence of Scavengers" by Martín Espada
   (*Alabanza: New and Selected Poems 1982–2002*)

"He rose on the surface of it like the layer of water on top of a wave"
   from "Pain" by Marie Howe (*What the Living Do*)

"I am like a man at twilight—bereft"
   from "A Cicada Sings to Me" by Luis Omar Salinas (*Elegy for Desire*)

"a crowd of echoes cries circling"
   from "Landscape" by David Wevill (*Solo with Grazing Deer*)

There are many fine places to start!

Pablo Miguel Martínez won the 2013 PEN Southwest Book Award in Poetry for his debut collection, *Brazos, Carry Me* (Kórima). His poems have appeared in *Americas Review, Borderlands, Comstock Review, Harpur Palate, Gay and Lesbian Review, Inkwell, New Millennium Writings*, and other journals. He has been anthologized in *This Assignment Is So Gay, Best Gay Poetry 2008, Poetic Voices without Borders 2*, and *Queer Codex: Chile Love*. Martínez has been a recipient of the Robert L.B. Tobin Award for Artistic Excellence, the Oscar Wilde Award, and the Chicano/Latino Literary Prize. He has received support from the Alfredo Cisneros del Moral Foundation and the Artist Foundation of San Antonio. A co-founder of CantoMundo, a national retreat-workshop for Latina/o poets, Martínez has participated in Sandra Cisneros' Macondo Writers' Workshop. He teaches English at the University of Louisville.

The Echo:
Same-Language Translation

Have you ever found yourself writing the same poem with the same tone and perhaps even the same tired, humdrum images over and over for weeks or even months? I have. Once, in a particularly muggy New York August, I wrote the same poem for thirty-one days. At least that's what it felt like. This pattern continued until I broke the spell by picking up a book of poems that I loved and figuring out how I would translate them into my own voice.

Not only did this exercise get me out of my ugly writing rut, it also helped me to home in on what was unique and weird about my own voice. But perhaps the most important thing this "echo" exercise taught me is how to really live in someone else's poem.

While I think of this as a writing exercise, it is in fact, first and foremost, deep reading practice. In workshops I teach and in my own writing routine, this exercise is somehow both thrilling and terrifying. When they say that the best way to write is to read, they are correct. But you also have to allow yourself to echo back the work. Give yourself permission to become the dark where the sound goes and toss that sound back into the air with your own strange voice.

Procedure

I. Find a poem to translate into your own voice. It doesn't have to be terribly different from your own work, but I find that if a voice interests me or feels as if it might be a stretch, the exercise becomes all that more exciting.

II. Absorb every part of the poem. Take in the title; take in each line—sounds, rhythm, and images. Live in the poem for a while. Buddy up to it at the bar. Get to know it. Does the poem use punctuation? If so, how? Where is the poem set? Does it give you a sense of safety, a sense of anxiety? What's the emotional life of the poem? Does it feel like it's generous or stark? Who is this poem, anyway?

III. Write your own translation of the poem. Think, "If this were *my* poem and I could choose a different image, what would it be?" You're not saying that the original image is wrong, or that yours will be better, but yours will be yours.

An Example

The real trick of this translation task is to take your time. It's a slow dance, and it's with a new partner each time. In my example below, I chose a fairly short poem, and still I had to mull it over for a while before I could even begin.

Note: My same-language translation is on the facing page. You can compare the original and the new poem—line by line.

Original Poem

Harbor

> The ice machine in the hallway
> Hummed a medicated noise
> But we heard a song
> Checked into the hotel
> Left the lights off for the night
> Watched the TV in the room
> Across the street
> Through a window
> In another hotel
> And bore with discipline
> What we saw there—
>
> A mountain pine beetle found alive in oak
>
> ~ *Adam Clay*

It's a beautiful poem, and I felt a little overwhelmed by it. First, there's the pacing. Because of its short lines, it moves directly but carefully. I had to do the same. Then, there's the syntax. The nouns are concrete and unpretentious. Let's take one example, Clay's two lines: "The ice machine in the hallway / Hummed a medicated noise." The ice machine in the hallway is a simple start; it doesn't make you work too hard. That's all there is: the ice machine. But things start to unfold with the second line: "hummed a medicated noise."

I knew I had to start simple, with a rock hard image that was something everyone could see, but I also wanted to make the image my own, something . . . living: "The stray cat." It had to be in a place that was odd or strange, not the poet's familiar place. Clay's "in the hallway" became "in the next lawn." His "Hummed a medicated noise" is such a perfect line, but I wanted to capture its essence without copying it too much. "Hummed" became "howled" because of the vowel sound as well as the auditory component. Then—because *medicated* is such a strange word, an unexpected word, and Clay is personifying the ice machine—I had to do the same. Instead of making the machine human, I made the cat machine-like with the word *electric*.

Same-Language Translation

Route

The stray cat in the next lawn
Howled an electric yelp
But we felt a purr
Opened the front door
Sat in the dark dining room
Listened to traffic on the road
By the neighbor's house
Over the fence line
Where another house
Bounced back the sound
And we took heed of
What noise we heard—

A rush of waves cresting here where it's landlocked

~ Ada Limón

As you proceed, the dance gets easier, you can see what the poet's intention is, and you can feel your words moving in tandem.

Tips

When you're working with a poem that you love, do not be frustrated if your translation doesn't come out as strong as the original. The point is not to out-do the original; let's face it, that's very rarely going to happen. The point is to walk outside of yourself and shake things up a bit. Rearrange your go-to images, your go-to way of writing a poem, and follow someone else's lead. I think you'll find it both harder and more enjoyable than you expect, like using your knees to steer a car. Look, Ma, no hands!

In the work on the preceding page, Adam Clay's poem is just stunning and my translation, well, is not, but I loved having the opportunity to work on it because it opened up in ways that kept surprising me. His minimal punctuation, his amazing mirror-quality of images, the silence in the poem—these made me want to work harder on the craft of poetry, and I could see how it might energize my work. May it do the same for you.

Echo, echo, echo.

Ada Limón is the author of three collections of poetry: *Sharks in the Rivers* (Milkweed Editions, 2010), *This Big Fake World* (Pearl Editions, 2006) and *Lucky Wreck* (Autumn House Press, 2006). Recipient of fellowships from the Provincetown Fine Arts Work Center and the New York Foundation for the Arts, Limón won the Chicago Literary Award for Poetry. She was a judge for the 2013 National Book Award in Poetry and will join the 2014 faculty for the low-residency M.F.A.–Latin America for Queens University of Charlotte. Limón is currently finishing her first novel, a book of essays, and a fourth collection of poems. She works as a writer and lives in Kentucky and California.

An Exercise in Derangement

Syntax comes from the Greek *tassein*, meaning "to arrange soldiers." We create meaning in a poem, but how do we create the beauty of that meaning? Word selection and order are a poet's stock in trade; they are the *original questions* of poetry. "Should I use a noun? If so, should I modify it? Should my modifier precede or follow my noun? Does my modifier need modification itself? Maybe I should use a verb instead. . . ." The poet's work is a chemistry of emotional and intellectual effects, but these raw goods must be processed to take on a consumable form. This processing phase distinguishes the proficient poet; the poet who can mold language to suit her vision of the world is the poet of whom we say, "She has a voice." But what does such processing entail?

Rationale

I find great value in the practice of releasing words from their grammatical constraints, moving words out of their normal positions in the sentence. The deliberate loosening-up of the typical function of words and word order can lead to new possibilities of meaning and beauty in language. Resisting, degrading, reducing, or minimizing syntax can be valuable generative practice.

This practice might be said to represent a violence on the poem in question, an unfair disturbance on the world of the poem's syntax, but I prefer to imagine deformations of this kind as ways to read and learn from a poem. My deformative practice involves a global, word-by-word inversion of a poem or an excerpt from a poem.

Inversion reveals, first, a number of idiosyncrasies in the English language. The first is the primacy of the relationship between the various types of modifiers (articles, possessive nouns, and adjectives) and their subjects. Articles shape their nouns very specifically, as Heather McHugh argues in her essay "A Genuine Article." "'A' is anchored in the unfamiliar," McHugh says. "'The' is anchored in the known. . . ."

Jerome McGann sees such deformative practices as critical tools: "Moving backward through a poem," he says, "we expose its reciprocal inertias in performative and often startling ways." But—it is important to remember as we perform—we also generate. The practice of word-by-word inversion generates hierarchical displacements that force us to rethink the power of each word. And nothing shakes a poem's plans looser than a shift in power. If we rid the poem of its plan, we are forced to invent a new plan, our own.

Procedure

I. Select a poem from which to begin the derangement. Laurie Ann Guerrero recently gave me permission to use one of her poems.

Original Poem

Babies Under the Skin

You come shy and unsure,
and we are strangers

but for the needing of each other.
I celebrate your births in water and wind.

Fish-mouths, rooting, even in death,
swallowing mouthfuls of air. Lipskin

papery, pink, wet, reaching to grasp
a nipple, a kiss. Your musty, meek fingers

reach for my hair—babies yearning
for mother muscle; my milk lets

at the thought of you. I stay living—
got to nourish the ones I can touch.

~ Laurie Ann Guerrero

II. Copy the poem, last word of the last line, second to last word, and so on, word by word, line by line—in reverse—until you get to the poem's first word.

With Guerrero's poem, for example, here's the first line of my transcription: "touch can I ones the nourish to got." While this is garbled English, it has potential for the poet who wishes to derange language.

III. Look at the poem in reverse as a new space; let go of the poem it once was. Now you can make the poem your own.

- Try to create new and strange phrases from the inversion. Use nouns as verbs and vice versa. The goal is to read the poem as a very rough draft that needs a translation. If the poem has a strong image system, consider how you could manage the reverse order of images.

- Any type of deformation in a poem can be generative, including switching the order of stanzas, lines, or sentences. Let yourself experiment.

An Example

By comparing my poem (below) with Guerrero's poem (preceding page)—word by word, line by line, in opposite directions—you can see how a deranged version of someone else's lines can become a poem in its own right.

Derangement

The Under Babies

Touch of nourish, turn us
living. Stay the thought of

milk as muscle, as mother to
yearning babies. To my fingers,

meek and musty, your kiss is a nipple,
a grasp to reach the wet pink and papery

lipskin air of mouthfuls swallowing
death in even the most rooting of mouths.

Fish, wind, and water birthed you, so I celebrate us
and also the other, each the need for

the strangers we are and for when
unsure and shy you come.

~ *Carmen Giménez Smith*

Carmen Giménez Smith is a 2013 National Book Critics Circle Award finalist for *Milk and Filth* (University of Arizona Press). The author of a memoir, *Bring Down the Little Birds* (University of Arizona Press, 2010), Giménez Smith has three prior poetry collections—*Goodbye, Flicker; The City She Was;* and *Odalisque in Pieces.* She is the recipient of a 2011 American Book Award, the 2011 Juniper Prize for Poetry, and a 2011–12 fellowship in creative nonfiction from the Howard Foundation. Formerly a Teaching-Writing Fellow at the Iowa Writers' Workshop, Giménez Smith currently teaches in the creative writing program at New Mexico State University while serving as Editor-in-Chief of the literary journal *Puerto del Sol* and as the publisher of Noemi Press.

Least Significant Object:
The Importance of Point of View

Acommon objective of **ekphrastic responses**—writing about art, regardless of medium—is to train the mind to write from a different point of view. Possibilities include the point of view of a participant in the work of art—perhaps someone of another gender—or even of an object in the picture.

In this exercise, the poet chooses the least significant object in a work of art and writes from this item's point of view. Within the poem the poet must define the item's role and importance in the larger scheme of the scene. In other words: why is the chosen object there?

This type of thinking helps break the tunnel vision that occurs in poems that describe scenes or events. Often, a poet will center on a single person or activity and leave out the granular texture of the picture, though this very texture might add immeasurably to the poem. One way of thinking says that each object has a path and purpose; another says that things happen randomly with no order to the universe. This exercise assumes that things are where they are for a reason, that each object has a role in a work of art or it wouldn't be there.

Procedure

I. The instructor will provide a selection of photos or paintings. Consider including these favorites of mine:

- *The Fall of Icarus,* a painting by Breughel, which inspired "Le Musée de Beaux Arts" by W. H. Auden. The way Breughel illustrates Icarus as a tiny figure in the corner of the painting actually ends up bringing ironic power to the story—and the painting.

- Just about any photograph by Edward S. Curtis of Native American people—writing from the point of view of a horse, an item of clothing, a warbonnet, the very chair an individual sat in to pose, etc.

- *The Syndics of the Clothmakers' Guild* by Rembrandt. What is the book they are reading? Why does one man not have a hat? What is the man on the right holding?

- *The Raft of the Medusa* by Géricault—a very busy classic painting with lots of smaller items to observe.

II. The participants have twenty minutes to write. No more than fifty lines. The poem can be in first or third person, although first person is preferred. At the end of twenty minutes the participant should be prepared to:

- Share the photo chosen for inspiration.
- Read the resulting poem.
- Describe the least significant object and how it affected the point of view.
- Defend the object's role in the artwork.

An Example

Cactus and a Beetle by Karla K. Morton

Destination

I do not see his Virgil here,
climbing backward up this green terrain.
And there are no small, miserable sinners
impaled on their own misery.
Perhaps this is not about overturned theology at all.
This might be how bugs view the world:
a flat geography, one surface after another—
It is all the same to them. There are no lessons
other than maneuvering around yucca, cholla,
and fleshy nodes.
I am not omniscient here. But neither
do I interfere. He has his steps
and I have mine and they have led
me here to watch. Is he watching me in turn,
deciding if he will have to navigate
around my boat-like foot?
Even the smallest leg has faith.
His journey might not end
when he climbs up to solid ground,
or mine when I detour around
this succulent.
We step. We step again
forward into our geography,
held confident and secure
by the great spatulate hand of God.

~ *Alan Birkelbach*

For a biography of **Alan Birkelbach,** see page 4.

Renegades, We Run

Since 2003, in conjunction with Urban Word NYC, we have team-taught at Bellevue Hospital's Adolescent Psychiatric Ward, leading workshops focusing on poetry and performance. Using Tim Seibles' poem "Renegades," we have developed a surefire approach to opening students to poetry. We have used the poem to teach poets of all ages and levels outside of the hospital setting as well. (See Seibles' exercise "The PoJack," page 149.)

At first we thought this poem would elicit from young poets a list of sensory details, but we found that our students were also inspired by the poem's themes, which center on race, class, and spirituality. Seibles' well-crafted poem perfectly demonstrates why each line in a poem needs to be perfect. It reminds us of what philosopher Frantz Fanon wrote about the tempo of racism: "Racism has not managed to harden. It has to renew itself. It has to change its appearance. It has to undergo the fate of the cultural whole that informed it."

Renegades

Dark until day
day into dusk
like elk
we run

We run like tumbleweeds
like water skeeters

Bright into late
Close until far
we run like
salmon   like radios
like kangaroos
we run

Day into dim
dim until dark
we run

like wolf spiders
like hammerhead sharks

We run like crickets

like moose
like hermit crabs
we run

Dark into dawn
dawnintodusk
we run like like

like tadpoles like
condors like
bacteria
we run

People say, "What?"
We run

People say, "But, but . . ."
We run

People say,
"Stoprunningoddammit!"

We run like fever
like smoke in a big wind
we run

Our knees pumping high and charged
as the round butts
of hard-bumping lovers
We run

moon into midnight
mist into fog
Carolina into California
We run
like witches like centipedes like
just-about's and maybe's
we run

past McDonald's
past the Chevy Dealer
past the synagogue
we run

Black into white
big into small
bad-ass into buffalo

Read us our rights
We run
like electricity
like frost like jazz clarinet

We run like honey
like blood and milk
We run like
We run like

Chameleons

Do into don't
Dabintosmack
Wouldacouldashoulda
we run

Wolf into woodchuck
Skin into sky

People say, "What?"
We run
People say "Huh?"
We run
People say, "Canyou   gettajob
doingthat?"

We run like meals
on wheels like spermatozoa
like shook-up soda

Hit into miss
Road into ditch
Shy into kiss

Like locomotives
like sandpipers
like termites
we run

We run like nobody's watching
We run like nothing's wrong
We run like jackhammers

We run like
We run like

We run like legs on legs
like flying saucers
Hold out your hand
we run

like a kid's nose on a cold night
Bring out the Koran

We run like a tongue up a thigh
naked as sunlight

Like a tattletale to the telephone
we run

You say, "Wait a minute."
We run

You say, *"Stopinthenameofthelaw!"*
We run

You say "Jesus IS Lord!!!"

We run
like a good sweat
like xylophones

like fleas chasing cheetahs
like swordfish
like watercolors
We run like elk
We

~Tim Seibles

Discussion

After reading the poem aloud but before any writing begins, discuss the following questions with students to get them in the mindset of the exercise:

1. Who (or what) is the "We" in "Renegades"? Are they a couple? A tribe? How do we form groups? What groups do you belong to?

2. What is the meaning of the term renegade?

3. What are things that "run" in "Renegades"? Do xylophones "run"? What liquids are in the poem? What are things that "run"?

4. Unpack the characteristics of the animals' differences/similarities. How does that imagery contribute to the tone of the poem?

5. Based on the poem, what is the age of this poet? Is he writing about a specific time in history? Could a woman have written this poem?

6. "Renegades" uses places, animals, instruments, and bits of dialogue. Which do you remember and why?

7. What are some of the places in the poem? What is significant about Carolina to California?

8. Find points of criticism. Who is criticizing whom?

9. Do you find the poem hopeful? If not, how would you characterize the narrator's tone?

Depending on the academic experience of our students, discussion can be vigorous, providing emotional stimulation for the writing to come.

Procedure

I. Brainstorming encourages all students to contribute as part of the group experience. Ask for a volunteer to list suggestions on the board: 1.) List groups or tribes. 2.) List things that run. 3.) List fierce and fast animals, real or mythic.

Using the brainstorming lists, choose one group/tribe and include at least three or more things/animals from the other two prompts.

II. Choose a real location—a specific street corner, for example. Imagine a crime, something forbidden that you commit with a friend, a lover, or a gang. Do you elope, hijack a car, rob a bank? Do you *witness* an explosion or some other violent act? Perhaps you're a vigilante on the run or Batman or Jean Valjean in *Les Misérables* or some other literary or historical figure on the run.

III. Start your poem with *We run* or *We run like*. Go from there. What do you see, hear, smell? This is an exercise in repetition and emotion; feel free to use rhyme, alliteration, rhythm—as Tim Seibles does—even onomatopoeia.

IV. After a few minutes of writing, we say: "You have superhuman speed. What cities and land masses do you pass? What do you hear? How do you feel?" These questions allow for new directions in the poem.

V. Finally, after a few more minutes, we say, "You are running so fast you can go through time, historical periods, events before dinosaurs, into the future. What do you see, hear, taste, brush past that's different from the present?"

Note: Although we emphasize using the prompts, we also remain open to writing that moves out on its own juice. We encourage a student-centered approach to our workshops.

An Example

> When the night's desire hangs
> like a slaughtered animal
> off of our skeletons
>
> We run
>
> wild
>
> like the feral tongues of two strangers
> tripping across the door jambs
> of each other's mouths
>
> We run like leaky faucets
>
> We run like ceaseless forbidden
>
> like all the wrong keys pushing
> into vacant locks, whispering,
> "break me open, break me open
> here, take everything I have"

We run on time catastrophes
like clockwork and then

your teeth are running out of your mouth
in that dream you keep having

and your nana's stroke smile is running right off
the foundation of her face

and your grandfather's fish out of water heart
is running right out of his goldfish bowl chest

and your father's love is running right out of your veins

and your mother's love is running right back into your cage

We run red lights and stop signs

We run like dead end streets
like dried river beds
like idling engines
like train wrecks

like the wind whistling through the night,
"everything is fine, everything is fine"

Like distracted playwrights
we run lines into the ground
like we are not, ourselves, reckless weeds
attempting escape out of a garden
sewn by domesticity

Envious of the trellis's view,
we run like clothes lines,
fishing lines, fault lines,
fate lines, love lines, life lines

trap lines

right back to the slaughtered animal of the night,
We run like:

here take this the loop of wire
caught snug around the wild beast's leg—

why do we name this wild after we have captured it?

Watch it begin to panic,
jerking, trying to escape

Watch it start to give up,
settle into complacency

Watch it begin to starve.

Will it chew off its own leg?
Is it strong enough to deny a part of itself,
just to be able to run again?

We have loved like we have run,
like the running of barely moving
borders across our bodies,

which is to say,
we have not gnawed off pieces
of ourselves to leave

which is to say,
we are barely running

~ *Mary Pinkoski*

Regie Cabico won the Nuyorican Poets Café Grand Slam and has appeared on NPR's *Snap Judgment* and HBO's *Def Poetry Jam.* He received The Writers for Writers Award from *Poets & Writers* and Barnes & Noble for his work at Bellevue Hospital. He co-edited *Flicker & Spark: A Contemporary Queer Anthology of Spoken Word and Poetry* (Lowbrow Press, 2013). A resident of Washington, DC, Cabico performs and teaches throughout North America and The United Kingdom.

Tina Jacobson has taught teenagers at Columbia University's advanced teen program as well as a variety of workshops through the high-octane after-school program Urban Word NYC, on whose board she currently sits. Under the auspices of Urban Word, she is the director of the writing program for the Adolescent Unit of Bellevue Hospital, a program she co-created with Regie Cabico in 2003. Jacobson is currently working on a memoir, *Chekov's Barn.* She and Cabico are recounting their years together in a teaching anthology they plan to publish in the near future.

Creating an Improvised Poetic Chorus

In my experience as a workshop participant, collaborative writing exercises create opportunities to work outside my comfortable habits and to experiment with alternative ways of making and seeing that help me learn about my own poetic processes when I'm back at my desk alone. Many of my beginning writing students are attached to their early drafts; they are reluctant about revision, unsure of how to approach it. I like to harness the collaborative energies, the wisdom of the group, in helping students re-vision their work.

The M.F.A. program I attended at the University of California–Riverside, included play-writing and screen-writing. The theater department invited M.F.A. students to submit plays for undergraduate directors and actors to stage as readings and performances—as a way for all to improve on their craft. As a poet whose work incorporates theatrical elements in the tradition of the choreopoem, I took advantage of this opportunity to see multiple poem-plays interpreted by directors and actors in early stages of development.

This process of re-interpretation involved seeing how directors and actors worked together to develop blocking and stage directions, fleshing out words and white space with their bodies. Seeing the choices they made in delivery and performance helped me see other possibilities for the words I put on the page. Their questions also pushed me to become more precise about what I wanted these words to perform in the world when I was not present.

This type of work laid the foundation for performance scripts I developed for my poems—often with multiple voices, sometimes as collage, sometimes as mash-ups, sometimes with audience participation, but always with the idea that, once released for performance, a script was subject to change and improvisation. I typically used boldface and italics in multiple fonts to differentiate voices and made use of white space to lay out phrases on the page. I learned by scripting varying numbers of performers, as well as variations in path and direction. As for directions, I often told my performers which voice they were to inhabit, but also that I was open to improvisation and multiple directions in a script—horizontal, vertical, or a mixture.

I also learned from other poet-performers who orchestrated scripts out of their texts. I witnessed Sharon Bridgforth conducting her performers and sought out opportunities to work with her. I was accepted into her Theatrical Jazz Institute at Links Hall in Chicago and was introduced to others who incorporated varied improvisations into their work, among them Daniel Alexander Jones, Helga Davis, Baraka de Soleil, and Lenelle Moise. Bridgforth introduced me to Lawrence D. "Butch" Morris and the chorus of poets that he conducted. Others introduced me to the Fluxus movement performances.

I developed this particular exercise as a way to encourage students to try out some of the techniques that have been helpful to my own process in revision and to consider multiple interpretations of their own work.

Preparation

I. Ask students to bring a page of their writing they would like to revise. If possible, have students bring their laptops or do this exercise in a space with computers available. If so, students are to bring a page of keyboarded writing, including the electronic file.

II. A mentor of mine, Juan Felipe Herrera, said that poetry is dance/movement, sculpture/the visual, music/song, and text/word all enacting simultaneously. I find it helpful to look at example poems, to discuss these elements and how they are engaged (or not) in the poems. Beforehand, you can assign these elements to student groups; each group can find poems that demonstrate the assigned element and bring them to class or workshop for discussion.

Poems I like to discuss include the following:

- "Doña Josefina Counsels Doña Concepción Before Entering Sears" by Maurice Kilwein Guevara—from *Poems of the River Spirit*. A video from the Poetry Foundation is readily available online.
- "A Natural History of My Disasters [Abridged]" by Yona Harvey—from the Natural Histories Project on the *Owls* blog
- "Arbor for Butch" by Terrance Hayes—from *Lighthead*
- excerpts from *The Vertical Interrogation of Strangers* by Bhanu Kapil
- "Swimchant for Nigger Mer-folk: (an aquaboogie set in lapis)" by Douglas Kearney—from *The Black Automaton*
- "Fast-Talking PI" by Selina Tusitala Marsh—from *Fast-Talking PI*
- excerpts from *from unincorporated territory [hacha]* by Craig Santos Perez
- excerpts from *Zong!* by M. NourbeSe Phillips
- excerpts from *and then entwine* by Jai Arun Ravine

III. Because this process is often outside my students' experience of poetry, it helps to show them examples of their predecessors' work. Videos of Sharon Bridgforth's work are readily available online, as are videos of Butch Morris conducting his Chorus of Poets. I recommend "Remembering Butch Morris, The Man Who Conducted Improvisation," from National Public Radio.

Procedure

Divide students into groups of no more than five. In the style of Morris or Bridgforth, each group will create a five-minute performance score based on a peer's page of writing. The score will include stage directions that can be easily understood by another group of students, who will perform the script.

I. Choose a page of writing by a member of another group. Read it aloud at least twice. Experiment with two different ways of reading (e.g., popcorn-style, where anybody in the group can read a line when he/she feels moved to; or taking turns, a member at a time, a line at a time) so that you can hear how words, lines, and other elements shift with changes in the reading.

II. For both readers and listeners, try to answer the following questions:

1. What is the artist's obsession or intention?
2. What is the style?
3. What emotions do the various readings evoke? What are similarities? What are differences?
4. Which lines really pop out to you?
5. Is there one line that you think is the heart of the piece?
6. How does this piece engage: dance or movement? sculpture or the visual? music or song? text or word?

III. Develop an interpretation/performance blueprint of the poem which highlights what the strengths of the piece might be. Then, develop goals for your performance score and notate your performance score with directions for your performers to follow. Consider the following questions:

1. What kinds of performance cues do you want to give to the performers and how can you represent them? Provide at least five. Examples could include volume level (soft, medium, loud); speed (slow, brisk, staccato); emotion/tone (angry, excited, happy, etc).
2. How many voices do you want? How will you represent them on the page? Are there lines you want to be spoken by more than one person? Do you want to make use of your audience? Consider using boldface, italics, and changes in font—with a key to what each indicates.

3. Do you want to retain the order of the original, or will you change it? Do you want to consider multiple ways to determine order? Setting text in columns, for example, can allow horizontal, vertical, or simultaneous readings.

4. How will the performers be conducted? Do you want to choose one person from your group to conduct the performance? Do you want to write up directions for performers to follow, or will you encourage some improvisation by having them self-direct?

Note: I do not recommend significantly re-writing someone else's piece. However, for the sake of the exercise, it is okay for the group to focus on a section of the writing they think is strongest or most engaging.

IV. Each group will choose another group to perform its score. The author of the original piece should not be among the performers so that she/he can observe. After the performance, all involved—original author, script writers and performers, audience members—will record their observations:

Original Writer: What surprises did you discover in the performance? Were there features of the performance that you especially admired? Features you did not like? How could you revise the piece with these new insights?

Script Writers: Did the performance meet the goals of your script? If you were to revise the performance score, what changes might you make?

Audience Members: How did the performance engage: dance or movement? sculpture or the visual? music or song? text or word?

V. The author of the original piece will compose an alternate draft that considers some of the insights received through the performance. If desired, this alternate draft could be her/his own performance score for the piece.

An Example

I wrote and choreographed all the original poetry text for the following script, which was performed December 18, 2012, at Woodland Pattern Poetry Center in Milwaukee, Wisconsin. It was created in the tradition of the Theatrical Jazz aesthetic, valuing simultaneous truths and experiences, improvisation, and the spirit/knowledge/creativity of what's in the room. To learn more, check out Sharon Bridgforth's *Experiments in a Jazz Aesthetic: Art, Activism, Academia, and the Austin Project* (University of Texas Press, 2010).

Following the Theatrical Jazz aesthetic, the piece is meant to "mutate" according to who and what else is "in the room." For this particular version of the performance, we proceeded in three stages:

1. A solo performance of the poem, with music for keyboard composed by Jessica Vega Gonzalez. Sung by Jessica Vega Gonzalez.
2. The first variation: a choral performance of rearranged lines from the original poem, with the audience reading assigned lines.
3. The second variation: a choral performance of rearranged lines from the original poem—by two featured readers and audience members.

Note: The stages of the performance were announced throughout by screens projected onto the wall facing the audience.

Part I: The Solo Performance

| **Emergency Mutations** |
[opening screen]

| music composed and performed by Jessica Vega Gonzalez text written by Ching-In Chen |
[2nd opening screen]

The answer is heat.
Because you know this night full of fish, this last night-milk—
  Roast two potatoes, taunt the bottle fly with sugar and glass.
Because last night, because the cloth cut,
  To clamp, silt, retreat, the surface of fantasy, turn from the face
    in front of you

  *

Organs have their own intelligence, she says.
What information is the body trying to gift you?

  *

I cannot sustain reading. I cannot make or break things. My skin
  sticks to my ribs, the ribs jump
through to the next condensed glass.

let's sit here these hours
our breath swimming
our story sand-stained
here here here
the heat breaks

here here here
the heat breaks

The answer is heat.

    ***

I am surprised at what the body
replies. Flare, rash,
gut. Sometimes you do not

know what you are, lizard river,
raspy pond.
The answer—a throat of moon
lighting up another
sky. You wonder

when she surfaces, who
she loves, who
she laughs. You wonder
if the body knows
how to construct
its granaries and wide fields
after the flash, all the branches.

fell down.

after the flash, all the branches.

fell down.

The desert also breeds
the living. The winter
also makes night.

The desert also breeds
the living. The winter
also makes night.

    ***

And what if the answers become monsters in your mouth
doors won't open into history   I don't know

much beyond what I can touch in the surface   Below,
the fish come again and I pretend not
to have vision, not
to have dream. The flatline
smooth under fingers.

A harmony which can't be sung
between teeth

***

The desert also breeds
the living. The winter
also makes night.

***

The answer is heat.

Note: At this point, the projected screen flashes the word *mutate* as a cue to the second stage of the performance, a choral rendition of rearranged lines from the original poem.

Part II: The First Choral Variation

Prior to the performance, volunteers distributed chorus instructions to the audience—included below. In addition, volunteers gave each audience member a line of text with a number on it. During the performance, text and visual art—incorporating numbers corresponding to lines of text—were projected onto the wall facing the audience. As conductor, I chose the speed and the intensity at which the projection would occur.

Instructions: There are several parts in the performance where you will be asked to perform the piece of text you have been given. Each text is numbered and you will be cued by numbers/visuals projected. When your number is projected, please perform your piece of text. As a conductor, I will observe the energy in the room and manipulate the speed of the projections. I may cue you to be louder or softer or to stop based on the energy in the room. For louder, I will turn my palms upward and raise them. For softer, I will turn my palms downward and lower them. For stop, I will use a flat-line gesture. Thank you for participating!

Note: Boldface numbers are projected as cues to audience members.

1 A harmony   A harmony

2 who she loves,   who she loves,   who she loves,

3 if the body knows
4 in the surface in the surface
5   Below, Below, Below,
6 what answer   what answer

10 Sometimes you do not know what you are

7 —a throat of moon makes night
8 after the flash, all the branches.

9 You wonder smooth under fingers sung

3 if the body knows
6 what answer   what answer

1 A harmony   A harmony
4 in the surface   in the surface

8 after the flash, all the branches.
10 Sometimes you do not know what you are

7 —a throat of moon makes night
9 You wonder smooth under fingers sung

10 Sometimes you do not know what you are

Note: At this point again, the projected screen flashes the word *mutate*—this time as a cue to another rearrangement of lines from the original poem, this time presented by two featured voices and audience members.

During the inaugural performance, Peggy Hong and Jessica Vega Gonzalez read the left hand column and the right hand column, respectively. I asked them to determine whether to read horizontally and/or vertically by listening to each other in the moment. They also determined whether to read simultaneously/in collision, or more coherently by waiting for one performer to finish before the next began. For this performance, they chose to read horizontally and more coherently. The audience was cued by the projected visual numbers where the numbers appear in the script.

Part III: The Second Choral Variation

Instructions: Dear audience, for this segment of the performance, please whisper your parts when cued by the projected numbers, repeating your lines until I ask you to stop or by listening to the room.

2 who she loves,
who she laughs.

6 The answer is heat.   8 You wonder
3 Because you know
       this night full of fish, this last night-milk   if the body knows
   Roast two potatoes, taunt
       the bottle fly with sugar and   how to construct
glass.   its granaries and wide fields
4 Because last night, because the cloth cut,   after the flash, all the branches.
5 To clamp, silt, retreat, the surface of fantasy,
    turn from the face in front of you   fell down.

      *   5 The desert also breeds
9 Organs have their own intelligence, she says.   the living. The winter
What information is the body trying to gift you?
                                                     also makes night.
      *   *

10 I cannot sustain reading. I cannot make or
    break things.
My skin sticks to my ribs,
     the ribs jump through to the next   3 what if the answers become
condensed glass.   monsters in
                                                     your mouth
7 let's sit here these hours   doors won't open into history
our breath swimming   6   I don't know
our story sand-stained   much beyond what I can touch
here here here   in the surface   Below,
the heat breaks   the fish come again and I

**

9 I am surprised at what the body
replies. Flare, rash,
gut. Sometimes you do not

10 know what you are, lizard river,
raspy pond.
6 The answer— a throat of moon
lighting up another
sky. You wonder

pretend not
to have vision, not
to have dream.
7 The flatline
smooth under fingers.

A harmony which can't be
1 sung
between teeth

when she surfaces,

Ching-In Chen is author of *The Heart's Traffic* (Red Hen Press, 2009) and co-editor of *The Revolution Starts at Home: Confronting Intimate Violence within Activist Communities* (South End Press, 2011). Chen is a Kundiman, Lambda, and Norman Mailer Poetry Fellow, as well as a member of the Voices of Our Nations Arts Foundation and Macondo writing communities. A community organizer, Chen has worked in the Asian American communities of San Francisco, Oakland, Riverside and Boston. In Milwaukee, Chen serves as Editor-in-Chief of *cream city review*.

The PoJack

This is an exercise I call The PoJack. It involves hijacking a poem for the purpose of studying and reworking the poem's inner operations. PoJacking also allows you to play with tone, image, sound, subject—virtually all the ingredients that help a poem do its work.

Materials

You will need a poem, preferably short. Generally, it is best to use shorter poems that can be seen and changed easily. Ultimately, though, this exercise can be used on poems of any length.

Here's a poem I made up for PoJacking:

Clarinet

The moon rises
like a child from her nap
and the dark sends a few stars.
Somewhere the sunshine
sounds its sleek clarinet.

The Set-Up

Before The PoJack, the poem must be appreciated as it is. It's useful to begin by discussing the sense the words appear to make. Consider:

- Is there a discernible subject?
- What is the tone of the poem?
- How do the images complement the tone?
- What do the line-breaks do for the reader?
- Are there any noticeable patterns of sound?
- Are the subject and the title the same thing here?
- How does the title work with the body of the poem?

Procedure

Now the PoJacking can begin. It seems best to start the process as a class with the poem on the blackboard or presented through a projector. Erase several words, so students see something that looks like this:

Clarinet

The   rises
like a   from her
and the dark a few stars.
Somewhere the
    its sleek clarinet.

Invite students to offer alternatives. This process immediately requires two things that can help someone become more comfortable with writing poetry:

1. It promotes playful invention with language.
2. It asserts the usefulness of revision.

Here is the result of one such PoJack:

Clarinet

The **man** rises
like a **wolf** from her **lair**
and the dark **buys** a few stars.
Somewhere the **moon**
chews its sleek clarinet.

From this point, the process can continue indefinitely until the text bears no resemblance to the original. Even the title can be changed. What happens, for example, if this poem is called "Zombie"? Students suddenly realize they've made a poem of their own with no fear of "doing it wrong." This is crucial to their development as poets. They've also been *revising*, but not thinking of it as a torturous process that requires them to reconsider their own hard-won poems. Additionally, as they discuss the original poem and the subsequent offshoots, they are becoming more fluent in the use of pertinent terminology.

Variations

After establishing the PoJack as a class endeavor, the exercise can be done individually, with each student taking his/her own approach to transforming the poem. Conceivably, the workshop leader could ask each student to re-do the original poem five times in five different ways, as Pilar White does in the five examples on the facing page. Follow up with a session of reading aloud, so the many possible variations can be shared while simultaneously building a deeper sense of community among the participants.

Examples

Beckoning

The sound rises
like a hiss from her lips
and the dark hides a few stars.
Somewhere the lover
tunes his sleek clarinet.

Lover's Song

Desire rises
like a mist from her hips
and the dark grasps a few stars.
Somewhere the moonlight
records his smooth clarinet.

Nocturnal Lamentations

The sun rises
like steam from a kettle's spout
and heat envelops the clouds.
Somewhere the night
mourns the sweet clarinet.

Linger

Evening falls meekly,
as dew swaddles the grass,
and bids the morning adieu.
Somewhere the dusk watches
and haunts the clarinet.

Convergence

Fists rise
like stars contracting

and grabbing idle space.
Somewhere the galaxy
mutes the sonata of the clarinet.

~ *Pllar S. White*

Tim Seibles is the author of several poetry collections. His first, *Body Moves* (1988), was re-released in 2013 by Carnegie Mellon University Press as part of its Contemporary Classics series. His latest, *Fast Animal* (Etruscan Press),was one of five poetry finalists for the 2012 National Book Award. A National Endowment for the Arts fellow, Seibles has also enjoyed a seven-month writing fellowship from the Provincetown Fine Arts Work Center. His poetry is featured in several anthologies, among them *Rainbow Darkness; The Manthology; Autumn House Contemporary American Poetry; Black Nature;* and *Evensong.* His poetry has been included in *Best American Poetry 2010* and *Best American Poetry 2012.* He has been a workshop leader for Cave Canem and for the Hurston/Wright Foundation, another organization dedicated to developing black writers. Visiting faculty at the Stonecoast M.F.A. in Writing Program, Seibles is a member of the English and M.F.A. in writing faculty at Old Dominion University.

Chapter IV:
Structure & Form

. . . forms create an almost bodily pleasure
in the poet. What you're doing is trying to
discover. They are not restrictive. They pull
things out of you. They help you remember.

~ *Marie Ponsot*

Alfred Nicol

List Poems & Syllabics:
Discovery through Form

> The formal structure of a poem is not something distinct from its meaning but as intimately bound up with the latter as the body is with the soul.
>
> ~ W. H. Auden

Some poets are put off by the mention of *form* in poetry. The word is too closely linked with *formalism* and *formality*, neither of which jibe with their idea of what poetry should be. They question why anyone should care about form in poetry. That's why I quoted W. H. Auden. I thought I might appeal to an authority greater than my own. But you may not be convinced by Auden's lofty rhetoric. Maybe "the soul," too, is an antique notion that we can do without, that doesn't help us estimate the value of form in poetry.

Okay, then, I'll try another authoritative voice:

> The real ideas of a poem are not those that occur to the poet before he writes the poem, but rather those that appear in his work afterward, whether by design or by accident. Content stems from form, and not vice versa. Every form produces its own idea, its own vision of the world. Form has meaning; and, what is more, in the realm of art only form possesses meaning. The meaning of a poem does not lie in what the poet wanted to say, but in what the poem actually says.
>
> ~ Octavio Paz

That's a more practical rationale for thinking about form. Paz talks about what form *does*. It makes things happen. "Content stems from form. . . . Every form produces its own idea." The poem's meaning collects in its form like spring water in a basin. I hope you'll agree that's an exhilarating way of thinking about writing. It makes the act of writing an adventure. By picking up your pen or sitting at the computer to write, you are setting out to *discover* meaning. It's not there when you begin. It makes itself known to you as you work.

Here's a more offhand way of saying much the same thing:

> It is part of the delight in poetry, too, that there are formal problems; going at these relieves you of a certain pretentiousness connected with what you are supposed to be saying; you let it say itself, if only because you are so blessedly busy getting things to fit.
>
> ~ Howard Nemerov

Nemerov makes the same point that Paz made, but without appearing to take himself seriously. What he emphasizes is the freedom that comes from working in form. You end up playing a little game with language. And it is play, but like true child's play, it's very serious play. You lose yourself in it, and the poem says what it means to say while you're kicking the words around. I find this approach to writing so much more interesting than *working* at it. And the wonderful thing is that you're likely to get more work done when you allow yourself to *play*. Once you're immersed in it, you'll be like a kid, willing to play all day and right past suppertime.

The List Poem

You can experience how every form produces its own idea—and how that idea gets the game started—by trying out one of the most rudimentary of poetic forms, the list poem.

Here are three lines from a poem called "Lines for the Fortune Cookies" by Frank O'Hara:

> At times, your disinterestedness may seem insincere, to strangers.
>
> The next person to speak to you will have a very intriguing proposal
>> to make.
>
> Your walk has a musical quality which will bring you fame and fortune.

You can imagine how easy it would be to continue this poem. The form gives you the idea; you only need to run with it. And though there is an element of play involved in writing in form, the results need not be as light, as seemingly frivolous, as in O'Hara's poem.

Not long ago *The New Yorker* published a poem by Vijay Seshadri called "Memoir," in which he writes, "The real story of a life is the story of its humiliations"; he follows with a searing list of what has embarrassed him most in his life.

Walt Whitman often made use of the list poem ("I Sing the Body Electric"), as did Allen Ginsberg ("Footnote to Howl," "Kaddish IV").

from I Sing the Body Electric

> The sprawl and fulness of babes, the bosoms and heads of women,
>> the folds of their dress, their style as we pass in the street,
>> the contour of their shape downwards,
> The swimmer naked in the swimming-bath, seen as he swims
>> through the transparent green-shine, or lies with his face up
>> and rolls silently to and fro in the heave of the water,

The bending forward and backward of rowers in row-boats, the
      horseman in his saddle,
Girls, mothers, house-keepers, in all their performances,
The group of laborers seated at noon-time with their open dinner-
      kettles, and their wives waiting,
The female soothing a child, the farmer's daughter in the garden or
      cow-yard,
The young fellow hoeing corn, the sleigh-driver driving his six
      horses through the crowd,
The wrestle of wrestlers, two apprentice-boys, quite grown, lusty,
      good-natured, native-born, out on the vacant lot at sun-
      down, after work,
The coats and caps thrown down, the embrace of love and resis-
      tance,
The upper-hold and under-hold, the hair rumpled over and blinding
      the eyes;
The march of firemen in their own costumes, the play of masculine
      muscle through clean-setting trowsers and waist-straps,
The slow return from the fire, the pause when the bell strikes
      suddenly again, and the listening on the alert,
The natural, perfect, varied attitudes, the bent head, the curv'd neck
      and the counting;
Such-like I love—I loosen myself, pass freely, am at the mother's
      breast with the little child,
Swim with the swimmers, wrestle with wrestlers, march in line with
      the firemen, and pause, listen, count.

~ *Walt Whitman*

The power of even this least prescriptive of forms is evident in this ageless masterpiece of Hebrew literature:

Ecclesiastes 3:1-8

To every thing there is a season,
and a time to every purpose under the heaven:
A time to be born, and a time to die;
a time to plant, and a time to pluck up that which is planted;
A time to kill, and a time to heal;

a time to break down, and a time to build up;
A time to weep, and a time to laugh;
a time to mourn, and a time to dance;
A time to cast away stones, and a time to gather stones together;
a time to embrace, and a time to refrain from embracing;
A time to get, and a time to lose;
a time to keep, and a time to cast away;
A time to rend, and a time to sew;
a time to keep silence, and a time to speak;
A time to love, and a time to hate;
a time of war, and a time of peace.

Procedure

I. Recruit a partner to do this exercise with you. You'll see why below.

II. Make a list of possible topics for a list poem. O'Hara's poem is a riff on the sort of line you're likely to find in a fortune cookie. Seshadri lists the humiliations he's experienced. Walt Whitman's great poem "I Sing the Body Electric" is nothing but a list of images of the human body—at work, at play, at rest.

III. Choose one of your ideas and begin to write a list poem: 10 minutes.

IV. Stop! Hopefully I've caught you in mid-stride: you feel you could have kept going. Let's look again at the quotation from Paz: "The real ideas of a poem are not those that occur to the poet before he writes the poem, but rather those that appear in his work afterward, whether by design or by accident. Every form produces its own idea, its own vision of the world."

Let's think about that. A form produces its own idea. The form doesn't tell you what to say; it gives you an idea of the kinds of things you might say. That limitation is the important thing.

G. K. Chesterton wrote that "Art consists of limitation. The most beautiful part of every picture is the frame." The artist doesn't have to paint the whole world, only as much of it as will fit inside the frame. The frame is what makes the endeavor possible.

V. Here is where you let the game come to you. Trade poems with your partner. Your task is to continue your partner's list. Now you really can't bring to it any ideas you had beforehand. You'll have to play the hand you're dealt! My goal in having you switch poems is to throw you off the beaten path, force you to go somewhere you would not have gone otherwise. With any luck you'll stumble on a place you've never been before.

Follow-Up

Sometimes poets have the wrong idea about form; they think of it as a box they can't get out of, they think it's something that will hem them in. I think of form as a roadblock that forces me to take a different route.

In a *Paris Review* interview, Kay Ryan, a recent U.S. poet laureate, brought her usual witty insight to bear on this idea of being forced to go a different direction: "The problem for me was that I willed my poetry at first. I had too much control. But in time the benevolences of metaphor and rhyme sent me down their rabbit holes, in new directions, so that my will—my intention— was sent hither and yon. And in that mix of intention and diversion, I could get a tiny inkling of things far beyond me."

At first "I had too much control," she says. She had an idea of what she wanted to say, and she was trying to force it, rush it along where it was *supposed to go*. A poem can't be in a hurry to get somewhere. It has to take its time and find its own way.

Robert Frost was clear on this point. He wrote that a poem "is but a trick poem and no poem at all if the best of it was thought of first and saved for the last." That would put the poet too much in control, would make a boss of him. The poem shouldn't take direction from anyone. No, Frost tells us, the poem "finds its own name as it goes and discovers the best waiting for it in some final phrase at once wise and sad." And he adds, "No surprise for the writer, no surprise for the reader." Why write at all, if we already know how it turns out?

The Syllabic

The form we've played with, the List Poem, is about as relaxed a form as there is. It has only one rule: Make a list. It doesn't prescribe a certain line length; it doesn't say how long the poem should be; it doesn't have a rhyme scheme— just one easy rule. That won't do for really forcing you to get out of your own way, to get out of the poem's way. We need something stronger. (For a list poem with rules and limitations, see the Keith Ekiss exercise "The World Without Us: An Exercise in Apocalypse," page 56.)

Form in poetry is closely tied to the idea of measure. A given form may determine line length, how many lines, when and how often a phrase is repeated, things like that. Let's consider just one of those elements, line length. Here's a sweet little poem by Kenneth Rexroth:

Raccoon

The raccoon wears a black mask,
And he washes everything
Before he eats it. If you
Give him a cube of sugar,
He'll wash it away and weep.
Some of life's sweetest pleasures
Can be enjoyed only if
You don't mind a little dirt.
Here a false face won't help you.

~ *Kenneth Rexroth*

What kind of measure is at work in the lines of this poem? You don't need a ruler to see that the lines are not all of the same length. (A friend of mine in college would write her poems on grid-paper, with one letter in each box, as though she were filling out a federal form, leaving a box empty to indicate a space between words, so that each of her lines was exactly the same length to the eye! She later became an accomplished novelist. I wonder what eccentric formal strategies she uses in writing fiction.)

This poem uses another kind of measure. There are seven syllables in each of the lines. If you choose to follow that *rule,* that kind of *measure,* in writing a poem, then you're forced to think twice about anything you choose to say, because you have to make it fit. It slows you down, it makes you reconsider words that may be unnecessary, it forces you to make little changes of phrasing that may suggest new things to say that you hadn't thought of; most important, it engages another part of your mind, what David Rothman refers to as "the numerical imagination."

Rothman's essay, "Lisping in Numbers," like the quotation from Octavio Paz, makes a case for measure in poetry because of what measure is able to *do* for the poet and for the poem. He eloquently expresses a near-mystical quality that counting brings to poetic composition, quoting Roy Harris from *The Origin of Writing:*

> Counting is in its very essence magical, if any human practice at all is. For numbers are things no one has ever seen or heard or touched. Yet somehow they exist, and their existence can be confirmed in quite everyday terms by all kinds of humdrum procedures which allow mere mortals to agree beyond any shadow of doubt as to "how many" eggs there are in a basket or "how many" loaves of bread on the table.

Writing syllabic poetry can engage the numerical imagination, and the result can be a kind of magic. The finest poem I can think of that is written in syllabics is "Fern Hill" by Dylan Thomas. Clearly, in that poem not every line has the same number of syllables, but the first stanza establishes a syllabic pattern that the other stanzas follow. It is a great poem to read aloud. (For another approach to the syllabic poem, see Brent Goodman's exercise "The Incredible Shrinking Poem: Using Syllabics to Inspire & Surprise," page 164.)

Procedure

I want you to try your hand at writing a syllabic, but it wouldn't be fair to tell you just to "write a poem with seven syllables in each line." I think you might find yourself at a loss for words. A prescribed line length by itself doesn't give you an idea of the kind of things you might say, which is what poetic form ought to do.

Kenneth Rexroth wrote another poem, "A Letter to William Carlos Williams," which brings together the syllabic and the **epistle**. That is to say it's a letter-poem in which each line has seven syllables. Rexroth's poem is too long to include in this exercise, but here are the opening lines:

> When I search the past for you,
> Sometimes I think you are like
> St. Francis, whose flesh went out
> Like a happy cloud from him,
> And merged with every lover—

Let me show you another epistle poem. This one is not written in syllabics, but it shows how writing an epistle poem is unlike writing an ordinary letter in that the intended recipient may be someone who doesn't have an address at present.

For My Great-Great Grandson the Space Pioneer

> You, What's-your-name, who down the byways of my blood
> are hurtling toward the future, tell me if you've packed
> the thousand flavors of the wind, the river's voice,
> the tongues of moss and fern singing the earth.
>
> And where have you left the rain? Careful: don't lose it,
> nor the moan of the seagull in her blue desert,
> nor those stars warm as caresses
> you will not find again in your nights of steel.

Watch that you don't run short of butterflies;
learn the colors of the hours;
and here, in this little case of bones
I've left you the perfume of the sea.

~ *Rhina P. Espaillat*

I. Okay, here's the exercise, the form. Where Rexroth combined two forms in writing "A Letter to William Carlos Williams," we'll add a third into the mix. The poet Ted Berrigan wrote a series of *postcard poems*. What I'll ask you to do is write a syllabic letter-poem that will fit on a postcard. That's a rather flexible formal constraint: your handwriting may be big or small, you can leave lots of white space in the margins or crowd your lines right to the edge of the card.

II. Address the letter to anyone you like, a friend, a parent, a child, an author, a saint, a deity, anyone in the community of souls—the dead, the living, and the as-yet unborn—with whom you have a connection. You might even choose to address a fictional or mythic person, or an animal that is good with language! (For another approach to the letter-poem, see Melissa Kwasny's "The Lyric as Letter," page 201.)

Examples

Dear Bill,

Saw your stunning show, Armed Chairs,
explosive black marks, coal grays,
rough scribbles, feral zigzags—
drawings moving on the page:
lines like iron, straight and strong,
velvet shadows, gentle curves,
form defined by vivid light—
thanks for teaching me to see.

All Best Wishes, Priscilla

Above: "Postcard to Bill Flynn" by Priscilla Turner Spada.

Do you remember the bus
to Bhaktapur-- that tin can
on wheels with old, burned-out brakes?
How we laughed, packed in place with
burlap sacks of mustard seed
and plump chickens for market!
And the trip down the mountain
riding on the roof with boys'
in tattered clothing, watching
terraced rice fields hurtle past?
How alive we were back then.
If you receive this postcard,
grab your passport and a pack.
meet me at the bus station!

To: My travel companion
c/o G.P.O.
Katmandu, Nepal

Above: "c/o G.P.O." by Julie A. Williams.

Alfred Nicol won the first Anita Dorn Memorial Prize for his poetry collection *Elegy for Everyone* (Prospero's World Press, 2010). Nicol received the 2004 Richard Wilbur Award for his first collection, *Winter Light* (University of Evansville Press). His poems have appeared in *Poetry, Dark Horse, The Formalist, The Hopkins Review,* and other literary journals. His most recent publication is *Second Hand Second Mind,* a collaboration with his sister, artist Elise Nicol.

Brent Goodman

The Incredible Shrinking Poem: Using Syllabics to Inspire & Surprise

Drafting a new poem while employing poetic restraint in form, be it rhyme scheme, meter, or shape, ultimately renders our first thought questionable, our second thought a close call, and our third a beautiful surprise. Some forms, such as rhyme patterns, are up-front to the reader's eyes and ears. Others, such as syllabics, function more like DNA to the poem's body: invisible, yet integral to the mechanics of its overall movement and expression.

In this drafting and revision exercise, you'll explore how condensation invites inspiration, forcing you to climb higher as the walls appear to close in, vaulting your lyric voice farther and farther into the heavens. You will invent your own personal poetic form based on two variables: syllables per line, and number of lines per poem. These templates will become the building blocks of whole series of future drafts and revisions. And within these new forms, little hurdles will appear for you to leap over, and in your leaping, to catch air.

To demonstrate, I chose to write a draft that was twelve lines long and twelve syllables per line. Then, to illustrate how a methodical pruning can help focus a poem's strongest moments, I condensed the poem, pruning to a 10 x 10—ten lines, ten syllables each. One thing this exercise teaches is how to let go of the weakest language, how to really tighten up what a poem needs to say. That becomes clearer and clearer as you revise further, shrinking the poem to an 8 x 8, then finally a wallet-sized 6 x 6, a mere snapshot of the first draft.

Procedure

1. Write a poem that is exactly twelve lines long, twelve syllables per line. It can be about any subject, in any style, narrative or lyric, photographic, impressionistic, or surreal; your freedom reigns. You might even use a poem-generating exercise from elsewhere in this book as inspiration for your own 12 x 12 poem.

When your draft is complete—typically 15–20 minutes—share it with a group or class. If working alone, ask yourself these questions: What challenges did this form present? What breakthrough ideas did it inspire? How did writing a twelve-syllable line influence your sense of **enjambment** (a line break that comes in the middle of a phrase or clause)? What word choices did the form force you to make that you wouldn't have explored otherwise?

Here's mine:

The Trees Can't Keep the Snow Secret   (12 x 12)

The trees can't keep the snow secret for long: the sky
falls to pieces, and even the birds tucked between
branches know how to stoke the smallest fires there.
To frame a pine tree in your gaze is to cradle
a constellation of half-dreaming birds. To dream
about this is to create a forest falling
upwards into a white cloud, where the thought of snow
never believes in love the same way twice. Surely,
every time I breathe, the little trees inside me
breathe inside me too. The sky knows the earth opens
in certain places, when we find them, when we plunge
like lost rivers into mist beneath the landscape.

I wrote this poem in early April in Northern Wisconsin, where yet another snowfall was trying to cover the first signs of spring peeking through after an already long winter. While the beginning of the poem began simply by looking up from my monitor to watch the second story view of our birch and pine backyard, by line nine, I felt I had to stretch myself to keep extending the poem in order to reach the twelve-line limit. But in turn, and by happy surprise, I discovered I had wandered all the way to where distant rivers plunge "into mist beneath the landscape."

Note: Syllable count can vary by individual—and by region. Here, for example, I'm counting the word fires as two syllables (fye-uhrs). Many writers—and readers—hear it as a single syllable.

II. Now, write the same poem, but this time, it will be a 10 x 10—ten lines long, ten syllables per line. Feel free to examine your previous version carefully, deciding what stays and what gets the cut. Strip out extraneous articles. Yank out any weeds. Put your adjectives on a diet. Get to the point.

When this draft is complete—typically 15–20 minutes—share and discuss it with a group/partner or examine the poem on your own. Notice how lines begin to migrate, the way ideas flow differently through the poem as the formal structure shrinks.

Here's mine:

The Trees Can't Keep the Snow Secret   (10 x 10)

The trees can't keep the snow secret: the sky
falls to pieces, even birds tucked between
branches stoke the smallest fires there. Frame
a pine tree in your gaze. To dream about
this is to create a forest falling
upwards into white cloud, where snow never
believes in love the same way twice. Surely,
every time I breathe, the little trees breathe
inside me too. Sky knows the earth opens
into rivers, mist beneath the landscape.

For me, this draft felt like upgrading the magnification power of my binoculars, everything growing more focused, sharper, the scene increasingly cropped. What disappears in this poem continues to flow beneath the landscape.

III. Now, write the same poem, but this time, it will be an 8 x 8—only eight lines long, eight syllables per line. Again, feel free to examine your previous versions, deciding what stays and what gets the cut. You're at the point now where you will need to make some seriously playful decisions. This poem cannot be the same poem as it was before; there is no room. What heart of the previous draft simply must continue beating? What new blossoms must bloom?

When your draft is complete—typically 15–20 minutes—share and discuss with a group/partner or examine the poem on your own. Explore what you've learned about where the poem wants to flow, through the very act of letting go.

Here's my third shrinking draft:

The Trees Can't Keep the Snow Secret   (8 x 8)

Trees can't keep snow secret: the sky
in pieces, even birds between
branches stoke the smallest fires.
To dream about this is to dream
a forest falling into a
white cloud, where snow never believes
in love the same way twice. Surely,
little trees breathe inside me too.

I love this draft for where it now ends: with the little trees back inside me. And how every time this poem shrinks into itself, the meaning of what it is to dream becomes something slightly stranger.

IV. Finally, write the same poem, but this time, it will be a 6 x 6—only six lines long, six syllables per line. Don't even try to remember the first draft, that pastoral. You are trimming a bonsai tree now with miniature clippers. Keep a steady hand and remember to breathe.

When your draft is complete—typically 15–20 minutes—share and discuss with a group/partner or examine the poem on your own. Hard for the final 6 x 6 pruning not to start feeling Zen and mysterious.

Again, here's mine:

The Trees Can't Keep the Snow Secret   (6 x 6)

Even the birds between
branches stoke the smallest
fires. To dream about
this is to never dream
about love the same way
twice. Little trees breathe too.

When I read this poem, I feel that I'm cupping a cloud inside a sparrow's heart, that the world only needs a few birds, a recurring dream, and the breath of tiny trees. And we could call this home.

Variations

- Compile shrinking drafts into a poem in stages. I decided to keep all four drafts above under the single title "The Trees Can't Keep the Snow Secret: Four Variations." Read aloud, the repetition of familiar images across gently changing syntax becomes hypnotic, obsessive, and dream-laden.

- Revive a stuck draft. Poem going nowhere? Turn the next draft into a syllabic poem with a shorter line count than the existing version and a smaller syllable count than the average line in the existing draft.

For example, if the stuck poem is twenty-five lines long with an average line length of thirteen syllables, make the next draft twenty lines long with exactly ten syllables per line. The fixed form will force you to make the revision choices you were hesitant to make before.

- Invent a form/create a series. Write a series of poems in a form you make up, determined by a set number of syllables per line, and lines per poem. Write ten or twenty poems; write a poem a day this way for a month!

- Build out a longer poem with varying syllabic stanzas. Invent a wire-frame form for a longer poem using a set syllabic count that varies between stanzas. The first stanza could be twelve syllables, the next six syllables, the next ten, etc. Keep each stanza the same number of lines, or vary that number as well. Use syllabics like varying scaffolds and see what grows from them!

Tips for Writing Syllabic Poems

- It's difficult to teach oneself slash-and-burn revision techniques, but assigning set syllable and line counts creates clear goals for pruning unwieldy poem drafts. (See also Alfred Nicol on syllabics, page 159.)

- Even though each line has a set syllable count, allow your lines to take shape on the reader's heart and tongue first. Avoid clunky line breaks unless you intend to create a clunky feeling. Balance all the reasons you'd write a perfect line along the invisible trellis of the syllable count.

- Allow every freedom to take flight. If one way to say something doesn't fit your syllable count, don't just try to say it in the correct number of syllables. Say something else entirely.

- Test your limits. Try to write poems of eighteen syllables per line as well as four syllables per line. Both stretch your muse muscle to the extreme.

- Learn to count syllables on one hand in the air like a pro. Go on YouTube and learn the American Sign Language (ASL) numeric system—or at least 1–20. You can sign the numbers for 1–100 with one hand! No more drumming desks or playing table piano!

Brent Goodman has taught poetry workshops at Purdue, the University of North Dakota, The Driftless Writing Center, and with the Dzanc Creative Writing Sessions. His books include *Far from Sudden* (Black Lawrence Press, 2013), featuring a syllabic sequence of "9 x 10" poems; *The Brother Swimming Beneath Me; Wrong Horoscope;* and *Trees Are the Slowest Rivers.* He lives and works in Rhinelander, Wisconsin, where he serves on the board of The Mill Paper & Book Arts Center and as a member of the Wisconsin Poet Laureate's Commission.

Writing the Bad Sonnet

As someone who has written hundreds of sonnets and has developed a huge appreciation for the form, I often teach writing the traditional sonnet in my workshops. When I do, students regularly tell me that they simply can't write a sonnet, that they can't write a poem that rhymes, that they can't write a poem that uses meter. Balderdash! What they usually mean is that they can't write a *good* sonnet that employs rhyme and meter—and *that* may initially be true. But they can write a bad sonnet; on that point they all agree. So I created the following exercise to help them write a bad sonnet, not only bad, exaggeratedly bad, the worst they possibly can.

Rationale

Of course, there's a method to this madness. By encouraging students to write a bad sonnet, they not only learn that they *can* write a sonnet, but they also learn quite a few tricks along the way—how to write in strict iambic pentameter that employs rhyme, how to use tone to their advantage in a poem, how to focus on the roles of metaphor, word choice, and syntax. I could stand there and tell them, for example, not to use convoluted syntax to force a rhyme at the end of the line. But when they actually create a tortured line themselves, they begin to understand what goes into writing a sonnet, good or bad.

The idea is that by learning how to write a bad sonnet students will be better prepared for their follow-up assignment, which is to write a good sonnet (or at least halfway decent!). And they have so much fun writing a bad sonnet that everyone is at ease—no pressure to prove anything and no fear of failure.

Preparation

As is evident from both *Wingbeats* and *Wingbeats II,* I am a strong believer in the use of examples or models as a teaching device. Before we begin the actual exercise, I show students a variety of sonnets, mostly Shakespearean. (Petrarchan sonnets employ fewer rhymes, making them a little trickier for beginning sonnet writers.) These examples are mostly traditional, too, since I think students need to know the traditions before they break away from them. Non-traditional sonnets by Rita Dove, Robert Pinsky, and C. K. Williams can—and do—come later.

Here are some of my favorite models:

- "Let's make a modern primer" from *33* by Julia Alvarez
- "The Cave" by Tony Barnstone
- "Contingencies" by Rhina P. Espaillat
- "Shakespearean Sonnet" by R. S. Gwynn
- "Anniversary" by Ted Kooser
- "Wedding" by Alice Oswald
- Sonnet 73 by William Shakespeare
- "The Egret Sonnet" by Scott Wiggerman

I almost always start with Gwynn's enjoyable sonnet because all fourteen lines of it are end-stopped, all of them are perfectly iambic, and all the rhymes are also perfect—making it an ideal choice as a starting point before moving into variations. Many students don't realize that each line in a traditional sonnet has ten syllables, five stressed, evenly spaced out (*daDA daDA daDA daDA daDA*), as in Gwynn's opening line: "A man is haunted by his father's ghost." The other sonnets listed here use enjambment and near rhyme, and most of them include some metrical variations, which is good for students to see—and *hear* (yes, read these aloud). I always include one of my own sonnets just to prove to students that if I can do it, they can too!

I also use the model poems to teach the structure of the traditional Shakespearean sonnet: three quatrains (rhyming *abab cdcd efef*) leading to a turn in argument or emotion (the volta) in the concluding couplet (*gg*). While the examples can overwhelm some students, I tell them that I'm not expecting any of them to write a good sonnet—not yet, anyway.

Procedure

I. On the board, write a truly bad line of iambic pentameter, which can come from your own mind or from a wretched poem. This will be the first line for all the students to begin their bad sonnets (or as Billy Collins' "Sonnet" proclaims, "All we need is fourteen lines, well, thirteen now"). Because it elicits a variety of responses, I often use the following line from Francis Saltus Saltus' poem "Posthumous Revenge" from the tacky volume, *Very Bad Poetry*:

> The one I loathed, my one malignant foe,

II. Divide students into groups of 2–3 to work on their sonnets together. Sharing helps those who don't quite have the rules down to learn from others, and it seems to bring out more hilarity. But all students should write down what the group composes. I usually provide a copy of my Iambic Pentameter Worksheet—provided on the following page—for those who find it helps them see and count syllables and stresses, with each line divided into five iambs, totaling ten syllables.

Their goal is to write a traditional **Shakespearean sonnet**—fourteen lines of iambic pentameter, three quatrains rhyming *abab cdcd efef,* a volta, and a concluding rhymed couplet (*gg*)—only to make it as bad as they can, using such features as:

- convoluted syntax
- extremely sentimental or lurid tone
- awkward or ridiculous rhymes
- overused alliteration or assonance
- archaic or absurd language
- excessive end-stopped lines
- laughable or trite metaphors

III. Allow about 45 minutes for students to write their bad sonnets. Expect lots of laughter, and encourage them to be over-the-top. You may have to close the door to the room because it can get quite loud, but that's the sound of learning. If there are tears in the room, they're tears from laughing so hard.

IV. When time is up, have groups read their sonnets aloud. After each sonnet, allow students to comment on the "bad" features incorporated in the lines.

V. Finally, give students their next assignment: take what they've learned about writing a bad sonnet, and try their hand at writing a good one (or at least a passable one) for the next class.

Examples

Here are two of the group sonnets that came from this particular exercise, where I actually made the initial line worse by changing it slightly to "The one I loathéd, my malignant one." Look at all the lines that include things such as convoluted syntax (e.g., "our nest did make"), lurid and sentimental tone (e.g., "My innocence besmirched in Papa's loft" and "love me true!"), ridiculous rhymes (e.g., Satan-toad/commode, pool/Tool), absurd, trite, and archaic language (e.g., "kaploosh," "greener pastures," "thou stolest"), laughable metaphors and similes (e.g., "Your eyes like Marfa lights cross and fade" and "Our love was oozing like a steaming brandy"). Remember, these sonnets were supposed to be bad; but notice how they've got the form down!

Iambic Pentameter Worksheet

Use the markers for unstressed (◡) and stressed (/) syllables to guide you as you write your sonnet:

						(rhyme)
◡	/	◡	/	◡	/	
1. ___ ___ ___ ___ ___ = 10						a
2. ___ ___ ___ ___ ___ = 10						b
3. ___ ___ ___ ___ ___ = 10						a
4. ___ ___ ___ ___ ___ = 10						b
5. ___ ___ ___ ___ ___ = 10						c
6. ___ ___ ___ ___ ___ = 10						d
7. ___ ___ ___ ___ ___ = 10						c
8. ___ ___ ___ ___ ___ = 10						d
9. ___ ___ ___ ___ ___ = 10						e
10. ___ ___ ___ ___ ___ = 10						f
11. ___ ___ ___ ___ ___ = 10						e
12. ___ ___ ___ ___ ___ = 10						f
13. ___ ___ ___ ___ ___ = 10						g
14. ___ ___ ___ ___ ___ = 10						g

140

Kaploosh

The one I loathéd, my malignant one
I hatest thou, O bloated Satan-toad.
Thou stolest my love and did me dirty wrong.
My fragile heart, kaploosh, down the commode.

You stomped my soul, you stole my horse and cash.
You shot my dog and hung him from a tree.
You told me lies. You're full of balderdash.
I should have guessed—you asked to see my knee!

Your legs, spaghetti, arms linguini-soft.
Your eyes like Marfa lights cross and fade.
My innocence besmirched in Papa's loft
the night you tricked me with your crude charade.

Betrayed, misused, yet still I dream of you,
and pray that someday you will love me true!

Bad Sonnet

The one I loathéd, my malignant one,
your mind dost wallow lower than a snake.
We started and our life had just begun
with hearts and flowers we our nest did make.

Gifts to me of jewels and chocolate candy.
Your lips that pump my ears with sweet nothings.
Our love was oozing like a steaming brandy.
For you I wore my raunchy sexy somethings.

Your cheating heart has torn our nest apart
while wading through your secretary pool.
That was bad enough but that was just the start:
you cashed in our 401 K, you Tool!

Henceforth I'm moving on to greener pastures.
You'll never hear from me again, you bastard!

Here are a couple of sonnets that were written after the bad ones and shared in class later in the week, a marked difference, to say the least.

Morning Trail

Above the mountains, bands of cirrus drift,
an archipelago backlit in tones
of rose and saffron. He hikes cobbly cliffs
in autumn's cold pre-dawn, sets out alone
propelled by hope of finding some renewal—
some splendor. Eagles gliding. Pastels
in spilling creeks. Firm shadows eased from view
by sunlight, jewel-like. Again, he tells
himself, be grateful for this glimpse; it's brief.
Be mindful, Nature heals—age-old wisdom.
But anger fouls his mood; old grievances
now sour him. His reverie is done.
He hears the granite rhythms of his heart
while following the trail back to the start.

~ Marilyn Westfall

Note from Marilyn Westfall: I admit to being one of those who added wretched vocabulary and sentiment to "Bad Sonnet." I don't know if others want to 'fess up or have their names attached to it. In my experience, the exercise helped to bring a random group together, with a range of writers—from the novice to the practiced. This wild exercise was a perfect icebreaker. Everyone could freely participate, let "freak flags fly," and not worry about decorum.

Little Traitors Everywhere

Blind eyes thrust down, I scanned the ground around
where tangled sticks and blackened branches fell
across my path in last night's storm. I found
fear tripping over forked twigs and half-shelled

hickory nuts or sunken holes that snag steps
and toss my fragile balance off; old bones
could break and leave me stranded there to beg
no one to help me limp my way back home.

What robbed the joy that came from trekking trails
to snuff clean scents of pine, drop gaze at hues
from lemon light through vines to brood-blue braille
of cedars pointing past white dogwoods' wounds?

I'd stepped around big logs that blocked my way,
but subtle, hidden, snake-like twigs betrayed.

~ *Charlotte Renk*

Note from Charlotte Renk, one of the contributors to "Kaploosh": Although I knew that sonnets followed formulas for rhyme and meter, I had avoided writing them because that form always felt stilted to me. Before this workshop, I didn't know how to create a more natural flow by creating mid-line stops (periods, semicolons, exclamations, etc.) and by enjambing end-lines, so that idea trumps form. By experimenting with these devices, I am able now to create a more natural flow in sonnets, and thus a more comfortable, effective sonnet. I won't avoid them anymore.

Scott Wiggerman is the author of two books of poetry, *Presence* and *Vegetables and Other Relationships,* and the editor of several volumes, including *Wingbeats: Exercises & Practice in Poetry* and *Lifting the Sky: Southwestern Haiku & Haiga*, both from Dos Gatos Press. His poems have recently appeared in the anthologies *This Assignment Is So Gay; The Crafty Poet; Forgetting Home: Poems about Alzheimer's;* and *Between: New Gay Poetry.* Wiggerman's sonnets have twice been nominated for Pushcart Prizes. He is chief editor for Dos Gatos Press in Austin, Texas, publisher of the *Texas Poetry Calendar,* now in its seventeenth year.

Angela Alaimo O'Donnell

The Sonnet Sequence & the Three S's: Story, Symbol, & Song

In "Poetry & Survival," poet and critic Gregory Orr names the three essential elements that make for good poetry: narrative, symbol, and incantation. I begin every course I teach with Orr's powerful essay, as it introduces students—especially those new to poetry—to the idea that there are clearly identifiable ways in which poetry works. It satisfies our hunger for story; it presents familiar objects from the workaday world in an unfamiliar light, charging them with new meaning; it does so in language that sings. For the sake of ease—and to provide my students with a mnemonic device—I call these elements Story, Symbol, and Song—The Three S's—and we use that shorthand for the remainder of the semester as we discuss the poems we read and write.

One might use any number of methods to encourage students to write poems that offer a satisfying combination of The Three S's, but the one that I have found to be the most challenging and rewarding, for both students and teacher, is to assign a sonnet sequence.

Rationale

Story: The sonnet offers students a compact space—fourteen lines, to be exact—within which to tell a story, leaving little room for explanation and elaboration, for unnecessary words (coordinating conjunctions, subordinators, adverbs, prepositional phrases), and for non-essential details. Every word must serve some deliberate function (which can include making music, as well as story-telling). This kind of brevity requires discipline; students must learn to make choices that writing in open form does not require.

In addition, the sonnet offers structure. Students learn to use the form as scaffolding for their story. With an Italian sonnet, apprentice poets discover the natural break that occurs around the eighth line as they realize that there are only six lines left for the conclusion. In writing a Shakespearean sonnet, poets find the three quatrains to be building blocks that allow them to "stack" events and then to summarize the invisible connections between the quatrains in the concluding couplet.

Symbol: The sonnet offers abundant limitation, requiring poets to load ordinary words and things with meaning. In the process of writing these compact stories, poets find it is easier to show than to tell. There is just no time or space to explain. Instead of exposition, they find themselves resorting to symbols— to images, to sensory impressions, and to concrete particulars—rather than abstractions. This process allows symbols to do some of the speaking.

Song: The sonnet is rooted in music. The Italian word *sonetto* means "little song." The strict rules of the form require writers to engage the sonic aspects of language—rhyme and meter—and provide a structure within which poets might amplify this music through alliteration, assonance, consonance, and other devices. There is both freedom and constriction here. Poets must focus on the sounds of words, as well as their meaning; this kind of attention leads them to lines and phrases they would never conceive without the restrictions. The desire to make music, then, often leads to delightful discoveries as poets unexpectedly find language to "say the unsayable."

The Sonnet Sequence

Writing an individual sonnet confines the poet to a necessarily limited terrain. There is only so much that can be said, and a good sonnet will take advantage of this focus and (seeming) narrowness of vision. The beauty of the sonnet sequence is that it allows the writer to exercise the skills discussed above and to open up the form's possibilities with a more expansive vision. In a fourteen-sonnet sequence, the poet tells not one story but fourteen, each of which stands alone yet also participates in the larger narrative arc of the sequence.

The benefits of this exercise are multiple, but I might mention a few:

- Practice makes perfect. The more sonnets apprentice poets write, the better they get at writing them. The first sonnet is almost always a humbling experience. But as the project goes forward, a teacher can actually see students' confidence increase as they learn to master the form.

- Writing fourteen sonnets takes pressure off apprentice writers. Not compelled to say everything in one sonnet, with multiple opportunities to shed light on the subject, student poets can focus more intently on each poem. In addition, after having written a number of sonnets, they find that the poems call and harken to one another in interesting ways, creating a unity and trajectory that is unconscious as well as deliberate.

- Since the subject of the sonnet sequence in my assignment is identity, poets have an unprecedented opportunity to explore key aspects of their being. Each poem invites entry into the mystery of the human personality, leading writers deeper into the darkness of the unknowable and the unknown. This work requires courage from both students and teacher. It also requires trust, leading to an extraordinary intimacy between poets and their readers—including the instructor and the other students in the class. In my experience, there is no better way to create community in a writing or literature course than to have one's students write sonnet sequences and to have them share them in a workshop.

Preparation

Since many of the students I teach have never read an entire sonnet sequence before, it's essential to provide them with a model. Daniel Tobin's book *The Narrows* contains a sequence that is autobiographical, contemporary, and—since it is set in Brooklyn—pleasingly local for my New York City students. Titled "Bay Ridge" (the name of the neighborhood where Tobin grew up), the sequence has fourteen poems, each focusing on a moment in the poet's childhood and young adulthood. The poems are full of pop culture references, historical events, and specific people and places. Tobin evokes not only the world of his childhood, but also the feel of it. While all of the poems observe the formal strictures of the sonnet, some do so loosely, using slant rhyme and the rhythms of conversation rather than strict iambic pentameter.

Tobin's poems provide apprentice poets with a world of possibility for their own sequence—in both content and form. Students can take their cue from his poems, substituting the particulars of their own childhood for his, or the poems can serve as inspiration, enabling them to imagine possibilities that are not in Tobin's. In addition, the ease with which he manages the form gives apprentice poets permission to play with the conventions of the Italian and Shakespearean sonnet. They do not have to adhere rigidly to those structures in order to create a satisfying "little song" or a powerful sequence of songs.

The first three poems reprinted here are the first three in Tobin's sonnet sequence. The fourth is the final one in the sequence. These poems provide a good sense of the lost world Tobin re-creates, as well as a glimpse of the sequence's narrative arc. They are both local and literary, the work of a poet who comes from humble origins but who has acquired much learning and experience since those childhood days. Thus, Tobin embodies in his poems at least two selves: the child he once was and the grown man he has gradually become.

Note: I also encourage students to read sonnets by other poets to get a feel for the form. Shakespeare's sonnets are readily available online, as are sonnets by John Donne, Gerard Manley Hopkins, Edna St. Vincent Millay, Robert Frost, and many others.

Prelude: The Narrows

"That's Dave Brown's house—do you remember?"
I feel the thin weight of my father's hand
on my arm, slow the car to Seventy-Ninth
and Shore where the two-story brick still stands,
though my father's friend is long since gone.
In his basement he kept guns, grenades,
his hat from the Spanish-American War,
the prize of a baseball signed by Babe Ruth.
All that afternoon we sat on his porch
and watched ferries churn across the harbor,
the Bridge rising slowly over the Narrows
at the round earth's imagined corners
where the Hudson opens into Gravesend.
Father, you asked if I remembered. I do.

The Avenue

French fries, burgers, baba, tabbouleh—
Smells that whir through the exhaust fan of Sally's,
acrid *mélange*, the blades furred with grease,
then across the Avenue where Frances Guariglia
walks with my mother, as she does each week,
past The Hutch and Sal's Salumeria,
to Frank and Albert's Beauty Salon
while my father tends bar at The Legion:

Though if it's Sunday we're off to Mass,
the scent of Danish from Lund's Bakery
tempting us as if it were the bread of life.
Even now, midway, I look back and see
the picture of a road aglow with signs—
Woods' Butcher's, Century's, Circles, Rose Glass.

A Scar

A crash that hammered through jet-black night
woke us to cries, our own, the fraught calls

of startled parents running down the hall.
Father, fumbling, flicked open the light.
So we found ourselves somehow still intact
under sheets smattered with ceiling debris
while our mother hugged us tight below the rift,
soothing us, even with her whiskey breath.

Now, on holidays, when we make it home
to strained hellos, petering talk—dull ache
of what has never healed—no one
wants to set the sky crashing, or wake
those two still asleep in quicksand beds,
the plastered-over scar stark above their heads.

Brown-Eyed Girl

Where did we go days when the rain came?
To Brody's, Skinflint's, Griswold's, Tun's,
Beard's, O'Sullivan's, every bar a station
on the March of the Wooden Leg. Just back
from college, we'd plan to make our way
the thirty blocks from Three Jolly Pigeons
to the Shore, a drink in each dive. No one
ever made it, stumbling into Howe's to hear
Jack Whitman belt out his covers of Van
and The Eagles, the crowd singing along
as they did each week. And me next to you,
so richly painted, tight blue jeans, the laugh
I loved—*Do you remember when?*—like an ad
for contentment. But I was already gone.

~ *Daniel Tobin*

Procedure

Phase I: Sonnet I

Approximately eight weeks before the end of the semester, I assign students
the first sonnet of the sequence, due two weeks later. I critique this sonnet and
make suggestions, then give students the opportunity to revise it, as well as to

work on subsequent sonnets. I should warn instructors who are considering this project that it can be labor intensive, involving multiple meetings with student writers seeking feedback on their work. On the other hand, these are among the most rewarding conversations one can have with one's students.

I. Write a sonnet about the experience of leaving or coming home. It may be about yourself or someone else. It may be about your literal home, a figurative home, or both—or even someone else's home. Remember this is only one poem in the larger sonnet sequence that describes, engages, and reflects on key moments in your life, the place(s) you call home, your family, and the ways in which these have contributed to your identity. Your approach to the question of identity may be oblique as well as direct, implicit as well as explicit. The rough model for your sonnet sequence is the "Bay Ridge" section of Daniel Tobin's autobiographical *The Narrows*.

II. Consider the following options for beginning your first sonnet:

- Focus on a particular event, a particular home-coming or home-leaving.

- Write the first line, and then see where the line takes you. As you grapple with the tension between saying what you want to say and trying to "stay within the lines" of the form, let the poem go in its own direction.

- Respond to what some of the writers we have read have said about home or the importance of The Local.

III. This sonnet—like the others in the sequence—must consist of fourteen lines, and each line should be approximately the same length (typically ten syllables). Like Tobin's, they may range between the formally tight and the formally loose. They may follow the form of the Shakespearean sonnet (three quatrains and a couplet) or the Italian sonnet (an octave and a sestet)—or you may invent another form of sonnet which you choose to follow.

The lines may rhyme, but they don't have to, and you need not develop a consistent rhyme. You may also consider using **slant rhyme** (or near rhyme) instead of true rhyme; for example, you could rhyme *broom* with *soon,* instead of *moon* and so on. However, if you would like to use rhyme, the typical pattern of end rhyme for a Shakespearean sonnet is *abab cdcd efef gg* and for an Italian sonnet, *abbaabba cdecde.* (For practice in writing a traditional Shakespearean sonnet, see Scott Wiggerman's exercise "Writing the Bad Sonnet," page 169.)

Phase II: Sonnets 2–14

I. Adapt the instructions, strategies and advice for Sonnet 1 to the remaining sonnets. After the first one, the rest will come more easily. Analyze the poems by Daniel Tobin for ways in which he approaches and develops his topics.

II. As in the traditional **crown of sonnets** (or sonnet corona), you may begin each subsequent sonnet with the final line of the previous poem (the first line of the first sonnet is repeated as the final line of the final sonnet in a crown of sonnets as a way of closing the sequence). Or, as in the traditional **heroic crown of sonnets**, you may write a fifteenth sonnet, consisting entirely of the first line of each of the preceding fourteen sonnets.

III. Your sonnets should form a unified group. Try to find a unifying principle or theme, such as chronology, geography, family structure, or numerology to tie the poems together. Each sonnet should stand on its own, yet taken together they should form a cohesive group moving in a particular direction.

IV. Try to find a specific focus for each poem—a distinctive event or subject. You may begin with an object, an image, a word, an expression, a person, a line from a favorite poem or song. Or you may begin with an epigraph about the subject of home and see where it leads. Examples might include Dorothy's mantra in *The Wizard of Oz,* a cliché such as "Home is where the heart is," or this from Robert Frost: "Home is the place where, when you have to go there, / They have to take you in." An epigraph can establish context or provide information needed by the reader to fully understand your sonnet.

V. Include at least one sonnet that features each of the following: your house, a favorite toy/object, a parent, a sibling/friend, a favorite song, a girlfriend/boyfriend, school, something lost, something found, and food. You may combine some of these in a single poem. Also, the poem can use or incorporate or allude to these in the service of exploring a related topic.

VI. Your sonnet sequence must have a title. It is likely that you will want to give titles to the individual sonnets as well.

Tips

- Use poetic license: Feel free to combine truth with fiction, especially if altering small details seems the best way to express a universal truth or to improve the formal quality of your poem.
- Avoid cliché and sentimentality.
- Find a voice in each poem that is appropriate to your attitude toward the subject matter. Feel free to combine the comic and tragic, the humorous, ironic, and/or irreverent with the dignified, solemn, and serious.

- Consider speaking in someone else's voice—imagining someone else's point of view.

- Allow yourself to be carried away by each sonnet in the composition stage. Robert Frost has this to say: "Like a piece of ice on a hot stove the poem must ride on its own melting. A poem may be worked over once it is in being, but may not be worried into being. Its most precious quality will remain its having run itself and carried away the poet with it."

- (Re)Shape your poem intentionally in the revision stage. Wordsworth defines poetry as "emotion recollected in tranquility." Use the tranquil state of reflection as an opportunity to shape the poem, to bring it into line with formal conventions you are adopting.

- Use a thesaurus, a dictionary, and a rhyming dictionary as ready sources of synonyms and diction variations. Regard these as banks from which you can draw as many words as you would like. Be sure, also, to draw words from real life. Slang, ethnic expressions, outlaw words belong in poetry as much as "polite" words, but use them consciously and deliberately.

- Carry a notebook—always. Write down and follow up on ideas as soon as they come to you. Inspiration—literally, *breath* or *wind*—comes and goes as quickly as breath or wind. If you don't write down an idea as soon as it comes to you, you will probably forget it.

An Example

Over the years since I first started giving this assignment, I have received a number of fine sonnet sequences. There is something about this project that engenders enthusiasm in the participants, and their passion for their subject comes through clearly in the poems. The four poems that follow come from a particularly accomplished sequence written by a student, Colleen Taylor.

Taylor's sequence echoes elements of Tobin's; she shares an Irish-American heritage with him and a deep interest in the history and landscape of Ireland as well as the private history of her family. Titled, "Mná Tí," Irish for "Women of the House," Taylor's sequence explores a woman's experience of growing up in an Irish-American family, harkening back to her female ancestors—those who are still with her as well as those from the distant past.

The first three sonnets reprinted here are the first three of Taylor's sequence, while the fourth poem is the final sonnet. As in Tobin's sequence, Taylor's demonstrates the poet's sense of the complexity of her own identity, the multiplicity of meaning conveyed in the concept of home, and a reverence for the mystery of how we come to be who and where we are.

Homesick

When I wade into the wood beside my everyday,
suburbanly normal house, when I step away
from television sets and sugar substitutes,
when I forget phones and hairspray and lightbulbs,
jokes that lack humor and music that doesn't speak,
when I adorn myself in a cape of green and air,
lapping up the raw scent of tree leaves and grass,
soaking in the sound of pine needles crunched with wood,
I believe in fairy hills and pirate queens,
in swan children and Gráinne and Deirdre;
I believe in the women before me, the stories
they told, mapping a magic trail to trace back time.
I believe in the smooth-cut isle jeweled in green,
and I believe those women were right to leave.

Ellis Island: January 1st, 1892

> *Annie Moore and her brothers embarked from this town on 20 December 1891 on the S.S. Nevada. Annie was the first person to be admitted to the new immigration center at Ellis Island. A statue of Annie Moore was also erected at Ellis Island, New York. This sculpture is dedicated to all who emigrated from Ireland.*
>
> ~Cobh Heritage Centre, Cork

Who knew the world made girls like you? Aflame
with strength at so young an age, for each one
of your fourteen years, ten more in dauntless deeds.
You stood a monument before they statued you.

First to cross the gates, christening a year
and a history, your small brothers trailing
your lead, you smacked your shoes into the tiles,
shoving a poor past behind, sprinting toward dreams.

The papers called you "rosy-cheeked," perhaps
they overlooked the red lining your blue eyes,
single source hinting remorse, tears shed for
the cottage behind you, the apartment ahead.

Now you face yourself across the sea, raise a hand,
mapping the watered path between your two lands.

Seeing Stories at Dún Aonghasa

There at the edge, sitting, foot dangling over the drop,
a wind-worn woman with years in her skin-creases
lilted a hushed tune that drifted in to me on waves.

Three circles of rock wall opening stage-like to clouds
and shining waters, the fort was alight with sun,
kindling a fierce peace among those atop the cliff.

I breathed in that whispered tune she made with magic,
yearning to match my own voice to its canter,
to take from that song, that sea, a story.

I strained to find my place as she had, and the walls
grabbed at me, stretching out a path to follow. My feet
sank into rock while pasts forgotten fogged my eyes.

I stood not knowing what happened there, but seeing remains—
in spaces between stone, shadows of grass, my own veins.

Kilkee

for Mom

Your toes splashed the water's foaming edge,
I watched gleaming waves greet their Maeve,
leaving you the space that molded to you,
in wave and wind, I heard your laughing voice.

Kilkee shone for you, beating its blue heart
so you might warm it with your tender touch.
Your eyes, the waters—a mirror of blue,

I joined you, ankle-deep in your soul's waves,
your smiles branding love for me, this place.

When time's jagged brush paints wrinkles on my skin,
when I return to this bay without you,
I will see you, clear as Kilkee water,
and soft, wet sand beneath my feet will cry

Here, here my mother lived a thousand lives.

~ *Colleen Taylor*

Summing Up

The poet Bashō once wrote of the experience of poetry, "It's like being alive twice." The apprentice poet arrives at this truth independently as he or she labors at the sonnet sequence, attempting to recreate the past, to stop time and capture in words fleeting moments of great meaning, and to convey that meaning to the reader through story, symbol, and song. With each reading, the life contained in those lines is renewed. In fact, to read and write poetry is akin to being alive many more times than twice. It gives us all a thousand lives.

Angela Alaimo O'Donnell teaches English and Creative Writing at Fordham University and serves as Associate Director of Fordham's Curran Center for American Catholic Studies. She has published three full-length collections of poems, *Waking My Mother* (2013), *Saint Sinatra* (2011) and *Moving House* (2009)—all three WordTech releases—as well as two chapbooks, *Mine* and *Waiting for Ecstasy*. O'Donnell's work has been published in many journals, including *Alabama Literary Review, America, Christian Century, Christianity & Literature, First Things, Hawaii Pacific Review, Mezzo Cammin, Runes, String Poetry,* and *Valparaiso Poetry Review*. She has been nominated for the Pushcart Prize, the Best of the Web Award, and the Arlin G. Meyer Prize in Imaginative Writing. O'Donnell also writes essays and reviews on contemporary literature; she is a regular columnist for *America* magazine. A memoir, *Mortal Blessings*, is forthcoming in 2014.

The Haikoum

If you have written haiku and mastered the pantoum, why not try a poem that is both a sequence of haiku *and* a pantoum?

Background

Pantoum: Of Malayan origin, the pantoum is an interlocking poem in quatrains in which all the lines are repeated:

1. The second and fourth lines of each stanza become the first and third lines in the following stanza:

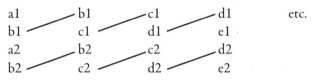

2. This interlocking arrangement continues until the closing stanza, which uses the first and third lines of the opening stanza as its second and fourth lines. If the pantoum has eight stanzas, for example, the final stanza will have two lines from the seventh stanza and two from the first, as follows: h1–a1–h2–a2

To visualize this pattern, read several pantoums. The following are readily available online:

- "pantoum" by John Ashbery
- "Stillbirth" by Laure-Anne Bosselaar
- "Iva's Pantoum" by Marilyn Hacker
- "Pantoum of the Great Depression" by Donald Justice
- "Parent's Pantoum" by Carolyn Kizer
- "Something About the Trees" by Linda Pastan

Haiku: Of Japanese origin, the haiku is a three-line poem focused on an image, often associated with a season, which in English traditionally follows a syllabic pattern of 5–7–5 syllables. Bashō is the best known of the ancient practitioners; a number of his haiku are available online.

Haikoum: A hybrid, the haikoum borrows from both of these forms, using the repeating pattern of the pantoum but with the syllable count and stanza breaks of the haiku.

Procedure

I. It is best to prepare the poem in quatrains, like the pantoum, so you don't lose track of the interlocking arrangement. Come up with your first four lines:

a1	five syllables	line 1 of first haiku
b1	seven syllables	line 2 of first haiku
a2	five syllables	line 3 of first haiku
b2	five syllables	line 1 of second haiku

Here's an example, taken from the published pantoum on the facing page:

a1	As blank as a stone,
b1	This young tabula rasa,
a2	And bad to the bone.
b2	His passage was clear—

II. Copy and paste b1 and b2 to the first and third lines of your second quatrain. Then compose lines c1 and c2:

b1	A straight tabula rasa	line 2 of second haiku
c1	Up to Salinas.	line 3 of second haiku
b2	But nothing was clear	line 1 of third haiku
c2	Thirty seconds from Cholame,	line 2 of third haiku

Note: Feel free to vary the lines, but you will need to edit your pasted lines, as in the second quatrain above. "This young tabula rasa" becomes "A straight tabula rasa," and "His passage was clear" becomes "But nothing was clear."

III. Continue, repeating the second step for each stanza, with two new lines (represented by the next letter of the alphabet) for each quatrain.

- Remember that you are writing haiku (a three-line form) in quatrains (a four-line form).

- You may write as many stanzas as necessary. There are no limits, except that your haikoum will end when the last line of a quatrain is also the last line of a haiku.

IV. When you reach your final stanza, use lines 2 and 4 from the preceding stanza as lines 1 and 3. Use lines 1 and 3 from the first stanza as lines 2 and 4.

f1	As the film slows down:	line 3 of preceding haiku
a1	He's blank as a stone,	line 1 of last haiku
f2	And blanker behind the dash,	line 2 of last haiku
a2	And bad to the bone.	line 3 of the last haiku

V. *Now* break the poem into tercets instead of quatrains.

An Example

Haikoum for James Dean

As blank as a stone,	**a1**
This young tabula rasa,	**b1**
And bad to the bone.	**a2**
His passage was clear—	**b2**
A straight tabula rasa	**b1**
Up to Salinas.	**c1**
But nothing was clear	**b2**
Thirty seconds from Cholame,	**c2**
Far from Salinas.	**c1**
He could see the fork	**d1**
As he floored it for Cholame,	**c2**
"That guy's gotta stop."	**d2**
He could see the fork	**d1**
From his low silver Spyder.	**e1**
"That guy's gotta stop.	**d2**
Why can't he see us?"	**e2**
Shadows blot out the Spyder	**e1**
As the film slows down.	**f1**
Though James can't see us,	**e2**
We see him behind the dash	**f2**
As the film slows down:	**f1**
He's blank as a stone,	**a1**
And blanker behind the dash,	**f2**
And bad to the bone.	**a2**

~ David M. Katz

Tips

Part of the fun of this form is generating **enjambment** (line breaks in mid-phrase or mid-clause), which is like playing that kids' game where you have various top and bottom halves of animals and you put them together to make weird and wonderful mixtures. Enjambment tends to work better (harder) if most of your first words are nouns, adjectives or verbs. Try to use slight deviations in words or phrasing, as in "Haikoum for James Dean," on the preceding page, and/or punctuation, as in "Haikoum" and "Triple Lutz," below.

Variations

As with contemporary haiku, don't feel bound strictly by the 5–7–5 syllable limits, but the final version in tercets should always demonstrate the short–long–short line pattern characteristic of haiku.

Examples

Haikoum

Red tulips bloom
beside wilting daffodils:
spring changes hands.

Storm-felled trees scattered
beside wilting daffodils:
the sky is too blue.

Storm-felled trees scattered
by winter's last big tantrum:
the sky is too blue.

Patched up, the fabric ripped
by winter's last big tantrum:
the quarrel is done.

Patched up, the fabric ripped
out of the family home.
The quarrel is done.

They have closed the blinds
out of the family home:
no one can reach them.

They have closed the blinds;
they will not come out again.
No one can reach them.

Red tulips bloom;
they will not come out again:
spring changes hands.

~ *Anna Evans*

Don't be afraid to vary the pattern of the typical pantoum either. In "Triple Lutz," notice that the *a2* line ("the skate blades, the ink"), which should close the poem, has been switched with the *b2* line ("skaters trace the ice") to good effect.

Triple Lutz

The ice, newly smooth:
a sheet of crisp white paper;
the skate blades, the ink.

Skaters trace the ice,
a sheet of crisp white paper,
with strange loops and whirls.

The skate blades, the ink
emptied into new poems
strange with loops and whirls.

All life's sadnesses
empty into new poems:
white anesthesia.

Our life's sadnesses,
erased by skating backwards:
white anesthesia.

Keep checking behind:
erased by skating backwards,
your first strokes forward.

Keep checking behind;
avoid others in your path.
You're first! Stroke forward!

The ice, newly smooth;
avoid others in your path,
skaters. Trace the ice!

~ *Anna Evans*

Anna M. Evans has poems in or forthcoming in *Harvard Review, Atlanta Review, Rattle, American Arts Quarterly,* and *32 Poems.* She has a new sonnet collection, *Sisters & Courtesans* (White Violet Press, 2014). With an M.F.A. from Bennington College, Evans is the Editor of *The Raintown Review.* Recipient of Fellowships from the MacDowell Artists' Colony and the Virginia Center for the Creative Arts, and winner of the 2012 Rattle Poetry Prize Readers' Choice Award, she currently teaches at West Windsor Art Center and Richard Stockton College of New Jersey.

Elizabeth Jacobson

Writing Renga Together

enga is an ancient form of collaborative Japanese poetry that inspires one participant to respond to a stanza written by another, building a linked chain of verse. The traditional length of a renga was one hundred stanzas, though thirty-six stanzas (a kasen) became more standard by the time of Bashō, and today renga are often of even fewer stanzas, especially in English.

A renga—like haiku, the term is the same whether singular or plural—starts with a participant writing a three-line stanza called a **hokku** that references the current season (traditional renga traveled through all the seasons according to very rigid rules). In fact, the hokku is the original source of the haiku prior to its evolution into a standalone form, thus their identical 5–7–5 syllable count, which these days is often regarded as short–long–short lines rather than specific numbers of syllables.

The next participant writes a two-line stanza known as a **wakiku** (syllable count of 7–7, or long–long), which connects in some way to the hokku. Thus the first two stanzas resemble the single-stanza tanka form:

stanza one (hokku)	5	short
	7	long
	5	short
stanza two (wakiku)	7	long
	7	long

From this point on, additional stanzas (verses) are added by other participants, alternating between three and two lines. But this is where renga becomes tricky, guided by a principle known as **link and shift**. *Link* means that each stanza connects in some way with the stanza before it; *shift* means that each stanza—through fresh descriptions—moves to a new topic, subject, or mood. According to William J. Higginson, author of *The Haiku Handbook,* the controlling idea behind renga is "to link your contribution to that immediately before, but to shift away from repetition of anything that has already appeared in the work." In the words of Martin Lucas of the British Haiku Society, "The overall effect of a renga is a scattered mosaic of images covering a broad spectrum of atmosphere and mood. Although narrative connection is one means of linking, there is no sustained narrative or logical thread in renga."

Here is an example of a renga section from the longer piece that follows:

dark pink hollyhocks
stand in the road dust, no rain
just fire ants swarming

fear fills my tender bare feet
sky so blue, so dry

Notice that the three-line hokku written by the first participant references the summer season with "hollyhocks" and "fire ants," while the two-line wakiku, written by the next participant, links back with "bare feet," then shifts to "sky so blue," anticipating the first line of the third stanza.

Procedure

You will need at least two people, but three or more works better. Decide how many stanzas you want to complete the renga. Ready to renga?

I. Choose someone to begin. Write the first three-line stanza, the hokku, and incorporate the current season.

II. When the first stanza is complete, pass it to the second writer, who will compose the two-line second stanza.

Note: These days renga are often composed electronically, with participants living in different towns, countries, or continents, so you may be "sending" instead of "passing."

III. With the first two stanzas—hokku and wakiku—complete, the developing poem will go to the next writer, who will compose the third verse (three lines) and pass the piece along again, where the fourth verse (two lines) will be added. And so on. Continue to read and reread all the verses during your turn to avoid repeating anything that's already been said. Don't forget to link and shift!

IV. When your group reaches the selected number of stanzas, read the renga and start another one—or revise this one.

An Example

Members of the Cut + Paste Society, a community of women artists and writers in the Santa Fe area, composed the following renga in a recent workshop. The group consists of Miriam Sagan (MS), Michelle Laflamme-Childs (MLC), Sydney Cooper (SC), Tamara Bates (TB), Elizabeth Jacobson (EJ), Edie Tsong (ET), and Monika Cassel (MC).

dark pink hollyhocks
stand in the road dust, no rain
just fire ants swarming

MS

fear fills my tender bare feet
sky so blue, so dry

MLC

as my son sings out
summer in present and past
burnished glare heat

SC

not forgetting how much time
changes when we stop moving

TB

each petal nods
toward the seasonless blaze of sun
even in clouds

EJ

that hide the earthly creatures
dreaming of thick icicles

ET

bare feet on floorboards
wondering if I forgot
to say: I love you

MS

tug and smack of sweaty skin
pulling against a smooth chair

SC

aching with her loss
my daughter touches the keys:
music can bring us home

MC

away from despair into
a time apart from grief

TB

shadows lengthen now
the pain wanes with the sun
relief cools the night

MLC

crane marking sky in pattern
black, gray, black as the sun falls

TB

it's time to block the sun ET
and sleep for several lifetimes
extra random letters, whatever

Variations

Two Stanzas (or more) Per Poet: Each writer composes two full stanzas consisting of both the hokku and wakiku, linking them to the full renga that the writer before him/her composed. This approach works well if participants are working separately—across states, or even continents—as one participant can e-mail the next participant his or her creation. *Crossing State Lines: An American Renga,* edited by Bob Holman and Carol Muske-Dukes (Farrar, Straus and Giroux, 2011), uses this method with poets across the United States.

Renga as Exquisite Corpse: Instead of passing the entire renga around so that each writer can read the developing poem from the beginning, fold the paper over at the top so the next writer only sees the stanza that was written prior to the one he/she is about to create, a version of the writing game known as Exquisite Corpse.

Writers who wish to collaborate on this version by e-mail can appoint a scribe for the group. As each participant completes a fragment of the whole, he/she e-mails it to the scribe, who assembles the developing poem and sends the most recent verse to the next participant.

An Example

This renga as Exquisite Corpse was written during a recent workshop of the Cut + Paste Society. Contributing poets were Miriam Sagan, Elizabeth Jacobson, Tamara Bates, Sydney Cooper, and Monika Cassel.

pay me what you owe **MS**
me—a kiss, a scratch, or laugh
at all my witty remains

things left over after summer **EJ**
seep into the earth like blood

bone mixed into soil **TB**
leaving behind pale, dusty
fragments. Moth wings

iridescent plaited sheen   **SC**
enfolding your hidden pulse

heartthrob, heartthrob, thump   **MC**
careful sunlight spreading far
abroad and along the riverbed

Elizabeth Jacobson is the author of *Her Knees Pulled In* (Tres Chicas Books, 2012), a finalist for the New Mexico Book Awards. Founding director of The WingSpan Poetry Project, which brings weekly poetry classes to the Esperanza Shelter for Battered Families in Santa Fe, New Mexico, Jacobson has taught writing for over twenty-five years, most recently as a teaching artist with Art-Works in Santa Fe. With an M.F.A. from Columbia University, she is the winner of the 2013 Western Humanities Review Mountain West Writer's Contest and the recipient of the Jim Sagel Prize for Poetry from *Puerto del Sol*.

The Landay

In English-language poetry, it's not so common to find poems shorter than eight lines, unless they are comic poems, satiric squibs. Yet other language traditions use very short forms—for example, the Japanese haiku, which distributes just seventeen syllables over a mere three lines.

In the June 2013 issue of *Poetry* magazine, scholar and writer Eliza Griswold discusses the landay, a poetic form practiced for centuries in Afghanistan, even by people who aren't professional poets. It's a popular form, composed by women as well as men; in fact, its popularity is attributed to Malalai, a woman warrior who lived and fought in the late nineteenth century. Landays have been published, but they are often spoken or sung at celebrations. They sometimes appear, unsigned, as graffiti on walls of villages and towns throughout the country. I recommend Griswold's article to anyone who wants to know more about the Afghani social contexts in which poems based on this form are composed. We can also adapt it for our own purposes here.

Procedure

The landay is short and simple. It consists of two lines only, a *folk couplet*, you can call it. The first line contains nine syllables, and the second, thirteen. The poem ends with the syllable *ma* or *na*. Sometimes the two lines rhyme, but more often they don't. Here is an example that sticks to all the requirements:

> Though I've just come back from Panama,
> I'm not going to start calling movies "cinema."

And another:

> My beloved's name is Diana,
> The wildest, prettiest, smartest fox in Montana.

Count the syllables: nine in line one, thirteen in line two. In the Panama landay, the last syllable is *ma,* and, since the couplet rhymes, the first line also ends in *ma.* Same thing for the one about Diana, though here the rhyming syllable is *na.*

Now let's look at a landay that doesn't rhyme:

> Oh, you want to know what a drone is?
> That dead guy can explain, or else go ask Obama.

In Afghanistan, landays often have political content, and they can be quite bitter. But not always. They can deal with love or the pain of love, with daily concerns, with the death of family members, or with current events. They can crack a joke, and the best jokes are short and blunt—for maximum impact.

Variations

In the Pashto language spoken in Afghanistan, a very large number of words end in *ma* or *na*. But there are not so many in English, and many of these are technical/scientific terms and proper names (see charts below). For that reason, you may discover, after writing a few landays, that you've run out of ideas. So, for our purposes here, you may make a substitution simply by reversing the letters and having the concluding syllable be either *am* or *an*. Doing so will open up a much wider range of possibilities.

English Words Ending in *ma:*

adenoma, Alabama, anathema, angioma, anima, anonyma, antepenultima, aroma, asthma, atheroma, blastema, Brahma, branchiostoma, Burma, carcinoma, charisma, chiasma, cinema, cinerama, coma, comma, condyloma, cosmorama, cyclorama, cyclostoma, cytoblastema, derma, dharma, diastema, dilemma, diorama, diploma, docudrama, dogma, drachma, drama, eczema, edema, endoplasma, endostoma, enema, enigma, epistoma, epithelioma, fibroma, firma, forma, gamma, georama, glaucoma, glioma, Grandma, hematoma, hematotherma, Hiroshima, hydrosoma, hypoderma, hypostoma, idioplasma, karma, kinema, kytoplasma, lama, leucoma, Lima, lipoma, llama, lymphoma, lymphosarcoma, Ma, magma, mahatma, Mama, Mamma, maxima, melanocarcinoma, melanoma, melastoma, melodrama, metastoma, miasma, Momma, monodrama, Montezuma, mycoderma, myeloma, neuroma, Norma, Oklahoma, optima, osteoma, osteosarcoma, ovoplasma, pajama, Panama, panorama, papilloma, penultima, peristoma, phantasma, phyllosoma, Pima, plasma, pleurotoma, pneuma, polyorama, prima, proforma, programma, prosoma, proxima, pseudostoma, psychodrama, pterostigma, puma, pyjama, rhizoma, sarcoma, schema, schisma, scleroderma, scleroma, shama, sigma, smegma, soma, spermoplasma, squama, stigma, stoma, summa, synonyma, Tacoma, teratoma, trauma, tristoma, ultima, xanthoma, Yokohama, zeugma, zygoma

English Words Ending in *na:*

alumna, Americana, angina, Anna, antenna, arcana, arena, Argentina, Arizona, Athena, avena, avifauna, ballerina, banana, bandana, Barcelona, belladonna, Bellona, Bologna, bona, Botswana, Bwana, cabana, campana, canna, cantina, carina, Carolina, cavatina, China, chinchona, cognomina, concertina, coquina, corona, Cremona, czarevna, czarina, damiana, Dana, Diana, diurna, domina, Donna, dracaena, duenna, dulciana, duodena, encina, entosterna, epiphenomena, episterna, etna, farina, fauna, fontina, galena, gena, Ghana, gitana, grana, guana, Guyana, gymkhana, Havana, Helena, hemina, henna, hosanna, hydrina, hyena, hyposterna, iguana, ikebana, Indiana, Indochina, interregna, jacana, kachina, kahuna, katakana, Katrina, Krishna, krona, lacuna, laguna, lamina, lantana, lasagna, legumina, liana, littorina, Louisiana, lumina, luna, machina, madonna, madrina, mañana, manna, marijuana, marina, medialuna, mischna, molybdena, Mona, monopneumona, Montana, na, nagana, nicotiana, nirvana, noumena, novena, ocarina, organa, ozena, parmigiana, Pasadena, pastina, patina, pedimana, penna, persona, phenomena, piscina, platina, plena, poinciana, polycystina, pomona, prana, quinquina, Regina, retina, retsina, salina, sauna, savanna, scarlatina, scena, semolina, senna, seraphina, sestina, sienna, sigñorina, sonatina, stamina, sterna, subpoena, sultana, toccatina, tsarevna, tsarina, tuna, tympana, tzarevna, tzarina, ulna, urbana, vaccina, vacuna, vagina, vena, verbena, vicuna, Vienna, vina, xiphisterna, zircona, zona

You don't want to be cramped with your landay. It is a spontaneous, shoot-from-the-hip form. The writer of landays jump-starts, gets straight to the point, wastes no time. Count your syllables, nine for the first line and thirteen for the second. Remember what the last syllable of the poem is supposed to be. Be bold! On your mark!

Alfred Corn is the author of ten poetry collections, most recently *Tables* (Press 53, 2013). Corn has also published a novel, two collections of essays, and *The Poem's Heartbeat: A Manual of Prosody* (Copper Canyon Press, 2008). An eleventh volume of poems, *Unions,* is forthcoming from Barrow Street; a second novel, *Miranda's Book,* is forthcoming from Eyewear. Corn's honors include a Guggenheim fellowship, an Award in Literature from the Academy of Arts and Letters, and one from the Academy of American Poets. He has taught at Yale, Columbia, and UCLA. Pentameters Theatre in London staged his play *Lowell's Bedlam* in 2011. In 2012, he was a Visiting Fellow of Clare Hall, University of Cambridge, preparing a translation of Rilke's *Duino Elegies;* he returned as a Life Fellow for a second residency in 2013. His first e-book, *Transatlantic Bridge: A Concise Guide to the Differences between British and American English,* was published in 2012.

The Lyric as Letter

Who among us has not, in moments of ambition, dreamt of the miracle of a form of poetic prose, musical but without rhythm or rhyme, both supple and staccato enough to adapt itself to the lyrical movements of our souls, the undulating movements of our reveries, and the convulsive movement of our consciences?

~ Charles Baudelaire, Preface to Le Spleen de Paris

As a poet who writes essays and whose last two books of poetry have consisted entirely of prose poems, I am interested in the borderlands between poetry and traditional prose. I like to read the cross-breeds, the hybrids, the genres that do not respect traditional boundaries. These boundaries are more fluid than we think; crossing them can move us toward a more imaginative prose and a more dynamic poetry, toward more possibility in either genre.

To that end, I have taught a workshop that includes the narrative poem, the poem sequence, the prose poem in its many forms, the parable, and the fragmented lyric. I begin with an exercise in writing the literary letter. Two reasons support this choice:

1. Everyone has written and received letters—texting and e-mail included.

2. The form allows for experimentation in voice, address, diction, image, narration, digression, and closure.

A **verse epistle,** or **epistolary poem,** according to *The New Princeton Encyclopedia of Poetry and Poetics*, is "a poem addressed to a friend, lover, or patron, written in a familiar style and in hexameters or their modern equivalents." In its earlier incarnations, the letter poem would take as its subject a philosophical subject or a romantic one. In later incarnations, it can be a way of exploring any kind of subject matter, whether poetic, romantic, philosophical, political, or historical. It can be a traveling travelogue of space or thought.

On the following page, for instance, consider a poem I wrote across the miles as a kind of spirit-missive to my close friend Patricia Goedicke, who was dying in a hospital far from me. In it, I was also able to reference the title of her book *When Earth Begins to End* and with it, some of our own conversations about death.

Nettle

Green clusters of soft beads, the nettle is flowering. When I disappear, you said, write and tell me everything. Snakes slide, when they hear my footsteps, further into the weeds. The tide shudders as it turns over each stone. Is this what it was like as earth began to end? It started out in loneliness and turned to poetry. Here: a scribble of seabirds, a peak across the Sound, so distant and vague, like your death to me. Last night, an Iranian doctor performed that tongue-cry she had heard the Arabs use at weddings and funerals. She had examined Fidel Castro and pronounced him fit, four times more charismatic than Clinton. Somehow, I thought you would want to know. Everyone is starting to take on the appearance of ghosts. Rain tips the needles of the cedar. If our days are the ritual we perform for the dead. *If our days are the ritual we perform for the dead.* I wade into the current and leave it open for you. I find excuses to say your name.

~ *Melissa Kwasny*

Preparation

There are many letter poems and poetic letters that can be used as samples for this exercise, depending on age group and objectives.

- Emily Dickinson's letters to Thomas Wentworth Higginson or John Keats' letters to various friends, in which he formulates his now famous notions of "negative capability" and "the chameleon poet," are poems in themselves.

- There are also beautiful poems written in the form of letters. Ezra Pound's "The River Merchant's Wife: A Letter" is one great example. ("The River Merchant's Wife" is re-printed on page 65.)

- Richard Hugo's book *31 Letters and 13 Dreams* is composed of letter poems, most of them addressed to other poets.

- One of my favorite series of letters is the compilation of letters Rainer Maria Rilke wrote to his wife Clara, while he was living in Paris and visiting daily a memorial exhibit of Cézanne's paintings. The book in which they are published, *Letters on Cézanne*, translated by Joel Agee, demonstrates Rilke's increasing perception of the artist's work, as well as what it means to his own sense of purpose as a poet. In my workshop, I ask students to read the entire book, but to pay particular attention to the letters dated October 9–15, 1907.

Procedure

Write a series of three to five letter poems or poetic letters. Think of the series as a narrative containing a developing story of character or idea or perhaps even plot. In Rilke's letters, the poet's developing sense of his own need to master his art form becomes explicit as he learns more about Cézanne. You may not recognize what your focus is until after the second or third letter. Adjust for this in your revision.

I suggest that students not write the series of letters all in the same day but revisit the subject matter over a period of days, as Rilke did, letting their perceptions grow and develop, letting time, as would be natural in letter writing, perform its changes.

Guidelines

- Make sure the letters are in sequence, i.e. chronological, dated, and placed.

- Establish the presence of a real or invented addressee. What are your shared concerns? What knowledge do you share that you do not need to explain? From Rilke's *Letters on Cézanne:*

  Yesterday, while I was admiring the dissolving brightness of autumn here, you were walking through that other autumn back home, which is painted on red wood, as this one's painted on silk.

- *Place* the narrator, i.e. use sensory and detailed imagery to let the addressee picture where you are—as in this example from *Letters on Cézanne:*

  You can feel what a light-green carriage can be on the Pont-Neuf or some red that can't contain itself, or simply a poster on the fire wall of a pearl-gray group of houses.

- Endeavor to establish a voice that is consistent and yet gradually reveals more and more of its character.

- Ask questions.

- Include anecdotes or excerpts from your reading. Here's one from Rilke:

  He ran back and forth in his studio with green apples scattered about, or went out into his garden in despair and sat. And before him lay the small town, unsuspecting, with its cathedral; a town for decent and modest burghers, while he—just as his father, who was a hat maker, had foreseen—had become different.

- A letter has a beginning (a salutation) and an end, though likely more letters will come. Don't aim for final closure; allow open-endedness.

- Allow for the digressions that occur in a correspondence.

Variations

- A series of letters in which you describe and respond to someone else's visual art (painting, sculpture, installation, ceramics), music, film, literature, or dance. The series should be a *developing* exploration of what you learn from your response, not a review or critique.

- A series of letters that serves as a kind of travel diary of a particular place and time.

- One side of an exchange of letters between people in a particular period of history (e.g., Einstein, a pioneer woman in Montana, the dancer Nijinsky in his insane asylum, Gertrude Stein's cook).

- Letters formulated as a kind of aesthetic argument with someone specific, not necessarily the addressee. That someone's views should be well known or, if not, made clear in the letters.

- Three different letters to three different poets, contemporary or otherwise, in which you pit your sense of poetics against their own, respond or praise or argue with their words. You can italicize their words to distinguish them within the letter. (See Hugo or examine how Rilke uses what he learns of Cézanne to think about his own work.)

Examples

Below are two letter poems by M. L. Smoker that can serve as excellent models for this exercise.

Letter to Richard Hugo (1)

Dick: The reservoir on my end of the state is great for fishing. Some of the banks are tall and jagged; others are more patient, taking their time as they slope into rocky beaches. If you were the kind of fisherman I imagine, then you might have considered it a great place to cast from. My family has gone up there ever since the water on the Mni Shoshe was dammed off. My grandparents put on their moccasins and beadwork and danced for FDR when he rode the train out to see the finishing touches of this great industrial project. I haven't yet decided if this is something I wish to be proud of. Maybe this summer I'll spend more time up there, on the edge of a lake that was never meant to be a lake, and form an actual opinion. Maybe too I'll write you again. But you have probably already figured as much. I almost thought of not returning to finish the writing program you began with your own severe desire for language. But I did. And now I'm at the end. Already though, I'll admit to you, I'm thinking of home. I have been this whole time.

Letter to Richard Hugo (2)

Dick: Once, in one of the small creeks that run from Fort Peck Lake I saw a catfish, swimming upstream, trying to make it back to the shelter of a larger body of water. It was late summer and there wasn't enough of the creek to cover the top half of his fins. Still, he pushed down into the mud and kept on. I did not envy him. Nor did I devise some plan to help him make it back to safety. I'll let you draw your own conclusions about what type of person this makes me. And since we're on this track: I have a sister I haven't spoken to in years. And the language my relatives spoke while getting ready for the dam's inaugural ceremonies is close to extinction, but I have always made up something more important to do, rather than take the risk of saving it. I am still angry at times with my father because I long for the type of mother mine could never have been. I go on mourning her, even though a medicine person has told me it was time to let her go to the other side. I wonder if she is still close, or if years ago she ignored me and went on. I certainly didn't know that today—when I'm a week away from packing up, leaving Missoula for good, and making my way east for home—I would sit here in the purplish light of the first real snowfall of the year and write to you. I could go on, tell you about my poetry, about how much it's meant to spend time with Ripley, about the influence Jim has been. (Thank you for telling him to write what he knew. That allowed me to write what I know, twenty-five years later, from another rez a little farther down the road.) I'll just close by saying the salmon are plentiful, even if they begin their lives in a hatchery down below the dam. For the time being, I don't mind this as much, and I have an idea you wouldn't either. There's just something about the remissible wave of a cast which feels like the biggest commitment of all.

~ *M. L. Smoker*

In Smoker's first poem, she acknowledges the connection between both poets as Montanans and as anglers. She then establishes their differences: Missoula and Fort Peck are on opposite sides of the state—one urban, one the reservation where she grew up, one white and one American Indian. Smoker also makes clear that she is only imagining Hugo's fishing skills. His death was before her time. There is only one story involved, but it is a story about her grandparents entertaining white authority and about a home that has existed for many generations.

In the second letter, there is the same "connection" with fishing and the dam, but different stories are told. Things deepen and darken. The plight of the catfish, which is struggling to make it back to the "shelter of a larger body of water," is caused by the human construction of a dam. This functions as a metaphor for a people, whose obstacles to returning "home" include their language being forcibly taken away from them. We see the first connection deepen into a more complex narrative of home, colonialism, and Indian-white relations.

Melissa Kwasny is the author of five books of poetry, most recently *Pictograph* (forthcoming, 2015), *The Nine Senses* (2011), and *Reading Novalis in Montana* (2009), all from Milkweed Editions. Her collection of essays, *Earth Recitals: Essays on Image and Vision,* was released by Lynx House Press in 2013. Kwasny is the editor of *Toward the Open Field: Poets on the Art of Poetry 1800–1950* (Wesleyan University Press, 2004), which was named as one of the best books for writers by *Poets & Writers.*

Mirror, Mirror: Inverting Stanzas

This exercise, though it can be challenging, prompts the poet to carefully devise and re-work syntax that will allow each sentence or fragment to work in reverse. When it is done well, the poet is able to discover something she might not have realized she wanted to say. It is an exercise that encourages surprise and invention.

Preparation

An excellent poem to study before you begin is "The Eldest Sister to Psyche" by A. E. Stallings—reprinted on the following page, alongside a second mirror poem, written by Allyson Whipple as an example for this exercise. Notice that the second stanza is a mirror image of the first, using the same lines as the first stanza (with minor variation) but in reverse order. Notice how the poet uses each sentence or fragment to build tension in both the sentence before and the one that comes after. Short sentences are also helpful. While Stallings employs frequent end-rhyme, you need not.

Procedure

The poem will contain two stanzas that mirror each other. Write the first stanza as an argument, choosing either an internal argument with the self or one with another person. The second stanza should answer or reply to that argument. The first stanza ends with a kind of assertion, and the second one starts with a kind of rebuttal, though the words are the same. The start of the second stanza is the line that ends the first stanza. The second line of the second stanza is the penultimate line of the first stanza, and so on, until you reach the first line of the poem, which also becomes its last line.

I encourage my students to write widely varied sentences as they compose the first stanza. When the first stanza is inverted to create the second, these varied sentence structures enhance the poem's movement.

Tips from Allyson Whipple: I found that the best way to write this poem was to write both stanzas in tandem. Once the first line is complete, write it at the bottom page of your notebook (or type it toward the bottom of the page in your word processor). Writing out each line in both directions will alert you early on to sticky spots that might not work out when you invert the order of the lines.

The Eldest Sister to Psyche

This palace, those invisible hands
That stroke the music from thin air,
Call it magic: everywhere
The haunted rooms obey commands,
And yet it sounds like loneliness.
Yes, I'm that ugly sister, true,
You'll say I only envy you.
The fact—I know your secret guess—
Surrendered blind to his embrace,
You dared not look. A human voice,
You thought. You never had a choice.
Perhaps a monster, face to face,
With scales and fangs and leathern wings.
What of the fetus that you carry?
For certain it is human? Very?
Doubt burns like hot wax; it stings.

Doubt burns. Like hot wax, it stings.
For certain, it is human, very.
What of the fetus that you carry,
With scales and fangs and leathern wings
Perhaps? A monster. Face to face,
You thought you never had a choice,
You dared not. Look, a human voice
Surrendered blind to his. Embrace
The fact. I know your secret. Guess
You'll say I only envy you.
Yes I'm that ugly, Sister True,
And yet ... It sounds like loneliness,
The haunted rooms. Obey commands:
Call it magic. Everywhere,
That stroke, the music. From thin air,
This palace, those invisible hands.

~ A. E. Stallings

An Example

Adulteress in the Mirror

My lover? Or my husband,
who says I must decide?
I seek counsel from a friend,
who thinks the choice is mine.
Why must I pick
just one, forever?
Love, a greedy thing.
Don't know how one can
believe in faithfulness.
A heart's quick to digress.

A heart's quick. To digress:
believe in faithfulness.
Don't know how one can
love a greedy thing.
Just one forever?
Why must I? Pick
who thinks the choice is mine.
I seek counsel from a friend
who says I must decide:
My lover or my husband.

~ Allyson Whipple

Cleopatra Mathis completed her M.F.A. in Writing at Columbia University in 1978. Her work has appeared widely in magazines, journals, textbooks, and anthologies. She is the author of seven poetry collections, most recently *Book of Dog* (Sarabande, 2013). Awards for her work include two fellowships from the National Endowment for the Arts, three Pushcart Prizes, state grants from New Jersey and New Hampshire, a winter residency fellowship from the Fine Arts Work Center in Provincetown, the Peter Lavin Award for Younger Poets from the Academy of American Poets, the Jane Kenyon Award, and a Guggenheim Fellowship. Since 1982 Mathis has taught English and Creative Writing at Dartmouth College, where she is the Frederick Sessions Beebe '35 Professor in the Art of Writing.

The Happy Blues Exercise

The blues is supposed to be about despair, right? Thus, the well-worn phrase "I got the blues" to describe any generic event from a family member's dying to burning the toast for this morning's breakfast. But the blues is more complex than just, "I'm having a bad day."

I have found that the blues is a very effective way to write a non-sentimental poem not just about a bad experience, but also, about a joyful occurrence. How many of us have cried over a sad movie and then felt wonderful and clear-headed afterward? Try thinking about that in reverse. In particular, the blues is a great form for writing about love, because most of us have a hard time avoiding sentimentality when depicting that emotion.

Procedure

There are seven elements to any blues poem. Your assignment is to use this seven-part "bluesprint" and write a poem about a happy event:

Pathos: Some sort of sadness must be apparent in the blues. An example might be the aubade, which describes a sorrow at parting—no matter how wonderful love shared the night before might have been.

A "Blue Note": In music, the blue note is a note dipping between major and minor scales. In poetry, this note can be compared to some sort of conflict or tension, which any good poem should contain anyway.

Three Movements: Every blues song and every blues poem contains a three-part structure:

1. identification of a problem or tension
2. exploration of a problem or tension
3. resolution of the problem or tension, though not necessarily in a positive way

Music: Because this poetic is based upon a musical form, there must be a sonic element to a blues poem. Free verse is fine for you to use; so is traditional form, such as the sonnet or villanelle. But there must be rhythm and overt sound working in the poem. It's up to the poet to "sing" however s/he wants to.

A Working Class Ethos: The blues did not start off as a parlor game for the idle rich. It started in the cotton fields of the American South, and the songs were composed by hardworking, racially oppressed African Americans. Now, that said, all folks of all complexions can write blues poetry, but a blues poem must focus on some aspect of the working class experience in order to reflect the original intent of the poetic, especially since so much latitude can be claimed with the line lengths, numbers, and meter.

Discussion

In "jonah," poet Lucille Clifton alludes to the Biblical prophet Jonah, who was swallowed by a whale and lived to tell the story: "Now the Lord provided a huge fish to swallow Jonah, and Jonah was in the belly of the fish three days and three nights. . . . From inside the fish Jonah prayed to the Lord his God." (Jonah 1:17 and 2:1)

jonah

> what I remember
> is green
> in the trees
> and the leaves
> and the smell of mango
> and yams
> and if I had a drum
> i would send to the brothers
> —Be care full of the ocean—
>
> ~ *Lucille Clifton*

God saved Jonah, but there are other trials after this supernatural event.

Despite these trials, God acts in compassionate ways, and in one of these acts, He causes a leafy plant to grow up over Jonah, providing shelter and shade. Its leaves are beautiful, and it is the tranquility of this utopian spot that Clifton recalls in her poem. But the pathos bubbles underneath, for despite this happy, serene moment, Jonah the prophet is never quite satisfied, and strangely, blames God for His compassion. In Clifton's rendering, Jonah takes a happy sanctuary (lines 1–6) and turns it into a point of departure for dissatisfaction (lines 7–9).

First, let's explore the meaning of "jonah" and then, connect it to the seven elements of the blues. "jonah" provides the yin and yang of the happy blues poems. The poem is a characteristically short one—Clifton's trademark, if you will—that nevertheless, is packed full of meaning; before we even read the lines of the poem, the title is allusive, and thus, does preliminary work.

We know that Jonah is a prophet of the Bible, but the title refers also to Zora Neale Hurston's novel *Jonah's Gourd Vine*, a germinal text in African American fiction, and there is a traditional Negro spiritual, "Didn't My Lord Deliver Daniel," that references Jonah; Clifton would have been familiar with both the novel and the song. Further: this poem has nine lines. In several syncretic African American spiritual traditions (such as Hoodoo), the number nine has great power and significance, and the choice of the number of lines could refer to the supernatural significance of Jonah's surviving his ordeal with the whale; often Clifton's poems treat Biblical stories within a black syncretic context.

Almost never does she provide notes for her poems, though; she assumes that her reader is smart. As a poetic form, the blues is highly allusive—as is much of African American poetry—and Clifton's work in particular relies on intellectual knowledge/research of Biblical lore, black syncretic spirituality, black vernacular(s), and African American history on both sides of the Atlantic, just to name a few. For example, in lines 5–7 the use of the words "mango," "yams" and "drum" refers to a West African setting and line 8 uses "brothers" to indicate black men. Because of this word usage, the reader may conclude that the "ocean" of line 9 alludes to the horrific Middle Passage of the Atlantic Ocean and to the transatlantic slave trade. In your own poem, you should consider how allusions might work, say, to contemporary popular culture or an event in American history that your readers might already know.

The seven elements of the blues rely on the reader's knowledge as well. As already mentioned, pathos is present in this poem in the allusions to the Middle Passage. The blue note of the poem lies in the conflict of the verdant setting provided by Jonah's leafy plant with the sad aftermath of his falling out with God.

The three movements identify Jonah's memories—"what i remember"— but also explore literally and emotionally a lost place of safety and happiness, for Jonah and the Africans who were stolen from their homeland; again, this African/Biblical location appears frequently in Clifton's work, in varying iterations. The last three lines of the poem represent the resolution; "Be care full of the ocean" references Jonah's water, full of man-swallowing whales, but unlike Jonah's (possibly) allegorical story, those kidnapped Africans that literally were thrown into the Atlantic Ocean were not saved by God—they were eaten by sharks following the slave ships. The ones who did survive are "the brothers," those who made it to slavery in the New World, the dystopia that stands in contrast to Jonah's utopia.

Music is present in the poem, both sonically and again, in an allusive manner. In terms of sound, the long vowel *e* repeats in "remember," "green," "trees," "leaves," and "Be"; the short vowel *u* joins "drum" and "brothers." There are slant rhymes with "mango" and "yam," and with "smell" and "send." Depending on (American) regional pronunciation, "ocean" will echo either "brothers" or "send." But the "drum" on line 7 of the poem alludes to a musical performance, as Clifton refers to an African talking drum; the phrase "I would send to" means "I would send a message with my talking drum."

The working class ethos in the poem relies on allusion. Given that this poem carries slavery connotations, it clearly works within an established working class context. And "the brothers" is a term of endearment used in certain African American communities to signify black men, usually of a working socioeconomic class; but the use of "brothers" also attempts to connect different classes in an affectionate manner by using "brother" as a (hopefully) unifying signifier.

Note: My essay "The Blues: A Craft Manifesto," which appeared in the *Kenyon Review,* goes into more detail about the seven elements of the blues poem—available online at the *Kenyon Review's* website.

An Example

Lush Life

Dixie Inn, a town over in Louisiana
Lunch at the Crawfish Hole
Waitress, name of Taylor

Blond girl
Talks like she got a mouthful
Of honey

Eating crawfish pie
Savory and brown on the plate
Catfish, hush puppies and slaw

Reading Alice Munro
As if I read a good book all the time
Heard she won the Nobel yesterday

Taylor's wearing short shorts
Skinny girl tight
Nothing showing pink or white

It's okay
Ain't supposed to be looking anyway
Turn the page with Alice

~ Oscar C. Peña

Honorée Fanonne Jeffers, poet, fiction writer, and critic, is the author of three books of poetry, most recently, *Red Clay Suite* (Southern Illinois University Press, 2007). Selected by Poet Laureate Natasha Trethewey as one of two 2014 Witter Bynner Fellows of the Library of Congress, Jeffers has received fellowships from the American Antiquarian Society, the Bread Loaf Writers Conference, the MacDowell Colony, the National Endowment for the Arts, and the Vermont Studio Center. Her poems, stories, and essays have appeared in *Angles of Ascent: A Norton Anthology of Contemporary African American Poetry* (Norton, 2013), *Common-Place: The Interactive Journal of Early American Life, Iowa Review, JENdA: A Journal of Cultural and African Women's Studies, The Kenyon Review: KROnline, Prairie Schooner, Virginia Quarterly Review,* and elsewhere. A native Southerner, Jeffers now lives on the prairie, where she has taught creative writing at the University of Oklahoma since 2002.

Fun with Fake Truths:
The *Wikipedia* Poem

For centuries, people have been drawn to poetry because of its ability to speak with beauty, wit, humor, wisdom, passion, longing, and insight about the self. In fact, many only write poetry in times of personal crisis, deep tragedy, or extreme joy. We turn to verse to help us make sense of our emotional landscape, whether it's in our diaries and journals or on Facebook or a blog. Admit it: you have reams of intensely rhyming poetry hidden under your bed, buried beneath yearbooks, ribbons, and bad photos, most of which laments the absence of justice in the world because _____ failed to return your love or because your _____ simply did not understand you. Don't worry. We've all been there. Most of us are still there.

Paradoxically, one of poetry's strengths is also its weakness: we want to write about ourselves, but we don't always know how to do it in a way that feels fresh and avoids cliché. The exercise that follows should help with that. In short, what I propose is this: write a poem about yourself in the form of a *Wikipedia* entry.

Rationale

Seriously, you might be asking, *Wikipedia*?

It may sound crazy at first and not particularly poetic, but bear with me. This practice is useful for a number of reasons. First, the form is familiar. We all rely on *Wikipedia*. We know what the entries look and sound like. They are direct, free of florid language and lush metaphors. They make references to external events and other *Wikipedia* pages. They tell stories but not in extensive detail. Best of all, the prose style of *Wikipedia* tends to be about restraint. This is great training for poets, who may, now and again, overwrite. You will also get the added advantage of immediate familiarity. Out of the gate your reader will know your reference and understand the context of your poem. It will be like delivering the letter of your poem in an envelope every reader will recognize.

Second, the form itself is liberating. As we all know, *Wikipedia* entries are written in prose (not verse), so you get to write a prose poem. Creating prose poems can be a lot of fun because they free you from the tyranny of the line. I often talk about readers of poetry feeling "poetry angst," but that can extend to writers as well. We feel pressure to deliver a big, gorgeous line; we want to knock out our audience with a turn of phrase or a singular image that will make readers weep with admiration and envy. And so we freeze up. Writing "poetry" is hard, in part because we only write in verse when we write poems. For better or worse, verse is a form that has a very limited use. On the other hand, we use prose for e-mails and essays and letters and fiction. We are fluent with prose; with that fluency expect for things to loosen up a bit.

Third, you get to write about yourself in the third person (Bob Dole would be great at this exercise). Why is writing about the self in third person beneficial? It allows you to detach a bit from your subject. When you write about yourself in the first person, there is very little distance between the speaker and the subject. That "I" pretty much collapses the two into each other. But if I am writing about "Dean Rader" in the third person, then both "Dean Rader" and the "author" are distinct—and perhaps even mysterious. We tend to be more willing to experiment and take chances when we jettison the "I." Put another way, when the subject of your poem is not you but "you," you will be bolder.

Last—and most important—*Wikipedia* entries are notorious for getting facts wrong. In fact, the actual *Wikipedia* entry on me is full of errors, both biographical and factual. To me, this is part of *Wikipedia's* charm. What it means for you is that it gives the writer license to get his or her own facts wrong. And that is a glorious thing.

Let me explain what I mean.

Every writer I know wants to write about the self in an interesting way, but almost no one wants to purposely mislead the reader. I know of no one who wants to produce fiction and pass it off as autobiography. However, Truth with a capital T is elusive and, to be honest, not always much fun. This is why writing a fake *Wikipedia* entry can be so freeing: we get to tell lies about ourselves alongside truths. Put another way, because *Wikipedia* entries are often incorrect, we are allowed to get our own facts wrong.

Preparation

If you are unfamiliar with prose poetry, you might also read a few prose poems to get an idea of what they do. Basically, a prose poem looks like prose: it starts at the left margin and goes all the way to the right margin, where it is right justified. You can make as many new paragraphs as you like. The point is to format your poem in prose, not verse.

Some examples of iconic prose poems include:

- "Be Drunk" by Charles Baudelaire
- "The Colonel" by Carolyn Forché
- "The Prose Poem" by Campbell McGrath
- "Goodtime Jesus" by James Tate

For more recent permutations and experimentations, check out an issue of the excellent magazine *Sentence: A Journal of Prose Poetics,* edited by Brian Clements.

Procedure

I. Visit several *Wikipedia* pages of famous people—preferably writers—to get a sense of how they are structured.

- Pay attention to each entry's writing style, and note the kind of data that is included (and not included) as well as the order in which this information is presented. Biographical details such as date and place of birth come first.
- Be aware of the length of the entries; you don't want your poem to be too long or too short.
- Consider using the standard headings in most entries. In the biography of Wallace Stevens, for example, there are category headings such as Education and Marriage, Career, Travel, Political Views, and Death. Imagine the fun you can have playing with these concepts in your own entry.

II. This is where the real fun happens.

- Make a list of true truths—actual biographical details you want to put into your entry.
- Then, make a list of fake truths—made-up details you also want to put into your entry.

III. Blend it all together. Write the poem, mixing your two notions of truths, trying to stay as faithful to the tone and style of *Wikipedia* entries as possible.

Tips

- Make your entry a funny, compelling mixture of facts you get right and facts you get wrong—just like a real *Wikipedia* entry. It is up to you how absurdly wrong your facts are, but I would have fun with this element of the exercise.

- Try not to stray too far from the style and approach of *Wikipedia*. If your language, diction, and syntax get too kooky, you will lose that sense of resemblance with the ubiquitous *Wikipedia* format. The more objective and rational your tone and prose style, the funnier and stranger the false facts will feel.

- In the first volume of *Wingbeats,* Lisa Russ Spaar offers up some very good suggestions for a self-portrait poem (pages 277–283). If you find yourself getting stuck, you might consult Spaar's suggestions for self-portraiture. You can then alter them as you see fit for your new Wikipediated self-portrait here.

Examples

My "Self Portrait as *Wikipedia* Entry" is a mash-up of details that at first seem plausible. It's only after you start reading through the poem that it becomes obvious I'm playing with concepts such as "truth," "fact," and "biography," as well as what kind of information comprises a biography of someone. Here is the poem as it appeared in *Zyzzyva*:

Note: As published online this poem, like *Wikipedia* entries, includes active links. They are represented here by underscoring.

Self Portrait as *Wikipedia* Entry

Dean Rader was born in Stockton, California during the Summer of Love. His sorrow is his own. He believes in star-sting and misnomer; he carries a toy whistle in his pocket. American by nationality, he was conceived in a Fiat near the Place du Châtelet. If asked, Rader will lie and say he doesn't remember it, but his lazy eyes and hunched back give him away. His left pinky finger, broken from basketball, has never healed, which he attributes to the caesura of distance and longing. His heart, the size of a normal man's heart, has been used as a model for a forensic mannequin. As a young boy, he once carried a small package to the river, but it was the wrong address. If asked to describe the river, he quotes van Heisenstadt ("die grenzen des wasser nicht vom errinerung"). Rader is not the little cricket. He is not a scissors for lefty. His soul, the size of a tiny condom, slides quickly onto time's blind spot. In 2004, he was asked about time's blind spot but responded only that "time, like a bandage, is always already wound and unwound." Once, as a student in college, he grew a third sideburn. Darkness, his maquette, darkness, his morning coffee. Rader's father studied to be a mortician; his mother was a therapist and, not surprisingly, Rader pursued both. His head, matted with crude sketches of <u>benches</u>, <u>nipples</u>, and flower <u>petals</u> is roughly the size of the <u>Place du Châtelet</u>. Strong at math from an early age, he helped develop what has come to be known as the <u>Osaka Postulate</u>, which proves that the square root of asyndeton is equal to the insphere of trespass, skin-spark, and elegy. As for his own spiritual beliefs, Rader is silent, though one of his recent poems, entitled "The Last Day of 34," suggests an <u>influence</u> of Simone Weil ("community is work. // For all I know, God may be in both. / For all you know, God may be both.) and Luigi Sacramone ("We want so much. // We only believe / in what we ask for"). Considered neither the lip blister nor the noodle wrenc, Rader has emerged, at least somewhat, as the repetitio rerum. In more recent work, he <u>denies</u> this (though indirectly) citing instead his commitment to interlocutory boundaries (bornage) through what he calls the "phatic interstice." At present his voice, the <u>pitch</u> and <u>timbre</u> of a young girl's, asks only for Tang. Consumed by his charity work with the NGO Our <u>Uncle</u> of Instrumentality, he has stopped writing entirely. When questioned about this at a 2007 <u>fundraiser</u>, <u>Rader</u> quipped, "Let my words say what I cannot." Since then, a <u>fragment</u> of an unpublished poem attributed to Rader has started appearing on the <u>Internet</u>:

Line up and line out
      says the moonwhittle.
Loss is the ring on our finger, the bright gem
compassing every step as we drop down.
Believe in what you know and you'll go blind.

Experts doubt its <u>authenticity</u>.

~ *Dean Rader*

The opening sentence of my poem is a fact. I was born in Stockton, California, during the Summer of Love. However, the second sentence, though also true, deviates from the objective information one finds in a typical *Wikipedia* entry. I would say this is where the text starts to become a "poem." By sentence three, the entry has moved slightly away from the dry presentational language of *Wikipedia* and slipped over into what I call "lyric-speak." Because of this move, readers don't really know where the poem is going, but they're probably along for the ride. The fourth sentence is completely made up, but it sounds like it could be strangely true. From here on, the poem modulates between true truths, fake truths, and sheer goofiness. But it never strays from the *Wikipedia* format. Structurally and tonally it never tips its hand.

If you are worried you are not famous enough to warrant a *Wikipedia* entry—even a false one—let me disabuse you of that notion. Everyone is famous enough for *Wikipedia*. But, regardless, you are just using the format of *Wikipedia*. It is the stencil, not the poem. How richly you color the stencil determines poetry.

For example, the poem below was written by an undergraduate at the University of San Francisco. This was his first poetry class. He was a theater major. I gave the class the *Wikipedia* assignment, and this is what he handed in:

Biographies Are Totally Factual

Sir James Carvallyo is a man on fire, a man with purpose. He was born on December 25, 1982 in a little village nestled in the Andes. Three years ago he made national news by taking Michelle Obama on a date without the Secret Service knowing. Sir James is wild indeed. In an interview with Oprah, he revealed that his primal side is aided by injecting snake venom into his arm. She then famously spit out her drink on accident once she heard his answer clearly. Sir James loves to make love with dragons not tigers, although he wants to be one. He struggles with depression and likes to roll a 24-sided dice to see how many pills he should take on a given day. Sir James once had an affair with Will Smith throughout the filming of *Men in Black II*. Once Jada Smith found out, the three of them engaged in a secret love triangle. This engagement lasted from the summer of 2003 to 2005. The trio publically addressed the issue prior to the Superbowl XL halftime show. Sir James had enough of the relationship, however, and decided to go another direction. Before the Queen knighted him for his brilliant efforts in social justice, Sir James would go to the ocean and write about how he would change the world. He would constantly put on the lens of greatness and would strive to eat it for breakfast, lunch, and dinner. Recently, however, Sir James has received enormous criticism. It all started in 2006 when having lunch with Pope Benedict XVI; he suffered a mental breakdown and slapped the Pope for not paying attention. As a result he was sent to the St. Vincent de Paul Wellness Center in Boston, MA, for three months to treat his illness. *GQ Magazine* asked the facility about

Sir James for their limited edition issue on him, and they said he loved to write poetry and smoke marijuana whenever he got the chance. He denies the facility's claim that he repeatedly snorted cocaine off a number of the nurses' buttocks. Sir James now resides in the California San Quentin State Prison for statutory rape.

~ James P. Carvallyo II

I don't love that last sentence (even though James is not, in fact, in prison), but I do like this poem. It is joyful and yet also punctuated with surprising moments of vulnerability and pain. For me, the revelation about depression stands out more in this poem than in would in an entire poem devoted to that subject.

One of the many reasons I like this exercise is that it gives the poet license to confess true personal details but because such details are buttressed by invented facts, humor, and the overall energy of the *Wikipedia* genre, the poet feels less exposed than he might in a traditional lineated lyric.

Variations

Hotlinks: To their credit, Laura Cogan and Oscar Villalon, the editors of *Zyzzyva,* published a version of my poem online at the *Zyzzyva* website, complete with hotlinks. So if you make your poem available on the Web, including hyperlinks can add a whole new element of interactivity—and wackiness.

Crowdsourcing: If you happen to be considering this exercise for a class, there is a variation of the *Wikipedia* poem that can enhance both the enjoyment and the verisimilitude of the project: consider crowdsourcing your poem. By that I mean, have two or three or four other authors contribute to the entry about you. Actual *Wikipedia* entries are compiled by groups rather than individuals. Yours could be the same. It works like this:

1. Let's say there are four people in your writing group. You will write four poems, one about each person in the group.
2. You will have to interview each person to obtain some basic biographical details, but that's easy.
3. Then you start writing four different poems simultaneously, with a different person beginning each poem. When the person who began the poem is done, another member of the group adds his or her sentences to the entry.

4. It can be chaos at first, and you never know what the final product will look like, but it can be incredibly thrilling. It is also a rare opportunity to collaborate on a group poem.

Alternate Realities. Other variations can expand upon the whole notion of fake truths. (For several possibilities, see James Harms' "Lying: A Series of Exercises," page 301.) You can write a *Wikipedia* entry for a book that does not exist, a record album by an invented band, or an actress you make up in your head. In fact, you could write a whole series of *Wikipedia* entry poems about some invented world. The possibilities are, literally, endless.

Dean Rader won the 2010 T. S. Eliot Poetry Prize with his debut collection of poems, *Works & Days* (Truman State University Press)—also a finalist for the Bob Bush Memorial First Book Prize and winner of the Writers' League of Texas Book Award. Rader's most recent collection, *Landscape/Portrait/Figure/Form* is part of the Omnidawn Chapbook Series. His poems have appeared in *Best American Poetry, Boston Review, TriQuarterly, Ninth Letter, Colorado Review, New American Writing, Cincinnati Review, Zyzzyva,* and many others. Editor of the blog *99 Poems for the 99 Percent,* Rader writes about poetry for *The Huffington Post, The Rumpus,* and *The San Francisco Chronicle.* He chairs the Department of English at the University of San Francisco.

Michael Theune

If They Can Do It, You Can, Too: The Dialectical Argument Poem

In *The Art of Syntax,* Ellen Bryant Voigt notes that the "sonnet's volta, or 'turn' . . . has become an inherent expectation for most short lyric poems." And in "Levels and Opposites: Structure in Poetry," Randall Jarrell notes that, while "making a great many structural analyses of poems," he "was astonished (and rather embarrassed) to find so many of the best-organized poems dialectically organized." Citing numerous poems by Yeats, Blake, Keats, and Hopkins, Jarrell goes so far as to claim that "anyone interested in such organization can easily find dozens or hundreds of examples."

If it is true that the **turn**—a major shift in a poem's rhetorical and/or dramatic trajectory—is a vital part of many poems and that dialectical structure—*structure* being the name for the pattern of a poem's turning—is at the core of so many poems, it would behoove any practitioner of poetry to become acquainted with, and perhaps even attempt, the dialectical argument poem.

According to John Beer, in "The Dialectical Argument Structure" (from *Structure & Surprise: Engaging Poetic Turns*), a **dialectical argument** is one "in which the speaker or speakers of the poem inhabit by turns the perspectives of two or more partial and unsatisfying positions before finding a resolution that transcends their limitations." Or more succinctly put, "In its most famous formulation, the dialectical argument structure is a three-part structure that turns, according to philosopher Johann Fichte, from thesis to antithesis to synthesis."

Discussion

Though all of this may seem impossibly complex, it need not be in practice. Consider this poem:

Back to the Body

If I'm arch, you're thrust. If I'm pocket,
you're muscle, kneecap, and skid. If I sit,
you're canvas, man, two eyes gone darker in the dark.
If I'm dark, you're insistent fingers.

I'm hinge to your lock and push, bare-toed,
uneasy in my skin and then the skin
forgotten. You're the bruise on my back
in half-circles of hunger, tongue, and hush.

If you're a spread of chest, I lay me down,
audience and song. If you're altar
I kneel before you. Here I am,
animal.

~ *Courtney Queeney*

In "Back to the Body," the dialectical argument structure is announced clearly in its repetition of "if I/then you." The relation between the *I* and the *you,* which often seems to be responsive, even electrically erotic, may not be purely antithetical; however, the *I* and the *you* clearly inhabit the perspectives of two partial and unsatisfying (unresolved) positions: if the *I* becomes one thing (the act of arching; a model; darkness; etc.), the *you* becomes another (thrust; artist and art materials; fingers; etc), and vice versa; however, the two keep becoming, seem stuck in becoming.

There is no resolution—that is, until poem's end, at which point *I* and *you* are finally joined. The poem's final sentence, "Here I am, / animal"—in which *animal* can be understood as a descriptor of the *I* (here I am, an animal) or else as a method of addressing the you (here I am, you animal)—joins both *I* and *you,* acknowledging their mutual physical existence and libidinous need.

Here is another "if I/then you" example:

Epithalamium

You're beeswax and I'm birdshit.
I'm mostly harmless. You're irrational.
If I'm iniquity then you're theft.
One of us is supercalifragilistic.

If I'm the most insane disgusting filth
you're hardly curiosa.
You're bubble wrap to my fingertips.
You're winter sleep and I'm the bee dance.

And I am menthol and you are eggshell.
When you're atrocious I am Spellcheck.
You're the yen. I'm the Nepalese pound.
If I'm homesteading you're radical chic.

I'm carpet shock and you're the rail.
I'm Memory Foam Day on Price-Drop TV
and you're the Lord of Misrule who shrieks
when I surface in goggles through duckweed,

and I am Trafalgar, and you're Waterloo,
and frequently it seems to me that I am you,
and you are me. If I'm the rising incantation
you're the charm, or I am, or you are.

~ Nick Laird

An **epithalamium** is a poem written to celebrate a marriage. Laird's "Ep-
ithalamium" seems, at least at first, to be about a couple, consisting of two
largely very different partners. The *you* is portrayed, mainly, as calm and state-
ly, as "beeswax," "winter sleep," "eggshell," "the yen," "radical chic." The *I* often
is frenetic, ugly, and/or debased: "bird shit," "the most insane disgusting filth,"
"the bee dance," "menthol" (a cigarette, one presumes), "the Nepalese pound,"
"homesteading."

However, this dichotomy does not hold throughout the poem. At
times, the roles are reversed: the *you* also can be "irrational" and "atrocious."
Additionally, the *I* and the *you* clearly have a good deal in common—as in
"iniquity" and "theft" (stealing is a sin), as in "the yen" and "the Nepalese
pound" (forms of currency), and as in "Trafalgar" and "Waterloo" (decisive
British military victories during the Napoleonic wars). In fact, their behaviors
also often relate and/or correspond to each other: "bubble wrap" calls out to
"fingertips"; someone's occasionally "atrocious" behavior might need correc-
tion (Spellcheck); "carpet shock" requires that "rail."

The interdependence of the *I* and the *you* achieves apotheosis in the po-
em's final stanza, in which the speaker admits that, in fact, there is little differ-
ence between the partners: "frequently it seems to me that I am you, / and you
are me." For all our differences, the speaker seems to be saying, *we*—in deep
union, an ultimate synthesis—are meant to be together.

A key feature, but also one of the great challenges, of the "if I/then you" version of the dialectical argument poem is keeping some real distance, some distinct difference, between the *I* and the *you,* at least initially. As Randall Jarrell notes, the "unity" that is often attributed to successful poems in fact "is generated by the tension set up between strongly differing forces, by the struggle of opposites; it involves not static things, but changing processes; it is a unity that is arrived at through heterogeneity, not homogeneity." If you can write such a conflicted, tense, yet also unified poem on your own, from scratch, then go for it. However, if this challenge comes a little less naturally, there is an easy way to take care of it: get both an *I* and a *you* to write the poem: collaborate.

Procedure

I. Team up. Get a poetry-writing partner, a *you* to your *I.*

II. To use time efficiently—and to create two poems with this exercise—each will start with her/his own sheet of paper. Each person will write down an "If I" statement. For example, if I were the one starting to write "Lake Muck" (see page 228), I would write, "If I am wheel."

III. Exchange sheets with your partner. Write the follow-up to that line: "then I. . . ." At this point, both partners are writing *I* statements. Later—Step VI— the individual who started a poem—with an "If I" statement—will take her/ his sheet of exchanges and make a poem of them, converting the other writer's statements into *you* statements.

The follow-up line almost never follows logically from the previous line, as logic removes all the tension and conflict from the poem. Rather, the follow-up line might relate only tangentially or associatively to the line preceding it, or else the follow-up line might be no follow-up at all. Instead, it could be a non sequitur. In fact, if it feels that you and your partner are having trouble breaking from easily fitting, logical connections, fold the page over backwards once a line has been written so that the partner cannot see the line, thus making the emerging relationship between the opposing voices totally random.

IV. Work to achieve variety both in terms of subject matter and in terms of form: write some long lines and some very short lines; write some abstract lines and some very specific lines; incorporate images from nature, sure, but also from technology, from real life and from fantasy, and so forth.

V. Go back and forth like this for a while—approximately twenty thesis-antithesis pairings.

VI. Working with their own texts, both poets will then independently select approximately 8–11 pairings from among those they have created and organize these statements into a back-and-forth exchange that has some arc, trajectory, or even jaggedness in it. Just as it is vital to have some tension between the *I* and the *you*, the different "if I/then you" pairings should have their own energy and occasionally come into conflict with or leap away from other pairings. (Notice, for example, how Queeney's second stanza begins with a "hinge" that seems to redirect the trajectory of the poem established in the first stanza.)

VII. Finally, try to come up with a synthesis—perhaps a statement about *we*. However, once again, don't allow the synthesis to be a mere synthesis. Poems largely are surprise-making machines. Try to create a synthesis that shocks, that astounds.

A Variation

If such intriguing synthesis is not possible, consider using the "if I/then you" pairings to create a different kind of dialectical argument poem, a poem of negative dialectics. Just as not all conflicts find resolution, not all dialectical endeavors invariably achieve synthesis. As John Beer notes, "One increasingly prominent variant of the poem of dialectical argument is what we might call the poem of **negative dialectics** . . . [which] sets up an opposition . . . but refuses to find a higher solution."

Instead of creating a statement of synthesis, consider transforming your dialectical poem into a negatively dialectical poem by concluding it with either an imperative (perhaps even an exclamation) or a question. Such an ending likely will not create a synthesis, revealing that, in fact, the *I* and the *you* do not or should not belong together in any significant way. Synthesis or not, what is important is that the final line be surprising even while feeling in some way connected with the lines that lead up to it.

Tips

Once you feel as though you have a draft of the poem, attend to the details.

- Consider revising line breaks. Collaborative work like this can often result in line breaks that are predictable (especially if each alternating line begins "if I" or "then you") or seemingly random (especially with lines of wildly different lengths).
- Additionally, consider revising syntax. You may decide you like the incantatory quality of the repeated "if I/then you" phrases, but you may also want to change things up, perhaps occasionally dropping the conditionals.

Examples

The results of engaging in such a procedure can be pretty terrific. The following is a poem created from the collaboration of two poets, Erica Kucharski and Jessica Rochford, and then edited by Erica:

Lake Muck

If I am wheel, you are eternal,
unafraid, and ever-pursuing.
If I am fumbling over my words,
then you are a trapeze swinger's safety net.
You're sway, and I'm constantly giving in.

If I am writer's block, then you are organic honey,
dripping from a hot teaspoon.
If I am off-white bed sheets,
then you are the cause of my anxiety.
I'm widespread panic, and you're doubtful.

You're tree sap, and I'm lake muck.
I'm cannibalism at its finest,
and you are waiting to consume me.
If I am hunger, then you are the flaky skin I pick.

If I am flesh, then you are stolen.
I am a bruised, discarded apple,
And you are the fruits of my labor.

If I am clay waiting to be molded,
then you are the whisper-kissed fingers
that hush me at night.

I am catatonic, steel, timber.
You are frustration.

If I am the crystalline edges of tomorrow,
then you are the ebbing tide.
Bring me in.

~ Erica Kucharski and Jessica Rochford

Of course, if you wish to try your own, solitary hand at creating an "if I/then you" dialectical argument poem, you should. Here is one, about the travails of a book lover (see how many literary references you recognize), created solely by Emily Susina:

Deuteragonist

> If I am a sixteen-year-old
> cynic, then you are
> my hunting hat. If I am a
> gypsy orphan, then you
> are the story of my revenge.
> If I remove the horns
> from a Viking helmet,
> you won't make a sound
> until everything is
> ruined. If I am trapped
> in a whale, then you
> are my salvation. If I
> receive a dollar
> for my birthday, then you
> are the last of five. If
> I am the boy who lived,
> you are made of
> holly. If I despise
> you, then you must be
> in want of a wife. If I
> am the leader of a savage
> utopia, then you are the sound
> of the sea in my ear. If I
> cannot fit through the
> door, then you are my
> REM cycle. If I am on
> a painted ocean, then
> you are the weight
> lifted from my shoulders.
> If I fake my death, then you
> are my dead boyfriend's

dagger. If my home has
been destroyed, then
you are my towel.
If I kill myself
in a swimming pool, you
are the green light that says go.
If I am the once and future king,
then you give light
like thirty torches.
But if I've been lost for years,
why do I still trust you to
carry me home?

~ *Emily Susina*

As the poems here reveal, incredibly interesting work can come from attempting to use the dialectical argument structure, an effort that offers poets the opportunity to become acquainted with and try their hand at employing a structure that is at the heart of so many great poems. For more information on and examples of the dialectical argument structure, see the *Structure and Surprise* blog and the *Voltage Poetry* website.

Michael Theune is the editor of *Structure & Surprise: Engaging Poetic Turns* (Teachers & Writers Collaborative, 2007) and the host of the blog *Structure and Surprise.* Along with Kim Addonizio, he co-edits *Voltage Poetry,* an online anthology of poems with great turns in them and discussion about those turns. Theune's poems, essays, and reviews have appeared in numerous publications, including journals such as *College English, Jacket,* and *Pleiades,* as well as books such as *Mentor and Muse: From Poets to Poets* (Southern Illinois University Press, 2010) and *The Monkey & the Wrench: Essays into Contemporary Poetics* (University of Akron Press, 2011). He is an associate professor of English at Illinois Wesleyan University.

Chapter V:
The Power
of Words, Names, Numbers

Poetry is all about nouns and verbs.

~ *Marianne Moore*

Natasha Sajé

Poems Aware of History:
Using the *Oxford English Dictionary*

Until our era, most writers learned Latin and Greek. They were trained, too, in the history and structure of English and in etymology. Even William Blake, who was not trained in classical languages, taught himself enough about Latin and Greek to use the devices of etymology in his poems. Times have changed, however. While many students do study a foreign language, only a small fraction study Latin, and fewer study Greek. Fewer still have exposure to the history of English. I myself never learned Latin or Greek, nor took a course in the history of English, but I've been obsessed with etymology ever since I stumbled on the *Oxford English Dictionary* (*OED*) and discovered its histories of word usage. Like me, most contemporary readers and writers must make a conscious effort to learn etymology by looking up words in a dictionary that lists word roots.

Samuel Taylor Coleridge said, "I wish our clever young poets would remember my homely definitions of prose and poetry; that is, prose = words in their best order; poetry = the best words in their best order." But what are the best words? And how do we choose? Most students, when asked, have not thought about choosing words; they merely use the words that come to mind.

Background

Conscious effort and dictionary work pay off for the writer who chooses words with an eye (and ear) to their history. Consider, for example, the word *inculcate*, which is sometimes used as a synonym for *teach*. The root of *inculcate* is *calx*, the Latin word for heel, so when *inculcate* is used as a synonym for *teach* it bears within it that image of a heel pressing something into the ground, and its metaphorical meaning is colored by that violence. The first listing for *inculcate* in the *OED* is a 1550 use by Coverdale: "This practyse dyd the holy elect of god in the olde time not onli inculcate and teach with words but also expresse and performe in dede."

Like Coverdale, contemporary writers can choose words from one or more families of our language. For example, the Anglo-Saxon word *woods* suggests something different from the Latinate *forest*, even though the two are equivalents. Imagine a Latinate version of Frost's poem "Stopping by [Forest] on a Snowy Evening": "whose [forest] this is I think I know." The Anglo-Saxon branch of our language is a boon to poets because its many monosyllabic words are easier to work into metrical verse.

Like French, German, and Italian, English has Indo-European roots, but English diction is less pure—and more interesting—not only because its synonyms have roots in both the Anglo-Saxon and the Latinate/Greek, but also because it has absorbed so many New-World and foreign words. By the time Samuel Johnson wrote his dictionary in 1755, the challenge was to standardize what had already become an unruly—or gloriously rich—language, infused with new words prompted by colonization, exploration, and technology. Meanwhile, as English entered the New World, it was further enriched by Native American words (such as *canoe* and *moccasin*) and borrowings fueled by British colonialism (such as *dinghy* and *pajamas* from Hindi). A writer can choose between these groups to achieve a particular effect.

Understanding etymology allows a writer to tap into buried or historical meanings of words, thereby amplifying the effect of a single image. For example, Linda Aldrich writes, "commonplace items in the house—in this case, a couch, a chair, a table—are similar to the many words we use every day without thinking." In her poem, "Deranging Furniture" (page 237), she notes that the word *chair* comes from *cathedra*, the bishop's throne, and thus connotes authority and exception. Aldrich's stanza on this word illustrates the history of the rise of the individual through the concept of a chair. In other words, in the Middle Ages, common people sat on benches, while chairs were reserved for nobility or ecclesiastics. The change to societies where everyone had a chair signifies a rise in individualism, yet the word still carries a trace of its former authority, as in "committee chair." In my poem "P" (page 239), *pakan* (a Cree word that means "nut which is cracked with a stone") calls forth the image of indigenous peoples harvesting this distinctly American nut, the pecan.

Etymology also provides access to history and inquiries about ideological change. For example, the word *silly* meant "worthy of sympathy" four hundred years ago; the change from a positive to a largely negative meaning today might serve as a prompt for a poem. Perhaps George Eliot knew that history when she complained about "silly novels by lady novelists." Conversely, the word *pride* has changed from negative to positive. It referred to the "first sin" during Milton's era but today connotes a badge of honor, as in "gay pride." A change in context appears to have risen from a change in thinking about individual power. Thus, a contemporary American reader might consider "man's first disobedience" as akin to taking initiative.

The exercise that follows is a quick lesson in etymology. I have found it converts some writers into dictionary users. At the very least it makes us aware that we must broaden our lexical field of choice and that word histories complicate that choice. The main purpose is to get students to think of word histories as both spurs to new poems and complicating factors worthy of our conscious consideration.

Materials

You will need access to the *Oxford English Dictionary*. Most universities and public libraries offer online access to the *OED* (under databases, "Arts & Humanities"); individuals can also subscribe to the online service. Students can bring laptops to class or access the *OED* from home. Today, the *OED* is also available on CD-ROM. Of course, the *OED* started in hard copy, but the latest edition (*OED3*) is available only as an electronic version. In hard copy, the searching can be truly random (open the book to any page), but online one has to enter a word into a search box.

Procedure

I. Make a list of five words that interest you or that you might want to use in a poem. Some might be very ordinary words such as *table* while others might be words you rarely use or whose definition you do not know.

II. Access the *OED* online. Read the full entries for the words and jot down the etymologies (dates, images, languages) that seem interesting. You may have to try several words before you find one whose history interests you.

III. Read the list of chronological instances of the word's use. Make note of the first time the word appeared in print in English; create a scene around this first use. Who uttered it? Where and why? Even if a quote is in Middle English, pronounce it and try to figure out what it means. Write down the quotes that intrigue you or that you disagree with, making sure to record the author and date. Note changes in connotation in the word's uses.

IV. Once you have a page or two of notes, connect the dots by asking questions. You may put the questions into the poem, you may speculate, or you may do research and arrive at an answer. For instance, the root of the word *peculiar* (*pecu*) means cattle, a reminder of the time when owning livestock was a primary form of wealth. When did owning cattle become an unusual situation? How many cattle did a person have to own to be considered wealthy? Make the leap, perhaps, to Ted Turner and his buffalo ranch or living in our era, when most of the wealth is held by a very few people. This investigative process should be playful and open-ended.

Variations

I. Invented Etymology: Write a poem creating a false etymology for a word, one that makes logical or sound sense, even if it is not historically accurate. For instance, *turkey* is a bird named after the country it was mistakenly thought to come from. *Peccadillo* sounds like an animal, perhaps related to *armadillo*. For examples, see Elizabeth Alexander's poem "Affirmative Action Blues," which explores the false etymology of the word *niggardly,* or Allen Grossman's "Sentinel Yellowwoods," which makes a false connection between *lute* (the musical instrument) and *lutea* (yellow).

II. Combinations: Outline three categories of words with similar meanings:

- Old English/Germanic
- Latinate/Greek
- "foreign borrowings"

Come up with—even by guessing, since process is most important here and there's no right answer—three similar words, for instance, *hope, expectation,* and *Esperanza.* This process will involve some toggling back and forth between the *OED*, a thesaurus, and a search engine. Then find quotes for each word and connect two of them. For example, connect Emily Dickinson's "Hope is the thing with feathers" and the story of the arson-set Esperanza fire in California in 2006.

Note: For other approaches that use the *OED*, see Joanne Diaz's "Digging for Names," page 247, and Marcela Sulak's "The New Yesterday: The Researched Poem," page 251.

Examples

The Greeting

> Masa tells me to ask about hamachi
> the yellowtail fish—some nights
> the restaurant has none.
> *And remember to write down names*
> Masa-kun says.
> (*-kun* the male equivalent of *-chan,* endearment

attached to a name—
a sheet of seaweed
encircling white rice.) The sushi chefs
adopt my middle name, my first too English
for their taste. *Mauri-chan*
they call, nudging sashimi my way,
take to table five.

Chan in old English sometimes meant
to open in fissures, to crack, or even
to burst. As in Japanese, a word
close to the heart.
And *kun* a variation of *con:*
to know.

My grandparents withheld their language, wishing
assimilation for their children,
though the food stuck: bento boxes
fragrant with pickled radish,
calm triangles of *o-nigiri* shaped
like the space between

my grandmother's palms. Home
from the restaurant, I find my father
at the kitchen table—
Bobby-kun!
He looks up quickly,
a strange recognition in his eyes.

~ *Anne Terashima*

Deranging Furniture

Not the Turkish divan—headless, footless bed,
reciting poems in Oriental alphabets,
and never in sofas, derived from desert
migrations and the cushioned camel's saddle.
Problems gather in the common couch, the one
without pretense, made to keep the carpet from flying.

The favored French are responsible for this instrument
of *coucher,* this lying down in layers: bourgeois secret
of loose change, mingled hair, wrinkled cigarette papers.
Keeper of phrases and men in exile. If couch could talk,
it would like psychiatrist's couch, unburden
threadbare nouns, run its recovered length
beneath our days before it is again put on the curb
for fraternity boys to find.

*

Chair has a singular sense of itself, as in *cathedra,*
bishop's throne, where stained glass and stone
provide a place for chair to dominate events.
However, four legs and a back sometimes have troubling
arms, as in dentist's chair, or electric chair, seat
of greatest shame, for chair is meant to be carried aloft,
separate and dignified, arms free to wave, certainly
not placed anywhere near the couch. No,
give chair some room, give it its own room, with steps
leading up, and, please, no games. No musical chairs,
no remote control organizer, no vaudeville
stacking act with plates and broomstick.

*

Table, raised and flat, comes from nothing more
than *tabula,* a slab on which to put or inscribe something.
Table cares not what shape or size it is, as long as things
are brought to it. Dinner, backgammon, a little hot toddy,
the ten commandments. A table of contents: first,
spread out the map and see everything from above,
nothing under the table. Next, put all cards on the table,
no second-guessing. Third, take everything with a grain
of salt or postpone until tomorrow. Flat does not mean
linear: good jokes bring out topography, and don't worry
where you sit, everyone is a member of the board.
Do a periodic table, pulling up a bench,
so as not to offend the sensibility of chair.

~ *Linda Aldrich*

P

Peccadillo. The animal I touched at age four, the rat I didn't recognize. I commit them every day. I am not the Pope, love like garlic emanating from my pores. Who would keep a pangolin for a pet? The pink fairy pichiciego dies in captivity. The serpent Python fell only after a thousand silver arrows from Apollo's bow, whose prowess changed Mount Parnassus into a place of music and light, transfixed him. *For the Lord has chosen Jacob unto himself and Israel for his peculiar treasure.* His "peculiar" treasure, privately owned, from *pecu,* cattle. When owning cattle meant being rich. Is ownership sin? Latin, *peccare,* to sin. Our peculiar institution produced slaves worth six billion dollars. There's a difference between owning human beings and owning cattle. The latter we eat, like pecans, from the Cree, *pakan,* that which is cracked with a stone. A New World nut, so rich in oil, undomesticated until 1846.

~ *Natasha Sajé*

Natasha Sajé is the author of three poetry collections, *Vivarium* (Tupelo Press, 2014), *Bend* (Tupelo Press, 2004), and *Red Under the Skin* (University of Pittsburgh Press, 1994), as well as *Windows and Doors: A Poet Reads Literary Theory* (University of Michigan Press, 2014). Her honors include the Robert H. Winner and the Alice Fay di Castagnola Awards from the Poetry Society of America, the 2002 Campbell Corner Poetry Prize, a Fulbright Scholarship to Slovenia, and a Camargo Fellowship in France. Sajé has been teaching in the low residency Vermont College of Fine Arts M.F.A. in Writing Program since 1996; she is a professor of English at Westminster College in Salt Lake City, where she directs the Weeks Poetry Series.

Weird Word Poems

When I was working on my second book, *Trouble with the Machine,* I stumbled on a website called *World Wide Words*, British writer Michael Quinion's weekly e-magazine on the English language across the globe. While perusing the site, I noticed one of its section indexes, entitled Weird Words. I immediately clicked on the link and was brought to a page that contained an alphabetized collection of, well, weird words. I clicked on *ataraxy* and found information about the word's origins, its definition, and examples of its earliest uses in English. I kept clicking, fascinated by word histories, intrigued by this opportunity to increase my vocabulary.

After a few hours, I decided to see if I could write a poem from one of the words. I liked the idea of using an obscure word for a title and letting it guide me. To add to the degree of difficulty, I told myself I couldn't use any of the word's definition in the poem. Eventually I wrote a poem about navel gazing:

Omphaloskepsis

At first, it seemed unnatural, like a mistake in my person, a thing of which to feel ashamed. After awhile, I understood its value, its meaning. It meant nobody's perfect. It meant a more adventurous type would be looking at the Grand Canyon. I conceded. Took a bath. Water pooled there. I felt a little better. I did not approximate anything near to God.

> ~ *Christopher Kennedy*

Pleased with the result, I began to write more poems using this approach. I ended up with about a half dozen I liked enough to include in *Trouble with the Machine.*

Note: You can sign up with the *World Wide Words* listserv, which will send you word histories, new words, the background to words in the news, and some of the problems of English usage—directly to your e-mail account on a weekly basis.

Procedure

That fall, I used this approach in one of my classes. I brought in words with their definitions, handed out one word to each student, and asked the students to write a poem that indicated what their word meant without using any of the definition. The words included *funambulist, sockdolager, gongoozler, humdedgeon, jobbernowl, lycanthropy, mournival, myphlolepsy, guillon, rodomontade, knucker,* and *thaumaturgy.* Students wrote for about twenty minutes, and then I had them share their poems while the rest of the class tried to guess the definition of the word.

I was impressed with the quality of the work (this was a graduate forms class), and the guessing-game aspect of the exercise was entertaining. I have had luck with it ever since.

Examples

One of the students in that first class, Erin Brooks Worley, used the exercise to write poems that were published in *Ninth Letter.* She ultimately took some liberties, in one case using a title other than the word itself, and in another case, using a word that may have been familiar to most readers. But the motivating factor was the same—to write a poem by trying to describe a word without using any aspect of its definition.

Bruxer

There are often avalanches in my dreams. Rocks collide and grate down to dirt. Other nights, machines break. Rusted gears wedge together and chains fall into piles of links. An engine chokes. Sometimes I am walking on glass with weights in my hands, or a child's bones are breaking. When they break loud, I open my eyes and watch your jaw moving. Unlike you, I talk in my sleep. You tell me I say quiet.

Copacetic

You never swung an arm across the bed and hit me in your sleep. I never hit you back, and you never called me a liar when I said you hit me first. There was never a car crash in the front yard of our first house; we never woke to the sound of shattering glass, and you never said the accident was an omen. Our daughter does not make finger paintings and paper ornaments for only one parent, or she does, but that parent is not you. Our air conditioner works so well that frost branches across our mirrors and windows; we are never so hot that we lie under the ceiling fan and call each other lazy. When we have sex, it is never complicated or cold. You would never move my hands to your throat and say please.

Night Shift

Others clean the trailers that circle outside. I watch their lights switch on and off through windows. I work alone in science classrooms, even during dissection units. The plastic containers of discarded frog stomachs and throats, the unwound small intestines of fetal pigs. The semi-light hour is saved for these tasks. Once I found a tiny lung on the floor. Geometry, geography, history? All those earlier rooms were the same: chalk dust and dirty carpets. Sometimes I sit at your desk to see the room that way. Sometimes I stand in your storage closet, turning objects upside down. Mugs, vases, other dusty and fragile gifts from your favorites. One night, I broke a small glass animal, the one with a red heart imposed on his chest. I put his halves in my pockets. I never expected you to notice he was gone.

~ *Erin Brooks Worley*

Note: In case you're wondering, *bruxer* is dental jargon for someone who involuntarily grinds his teeth. *Copacetic* is an adjective used to describe something in excellent order. And *janitrix*, which is the word "Night Shift" riffs on, is a female janitor.

Christopher Kennedy is the author of four collections of poetry—*Ennui Prophet* (BOA Editions, 2011), *Encouragement for a Man Falling to His Death* (BOA Editions, 2007), which received the Isabella Gardner Poetry Award, *Trouble with the Machine* (Low Fidelity Press, 2003), and *Nietzsche's Horse* (Mitki/Mitki Press, 2001). Kennedy is the translator, along with Faisal Siddiqui and Mi Ditmar, of *Light and Heavy Things: Selected Poems of Zeeshan Sahil* (BOA Editions, 2013), as part of the Lannan Foundation Translation Series. Kennedy's work has appeared in numerous print and online journals, including *Ploughshares, McSweeney's, The Threepenny Review, Mississippi Review, New York Tyrant,* and *Plume*. A recipient of poetry fellowships from the National Endowment for the Arts and the New York Foundation for the Arts, he is an associate professor of English at Syracuse University, where he directs the M.F.A. Program in Creative Writing.

Tony Hoagland

The Poetry of Multiple Naming

In Shakespeare's *Henry the Fourth Part I,* the character Falstaff is talking to Prince Hal, the future King of England:

> when thou art king, let not
> us that are squires of the night's body be called
> thieves of the day's beauty: let us be Diana's
> foresters, gentlemen of the shade, minions of the
> moon; and let men say we be men of good government,
> being governed, as the sea is, by our noble and
> chaste mistress the moon . . .

Thieves of the day's beauty. Diana's foresters. Gentlemen of the shade. Minions of the moon. Falstaff is practicing the comedic art of renaming, using naming as a mode of imagination and re-invention; he and his friends are a bunch of thieves, and he is trying to romantically elevate their profession.

Discussion

Multiple naming is a device which many poems use, in different ways, to increase their energy and drama. Such artful renaming requires the skills of diction and of rhetoric, the art of raising and lowering levels of vocabulary, the warming and cooling of word choice and attitude. Renaming is also related to skills of idiom and speech register. One might even say that some poems create their narrative entirely from the naming and renaming of a thing.

Consider the prose poem below:

The Beautiful American Word "Guy"

The beautiful American word "guy." It always gets me. For one thing, a guy is never alone. What if your name were Guy? Then you'd think that all the men behind all the deli counters on Ninth Avenue were talking to you. "What'll it be, Guy?" "Mayo, Guy?" "We're outta sesame, Guy, how about onion?" "Guy" is friendly, whereas "man" is hostile and competitive. "I hear you, man," actually means, "Back off, Dickhead, I'm in charge here."

"Dude" is useful, but thanks to Bart Simpson it's never sincere. "Buddy," "buster," and "pal" are sturdy but tainted by camp, like dialogue from old

Hollywood movies. "Boss" scares me, and "chief" sounds undemocratic and maybe politically incorrect.

I like "brother" sometimes. "Brother, you gotta be kidding," a truck driver yelled at me once on Eighth Avenue, because I was reading a book and crossing the street against the light. He twisted the word around to mean, "Die, motherfucker," but I'm a romantic, and I heard him saying, "Cling to me as we plunge together manfully into the abyss."

Still, "guy" is the most inclusive and universally tender, taking the back of your neck in its creased palm and saying, "I'm counting on you." It's a promise and a threat, a stroke, a supplication, and a plea. If there were an epic poem of America in muscular four-beat Old English lines, its first word would not be "Hwaet," but "Guy."

~ John Weir

Weir's poem rejoices in and agonizes over the wealth of alternative nouns by which one man can address another in America. His poem is very funny, in part because it expresses a very real and familiar anxiety felt by men about the many relative degrees of masculinity represented by our everyday speech.

Looked at as a dilemma of vocabulary, the poem can be seen as simply a catalogue, or rehearsal, of available synonyms—each one with its own history, baggage, and connotations: *man, dickhead, chief, motherfucker, buddy.* Looked at as a dilemma of psychology, of masculinity or politics, and we are deep inside not just the psyche but the history of the world.

In other words, language has baggage—and a skilled writer can play on the scale of inferences and tones as if English were a music hall piano.

As another example, here's a short poem that uses multiple naming to explore the broad range of perspectives one might have on a common modern appliance:

Boob Tube

Jillian says that television is the great blue bosom
through which Americans like to suck forgetfulness.

Joey says that if you have HBO, the moon
comes to seem over-rated.

Emily Dickinson never wrote a poem that begins *Because I did not stop*
> *for death,*
I turned to CNN.

Robert says that TV is a true friend to the sick and the afflicted.

But Dorothy Parker said *If I can't eat it, drink it or sleep with it,*
what good is it?

Travis says television can't compete with beer
and Phil says the Iroquois call it the last hope of Native People,

a remark which nobody understands;
and which the Iroquois, those mysterious people,

refuse to explain.

> ~ Jill Eisenbaum

Eisenbaum's poem bears a distant resemblance to Wallace Stevens' canonical poem "Thirteen Ways of Looking at a Blackbird." It is easy to imagine some later poet writing "Thirteen Ways of Looking at a Cell Phone" or "Thirteen Ways of Looking at the Iraq War." Almost any topic or theme can be approached through the technique of multiple naming.

Here's a short list of poems that do this infectious riffing (book title included for those not readily available online):

- "Idiomatic" by Billy Collins (from *Sailing Alone Around the Room*)
- "betrothal in B minor" by Barbara Hamby (from *Delirium*)
- "A child said, What is the grass?" by Walt Whitman (from "Song of Myself")

Procedure

Write a poem in which the principle linguistic activity is naming and renaming. Let yourself use exaggerated metaphors, euphemisms, ornate styles of speech, real or invented synonyms for referring to the object of discussion. You can have a single speaker renaming a thing (your dog, your brother's old Chevy Nova, the government, a gun, a desert, a cocktail . . .). Or you can have multiple speakers each taking a turn at renaming, as in the poem that follows.

An Example

Breaking Up Is Hard to Do

On Friday afternoon David said he was divesting his holdings
            in Stephanie dot org.
And Cindy announced she was getting rid of all her Dan-obelia,
            and did anyone want a tennis racket or a cardigan?

Alice told Michael that she was transplanting herself
            to another brand of potting soil
And Jason composed a 3-chord blues song called
            "I Can't Rake Your Leaves Anymore, Mama,"
then insisted on playing it
            over his speakerphone to Ellen.

The moon rose up in the western sky
            with an expression of complete exhaustion,
like a 38-year old single mother
            standing at the edge of the playground. Right at that moment

Betty was extracting coil after coil of Andrew's
            emotional intestines
            through a verbal incision she had made in his heart,
and Jane was parachuting into an Ani Difranco concert
            wearing a banner saying, Get Lost, Mark Resnick.

That's how you find out:
out of the blue.
And it hurts, baby, it really hurts
because breaking up is hard to do.

        ~ Tony Hoagland

Tony Hoagland teaches creative writing at the University of Houston. His books of poems include *What Narcissism Means to Me, Unincorporated Persons in the Late Honda Dynasty,* and *Donkey Gospel.* Hoagland's work has received the Mark Twain Award, a Guggenheim Fellowship, the Jackson Poetry Prize, and others. He has written two collections of craft essays, most recently *Twenty Poems That Could Save America* (Graywolf Press, 2014). Several years ago he founded *FivePowersPoetry.com,* a program for coaching high school teachers in the teaching of poetry in the classroom.

Digging for Names

My interest in the archaeology of our language and how it has transformed over time has led me to search for countless words in the *Oxford English Dictionary*. Recently, though, I've started to narrow my search in order to focus on people's names. These searches provide fascinating ties to ancient stories, myths, and religious allusions. For example, *Jason* has roots in the great Greek myth of Jason, Medea, and the Argonauts; *Lauren* carries the echoes of the story of Daphne and Apollo (in Ovid's story, Daphne is transformed into a laurel tree); and *Adam* is a reminder of our humble origins (the name means "of earth") and our fallen state. This awareness of the archeology of names allows a poet to initiate a journey into identity that can be very compelling.

Procedure

I. Look up your first name—or the name of a friend or loved one—in any one or more of the following resources:

- The *Oxford English Dictionary* (*OED*), the greatest repository of definitions, etymologies, and usages of words in English, can be especially useful for names that also function as common words (e.g., ivy, warren, daisy, or chuck).

- If you don't have access to the *OED*, Douglas Harper's *Online Etymology Dictionary* is also an excellent resource.

- Dozens of websites are devoted to baby names and their meanings. Use any one of these sites to search for names.

- The Hebrew Bible and the New Testament provide remarkable stories of figures who overcame seemingly insurmountable obstacles, heard the voice of God, or performed superhuman feats of strength. Look here for hundreds of Judeo-Christian names, including Noah, Sarah, Rebecca, Benjamin, James, Thomas, and Peter.

- Books of saints provide the stories of saints' lives, many of which are remarkably interesting. Looking up the stories of Augustine, Benedict, or Teresa of Ávila will provide any poet with reams of great information.

II. Look up your last name, too. Surnames can be the key to our linguistic and ethnic origins, and, once translated into English, can provide terrific language imagery. In recent years, I've had students with last names that, in various languages, mean shoe maker, field, thirst, sugar mountain, oil striker, and ditch. Any one of these words could be useful in creating a ghazal's final signature couplet, which often includes the poet's name—or in developing a poem in any shape or style.

III. Use the material you find as raw material for a poem. In truth, you can do this exercise any way you like, as long as your engagement with your name(s) brings you to the strangeness of the name, and of the English language. You can refer to the translation or origin of your name in passing; it can be the launching pad for the poem's central concerns; or, as the poem that follows will demonstrate, it can be the primary source of interest for the poem. (For an approach that uses names grounded in history/tradition/culture, see Marcela Sulak's "The New Yesterday: The Researched Poem," page 251.)

An Example

Passive Insults from the *Oxford English Dictionary*

You were named after a common plant
with dark green leaves, tough gloss,
and serrated edges.
The berries that glow vermilion are toxic to humans,
causing vomiting and diarrhea.
But they feed the birds well,
especially in colder times.

You were named after the bark that people in 1728, England,
boiled for ten to twelve hours to make birdlime.
They spread it thickly on branches, trapping the birds
and letting them die from exhaustion,
all for an afternoon snack.
During World War II that same birdlime made sticky bombs.
They often stuck to the soldier's uniforms
instead of the enemy's tank—
after the pin was pulled.

You were named after Celastrina Argiolus,
the azure butterfly that looks more like a spray-painted moth.
Every five years it dies out almost completely, but comes back.
Lucky enough for the parasitic wasp that eats its larvae.

You were named after an effigy children would burn
during village games, East Kent, 1779.
You were also an integral part of Bonfire Night,
where you were roasted next to a straw Guy Fawkes
for hundreds of years and counting.

Your name used to be for men,
and now ranks approximately #380 for most popular girl's name in
      the U.S.

In Celtic, it means to rule with dignity and honor,
even in the midst of a great challenge.
Your parents must not know you as well as I do.

In Turkish, it translates to Özgü, meaning "characteristic."
As in, it's very Özgü of you to know you're making a mess of me,
and leave me to fix myself up.

My favorite definition, though, is in Urban Dictionary:
lacking volume control, slag, whore, loose, kinky, blonde.
The one you will always want, but will never want you back.

Examples:
I thought she was the one who would follow through on her
      promises, but . . .
I thought that because she was almost thirty, she must be mature,
      but . . .
I thought that because she wasn't always the drunkest one at the bar,
      she was a good person,

but . . .

she was just another Holly.

~ *Amy Werner*

Amy Werner is a history major at Illinois Wesleyan University. Here, she fuses her interest in the history of a word with her exploration of a person's character. From the opening stanza, the reader can see that the *you,* by virtue of her name, is capable of causing real harm. The speaker engages with the strangeness of Latin, Turkish, and the English of another century. Then, by the sixth and seventh stanzas, the reader starts to see the relevance of this research: the speaker is trying to use the dictionary to understand how the *you* could be so hurtful, so unkind, so careless. Toward the end of the poem, the speaker registers her dissatisfaction with the *OED* and insists on more research—this time at the *Urban Dictionary* website, where she finds usages of the word that seem to suit the addressee. By the final line, the speaker has revealed the name that she has been investigating throughout the poem, a surprise that rewards tenacious, curious readers and makes them want to read the poem all over again.

Joanne Diaz won the Brittingham Prize for *My Favorite Tyrants* (University of Wisconsin Press, 2014). She is also the author of *The Lessons* (Silverfish Review Press, 2011). Recipient of fellowships from the Illinois Arts Council and the National Endowment for the Arts, Diaz teaches in the English Department at Illinois Wesleyan University.

The New Yesterday:
The Researched Poem

For about ten years I found myself living and working in a different country every two years or so. In each temporary home, the histories of the local textile factory, castle, cathedral, synagogue, train tracks, or cacao plantations revealed more to me than the current newspapers. A country such as Israel, where I have lived for the last three years, can be daunting, though. Every hill and stone is already inscribed in poems, songs, histories, and the religious texts of three major religions. Often there are multiple versions of everything.

Especially when poets feel strongly about a political or cultural situation, researched and documentary poetry allows them to make a point effectively, without turning poetry into propaganda. I designed the following set of exercises for a graduate workshop in documentary poetry—to help my students and me gain a toehold on the local landscape.

Preparation

Choose a single object or person about which to become temporarily obsessed. My students have had success with the topics of tear gas, Herod the Great, and a Rio de Janeiro favela. I chose Puabi, a powerful Semitic Akkadian woman from the city of Ur in Sumeria.

Procedure

The individual approaches that follow can be done in any order to produce six different poems, or they can be combined to produce more complex poems. While I have never used all six approaches to produce a single poem, I have used various combinations of the six to produce a poem, "Hebrew Lesson: Avera" (page 255).

Approach I: The *OED*

Locate your object/person—or a word that characterizes your object/person—in the *Oxford English Dictionary*. List definitions and usages you've never considered before, including the oldest usage and the most recent. Write a narrative connecting the oldest use of your word to the most recent. (For other approaches that use the *OED*, see Natasha Sajé's "Poems Aware of History: Using the *Oxford English Dictionary*," page 233, and Joanne Diaz's "Digging for Names," page 247.)

An Example

One of my students chose tear gas. She looked up *panic,* which derives from the name of the Greek god Pan. Commonly depicted as half-man, half-goat, he would seem at home among the herds of goats witness to the demonstrations Joanna had been following in the West Bank, at which tear gas was sometimes dispersed. Pan was surely present there during the Greek occupation, as well.

Panic at the Demo

You panic southward
    into the wind.
The canisters catherine-wheel
    through the air
sputter-whistling
    bouncing landing
with sharp bang-bangs
    one under an olive tree one
on the path

        that snakes up the hill

one just beyond
    the fence falling with
a ping rising like
a rain-cloud spreading pale
    gray pillows of burning.
Pan sees it   he
    tosses his head back and
laughs at you all   scattering
    like fistfuls of shells
thrown back
      into the sea.

~ Joanna Chen

Approach II: A Dual-Language Dictionary

I. Find a word that you associate with your object/person, and look it up in the language from which your object/person originates. For example, I chose the verb *to cross* since all we know of Puabi was found in her burial chamber, along with dozens of maidservants killed in her tomb and buried with her to serve her after they "crossed into the next world." I also chose this verb because Puabi comes from Ur, the same city as Abraham, who "crossed" into the land of Canaan. I looked up the verb in Hebrew, since both Puabi and Abraham spoke Semitic languages. In Hebrew "to cross" is עבר.

II. Now take the non-English language word and look it up once more—in English. Pick out 2–3 diverse definitions. For example, the root עבר can mean, among other things: to cross, to pass, to advance, to move, to violate, to breach; embryo or fetus. It is also a root of *Hebrew* and *Abraham*.

III. Connect the disparate definitions into a single narrative.

Approach III: Mapping

After you've looked up the definitions of your word in the *OED* and a dual-language dictionary, trace the word/object/person's trajectory, or at least a portion of it, on a map. Create a narrative that explains the word's journey from one language to another, from one land to another, one religion to another. . . . Alternatively, you might focus on a single point on the map.

Approach IV: The Internet

Find the most recent internet entry you can for your word/object/person. If it is a video, transcribe it. If it is an image, translate it into language.

Approach V: Walking

This approach is designed to help the writer learn to trust simple observations to convey messages or states of being. It can also produce a poem to serve as the wide angle, or opening shot, in a documentary poem series. I came up with it after reading Muriel Rukeyser's *Book of the Dead,* as well as Jon Cotner and Andy Fitch's *Ten Walks/Two Talks.*

- Commit to taking one sixty-minute walk every day for a week. Write down sixty observations.

- Try to refrain from writing reflections. Instead, focus on sensory detail, overheard conversation; pay deep attention to the environment.

- Try to recreate the physical walk while refraining from the mental soundtrack that accompanies it.

- Avoid value judgments and loaded adjectives (e.g., *gloomy tree*); describe the scene as objectively as possible (e.g., *gnarled tree empty of leaves*).

When reading the results of this exercise in a group, one woman was astonished that every member realized that the walker was having a difficult time with her mother. Nothing had been mentioned about the mother explicitly. But nearly every detail in the physical world that the walker had noted pointed to the fact she was thinking about her mother, and the thoughts were uncharacteristically ambivalent.

Approach VI: A Local Business, Site, or Museum

If your object is made locally, or sold locally, go to manufacturers or retailers and talk to them—not about the object, but about their lives or their customers, or the process of opening the place of business. Find customers and talk to them about themselves.

Alternately, if your object of obsession is a historical or mythic figure or legend, go to a museum, look up the object, and note all that is associated with it. In the poem I've provided on the facing page, "Hebrew Lesson: Avera," I focused on Puabi's beer straws, which I found in the ancient glass exhibition at the Eretz Israel Museum in Tel Aviv.

An Example

This series of exercises should simply start you out. Once you've sampled from among them, you'll probably have discovered many others you'd like to explore. The combination of approaches II, III, and VI above produced my syllabic poem "Hebrew Lesson: Avera."

Note: A **syllabic poem** is one in which lines are broken according to syllable count, not stress. There are two kinds—**normative**, in which each line of a poem has the same number of syllables; or **quantitative** (line-mated), in which each stanza has the same number of syllables, and each corresponding line of each stanza has the same number of syllables (e.g., each first line has the same number as every other first line; each second line has the same number as every other second line, and so forth). Like Marianne Moore and Robyn Schiff, I find that researched poems work well in syllabics, for, by their very nature, syllabics force us to pay attention to the act of perceiving.

"Hebrew Lesson: Avera" is a quantitative syllabic. For examples of a normative syllabic, see Alfred Nicol on the syllabic (page 159) and Brent Goodman's exercise "The Incredible Shrinking Poem: Using Syllabics to Inspire & Surprise" (page 164).

Hebrew Lesson: Avera

crossing, violation

In Venezuela, we could whack the heads off these empty wine bottles,
     plant
their bottoms in fresh cement so their jagged teeth would flash between
     the rich
and those of the poor unemployed by the rich. If we were still
in Germany, there'd be a pragmatic plastic bin labeled *colored glass,* and
     there
they'd sleep it off, till someone hauled them to the rubber belt
they'd ride for free, be scrubbed and dried. They'd open
their mouths and be filled again. If we were still in Austin
or South Philly we'd be laughing so hard when they fell, we'd
gather their shards, and with mirrors (because the more
the merrier) and plastic glo-in-the-dark saints
we'd make the guys who piss against the walls at night
something nice to look at;

as Henry Ford said, art should be something for every day. Most workers
     on
large public projects in Mesopotamia got one liter of beer
a day. On the occasion of Queen Puabi's death (daily
allotment, six liters, with silver, gold and lapis straws, cased with marsh
     reeds)
twelve chamber maids, five male armed guards and two groomsmen
     were thrown
a banquet to die for. Literally. Had
I been there I would have looked longest at the rams rendered
in gold, silver and lapis lazuli—each raised on hind
legs, nibbling a shrub—coffee? At some point that
night, I would have dipped my cup into a copper
pot, like everyone else, and drunk it. The effect
was irreversible.

It's true my mother's angry children made me keep their vineyards while
     my own

I had not kept. But lately I've found myself possessed of stone jars full of
sweet and of breath that hovers just above the earth awhile. When
I taste it I don't know what is earth and what air, what is water, what fire,
    who
my mother's angry children are, where never ends where I
begin and what Puabi did with the key
to the death pit where the banquet was. The only thing worse
than being unloved is being loved above all others.
Ayin-bet-reysh—pronounced *Avera*—means violation,
means moving, since at a certain point it's hard to
stop. Moving, from one word to the next because *ayin-bet-reysh*—
pronounced *Ivrit*—is language

or "Hebrew" and a state of existence if you happen to be Avram,
the first Hebrew, crossing a river from his and Queen Puabi's
hometown Ur into Canaan. Since then every age of wonder
has its own body of water, and the inconsolable who discover what
they crossed was sometimes only the usual kind of water,
which is why Baudelaire said *always be drunk;*
be drunk means be emptied or else filled, almost all the way,
but never at the same time. A tooth in the mouth of the
Gulf of Mexico, my grandfather reminds me
of Noah. First thing upon disembarking, his
native village obliterated, he planted
himself a vineyard, too.

~ *Marcela Sulak*

Marcela Sulak is the author of *Immigrant* (Black Lawrence Press, 2010) and
the chapbook *Of All the Things that Don't Exist, I Love You Best* (Finishing Line
Press, 2008). Sulak has translated three collections of poetry from the Czech
and the French. She directs the Shaindy Rudoff Graduate Program in Creative
Writing at Bar-Ilan University, where she is a Senior Lecturer of English.

Carol Dorf

Writing the Mathematical Poem: Two Approaches

There are many starting points for beginning mathematical poetry. Some begin with syllabics. Fibonaccis following the Fibonacci sequence—1/1/2/3/5/8/13—are a favorite. Others emphasize the visual symbols of mathematics as Louis Zukofsky did with the integral ($\int$) and Bob Grumman does with the division sign. However, the mathematical poetry that I find most fascinating has both mathematical content and form.

I. The Counting-On Poem

Procedure

I. To begin a counting-on poem, acquire or create a list of numbers and connections to those numbers. For an activity with my students I call "What Is the Probability of Love," I use the U.S. Census Bureau website to give my students a set of numbers to incorporate into their poems. The Bureau has statistics about marriage and divorce, candy and flower sales, and the fact that as of 2007 there were 393 dating services nationwide. Similar data can be accumulated about other holidays or situations, or you can create a list of more personal data—e.g., the number of times a sweetheart texted you per day when you first met, the number of times you went out to the movies, and so forth.

In a recent workshop, for example, one of the participants made a list of odd numbers and let each one suggest a sentence or phrase beginning with the number in question:

1 is the only number
3 Gods in one
5 dollar hot dog
7 days, 7 dollars

II. Once you've created a list, choose one statement as your starting place and write for ten minutes. Take a break, and then start again with a different fact/group of facts. Or choose the most intriguing line from your freewrite as your springboard. After three to five short writing sessions, you will have a draft to revise.

Examples

If a Garden of Numbers

If a garden is the world counted
       and found analogue in nature
One does not become two by ever ending
         so the stairs must be uneven
   in number
and not exceed
thirteen without a pause
of two paces' width, which
       for instance, the golden section
     mitigates between abandon
and an orchestra just behind those trees,
gradations of green that take a stethoscope: we risk:
Length over width
     to make the horizon run straight
equals
   to make the pond an oval:
        Width
         over length minus the width
     in which descending circles curl
into animals exact as a remainder.

     Which means excess. The meaning of the real
always exceeds that of the ideal, said someone.
         He was speaking of Vaux-
  le-Vicomte,
but it's equally true of parking, or hunting, or wishing you could take it
  back. He

     who is Allen Weiss, actually said, "The meaning
of a plastic or pictorial construct always surpasses the ideal meaning of
  that work."
Which is something else entirely. Said
the axonometric
divided by
the anamorphic.

There is nothing that controls our thoughts
more than what we think we see,
which we label "we."

~ *Cole Swensen*

Here, Swenson's larger topic is the nature of the world and what that means in terms of our risks. She begins by implicitly contrasting analog, the world of nature, with digital, the world of devices. Next, the description of particular analog stairs takes the reader to the complex mathematical idea of the golden section. Euclid, in his *Elements*, defines the golden ratio as the ratio when a line is divided and the whole line is to the longer segment as the longer segment is to the shorter segment. We can write that as follows:

$$\frac{a + b}{a} = \frac{a}{b} = \emptyset$$

This ratio is approximately equal to 1.618. Swensen's poem talks through other mathematical ideas including ovals, spirals and remainders, "in which descending circles curl / into animals as exact as a remainder." The final mathematical image is that of dividing axioms, the fundamental starting points of classical geometry, by anamorphic perspective where the viewer can only see the image from a particular vantage point.

A more direct example of the counting-on poem is "I Am a Number" by mathematician Sarah Glaz. Here is one section of that poem:

5   Forged in time's fire
my golden figure
rises
open
to the past
and the future
I count my digits
All Present
yet only
half way there

~ *Sarah Glaz*

This poem captures the way numbers in and of themselves can have meaning for many of us. "All Present / yet only / half way there" uses the concrete metaphor of one hand to show how objects can be complete in themselves, yet also part of a larger set of objects, in this case, the hands. Part of what makes the number five significant, for example, is that we have five fingers on each hand, five toes on each foot. Double the number five and you have ten, which is the basis of our decimal number system.

II. The Context-Shift Poem

Procedure

I. The context-shift poem uses mathematical language to discuss personal life. To begin one of these poems, fold a piece of paper in half vertically. In one column, list a few things in your life that you obsess about. In the other column write some mathematical words, symbols, or ideas. Sources for these ideas could be textbooks, web articles (in this case *Wikipedia* is an acceptable source), or odd facts you remember from school. Don't worry too much about understanding every aspect of the mathematical ideas.

Here's an example of context-shift notes written by a high school senior.

Auditioning for the musical	infinity
Emily being depressed and feeling	
bad for her but also a little irritated	limits
The cat running away	imaginary numbers
The Common App	pi
Uncle Will's death	zero

II. Choose a situation from the first column. Then see how much of the language from the second column you can include in a poem or freewrite about that life event. One way to think about this is to imagine the mathematical words you generated in the second list colliding with your situation. This juxtaposition creates new images for expressing event and emotion.

An Example

In one of my own context-shift poems, I used information I was reading about chaos theory—in Ivar Ekland's *Mathematics and the Unexpected*—to write about the unexpected in my own life.

Dear Ivar,

I read your book on the unexpected.
Like most poets, I opposed mathematics

when I was young, seeing it as the converse
to feeling. The previous statement is false.

When I was very young I loved counting
and zero and even numbers. At sixteen,
I wanted to imagine calculus as a novel
of limits and motion. Yet by college,
I had learned mathematics could not correspond
to poetry in a one-to-one intensity.
Would your book have mattered to me, then?
Most likely, I would not have read it.

Today, I am sending this fan letter. Thank you
for explaining catastrophe and instability.
I spent so many years writing my way
through them. And boundaries, I kept insisting
they were psychological or geographic,
unwilling to see them as breaks
between states of matter. Your words
matter to me, a language as precise as poetry
to delineate universe and being.

Sincerely,
Carol

~ Carol Dorf

Summing Up

Mathematical poetry happens when ideas from worlds we usually consider
distinct collide. In her poem "Pi," Nobel Prize winner Wislawa Szymborska
confronts questions of scale by exploring the expansion of pi: "How feeble the
star's ray, bent by bumping up against space!" Later, she says pi does not "stop
at the page's edge." In other words, the small symbol π holds within it a sense
of infinite meanings.

For your further reading pleasure, and to suggest future mathematical po-
etry prompts, I suggest the following poems:

- "Auguries of Innocence" by William Blake, which begins: "To see a World
  in a Grain of Sand / And a Heaven in a Wild Flower / Hold Infinity in the
  palm of your hand / And Eternity in an hour."

- "Meditation on Statistical Method" by J. V. Cunningham, which takes a humorous approach to the mathematical poem.
- "Comp. Mem." by Catherine Daly, which uses the language of computing in an open form structure.
- "Geometry" by Rita Dove, in which the poet says, "I prove a theorem and the house expands . . ."
- "The Old Poet Moves to a New Apartment 14 Times" by Louis Zukofsky, which has fourteen sections, many of which are rich in mathematical connections.

In the exercises I've described, mathematical ideas act as triggers for poems. For the mathematically inclined, these exercises can be a way of bringing your worlds together. For those who are made nervous by mathematics, I hope that as you encounter mathematics, instead of saying, "Oh, no," you say, "What can I write from this starting point?"

Carol Dorf has led workshops on mathematics and poetry in a number of venues, including the Bridges: Art and Mathematics Conference in Enschede, Netherlands, and at the Northern California Math Council Conference. Dorf's poetry has been published in *Spillway, Sin Fronteras, Antiphon, Composite, Occupy SF, Fringe, About Place, The Journal of Humanistic Mathematics, Maintenant, OVS, Best of Indie New England Lit,* and elsewhere. She has a chapbook, *Every Evening Deserves a Title* (Delirious Nonce, 2013). Poetry Editor of *Talking Writing,* Dorf teaches mathematics at Berkeley High School in Berkeley, California.

A Different Dictionary

This exercise focuses on the word. I often introduce it by pointing out that poetry is based on the word, just as prose is based on the sentence. On the one hand, poetry plumbs words to their very depths, searches out their corners, and uses every scrap of their potential, and in doing so, intensifies and sharpens them. By sharpening your own words, then—being aware of each word's field of association, as well as its sound and speed and tone—you inevitably sharpen your poetry.

I use this exercise to teach two specific things:

1. the difference between connotation and denotation, thus the difference between a personal definition and a public definition

2. a way to get past the automatic editing function that hampers many early (and late!) writers

Procedure

I. First, I pass out a sheet—as on the following spread—with lots of *different* definitions on it. When I make up the sheet, I avoid making a list; I scatter them all over the page, going in all directions, so that students don't read them in the same order. They have to do a bit of exploring to see what's there.

II. After a couple of minutes of their reading silently from my Different Dictionary sheet, I ask students to mention ones that they particularly enjoy or that they find especially striking or fitting. We don't do any analysis here; I think analysis would be destructive at this point. I just want students to get more engaged with the material. I'll often remark on a student's choice—"Yes! Isn't that a stunning image!" or some such—just to reinforce one choice and make a bridge to the next.

III. After students have volunteered five or six examples from the sheet, I ask them what's different about these definitions. Depending on their age and experience, they may or may not have much response here. I encourage what response there is and move toward a brief talk on the difference between denotation and connotation.

IV. I start with the dictionary definition, the word's **denotation,** and point out that it's devoid of personality; it is, in fact, intentionally impersonal. It's a common denominator—a lowest common denominator. It can only include

A Different Dictionary

STORM: grace gets angry

STAR: an eternity staggering alone

BUMBLEBEE: a daisy flying

HANDS: tools of the soul

WAVES: the rocks caught in curlers

SHADOW: a ghost sunbathing

CANDLE: time on fire

FEATHER: the sky's hair

ROSE: a heart shaped like a maze

PEOPLE: animals in disguise

FIRE: fury learns to fly

MIDNIGHT: ebony houses carrying us away

ELECTRICITY: minds assimilating memory

PEARL: moonblood

LIGHTNING: fingernail scraping down the silent black

TWILIGHT: the curve of a closed eyelid

DOG: a distinguished-looking fuzzy face

FORGETTING: having a relationship with a wild animal

HARBOR: arms grow larger in the sun, in the wind

BOOKS: *freeze-dried astonishment*

OCEAN: *joy freed from its person*

MIRROR: *the past burning itself down*

FOREVER: a man not being able to find his car keys

KNIFE:
waterfall of life

FLOWER:
periscope for the dead

OUTSIDE: *a paradise in disguise*

LIGHTBULB: *a volcano in a fist*

FOSSIL: *early photography*

FACE: *a symbol of two people's love*

ROSE:
your heart on a stick

KITE: *a childhood in flight*

MIRROR: *light built of faces*

AIRPLANE: *an accent aigu on time*

TOUCH: *talking radar*

ECHO: *memory whispering itself into distance*

RUBY:
a spark stopped in time

DIAMOND:
a fox's footprint in the fresh snow

STAR: one of those things that slipped your mind

what we all can agree on about a word. At this point, I use a simple example, such as *thimble*. The dictionary says, "An object made of a hard material, such as metal or bone, designed to protect the finger when sewing."

This is the public definition of the word, but most people will also have a private definition, something additional that this word means to them. It may make one person think fondly of a grandmother and the warm atmosphere of the room in which she used to sew at night; to another it may represent the grueling labor his mother had to suffer in a sweatshop in China.

This additional meaning is the word's **connotation**—the wide field of association that every word has. This field has different layers, from the most private, based on the individual experience of a single person, to a local, social layer, dependent on the cultural assumptions and habits of a given area, to the general human. A snake, for instance, has connotations of danger for all peoples, while only for some is it a metaphor for a traitor or for virility.

This exercise asks writers to become aware of the difference between denotation and connotation by separating them and concentrating, for once, on connotation only. I point out that just as poetry concentrates more intensely on each word than other types of writing, it also concentrates more on words' associations and private meanings. These are rich raw materials for poetry; however, because they tend to cloud expository writing, we're often trained away from using them. This is an exercise that trains the mind back toward its private definitions and to the associative field of each word.

V. I accomplish this training by giving my students a kind of verbal Rorschach test. I have a list of ninety-some words, as on the facing page. The Word List is for my use; I do not distribute it. I tell students that I'm going to say the words one at a time and that as soon as they hear one, they must start writing. I emphasize that above all, they must not think about what they're writing, and they must keep on writing until I say stop. I allow about twenty seconds per word; this exercise works best with a bit of time pressure.

I explain that what I'm trying to do is to get students to turn off their automatic editing faculty. When we're writing straightforward prose, that automatic editor can be very useful because it keeps us writing in standard, easily grasped modes. But it's the death of poetry. When you think about what you're writing as you're writing or before you write it, you limit yourself to what you already know, quashing all true insight, all impressions and sensations beyond the already said. Language only really gets exciting when it's saying something new, when it's creating the thought, the knowledge, through saying it.

Word List for the Different Dictionary Exercise

You'll quickly grasp the pattern: concrete nouns that have a strong emotional charge and a large associative field. I like to include a few whose physical images suggest other things, such as *sunflower* or *streetlight,* and at least one proper noun, usually a place, and at least one word that's highly ambiguous, such as *figure* or *silhouette.* But you'll no doubt come up with your own list of words that work.

Note: I never worry about using words that appear on the initial Different Dictionary sheet. That doesn't seem to influence or dampen writers' responses.

piano	river	twilight	lake
wave	silver	movie	music
moon	mist	paintbrush	fire
winter	airplane	match	book
gold	ceiling	memory	train
window	journey	globe	sunflower
garden	feather	cloud	sunrise
wonder	rose	India	red
sailboat	China	figure	radio
shadow	lightbulb	photo	mirror
star	lightning	forgetting	electricity
anger	ocean	midnight	whisper
flute	fountain	legend	dream
silhouette	Paris	dawn	hands
eyes	never	pearl	laughter
blue	grace	smile	streetlight
sky	snow	echo	eclipse
waterfall	clock	diamond	crystal
journey	freeway	bridge	firefly
kite	time	key	rain
cyclone	rainbow	firecracker	candle
ruby	eagle	fog	flame
evening	rage	starfish	forever

Before calling out the first word, I remind students not to think and, above all, not to give a dictionary definition. Instead, they must give their own. Then I call out words from the list. Most students really enjoy the exercise; it's very active and closely controlled. They know exactly what they're supposed to do. Responses are short, and with each word they know they'll have another chance in less than a minute.

I walk around the classroom or around the table as I'm saying the words, discreetly reading over my students' shoulders. During the first few words, when I spot a good response, I say, "Hey, here's a good one!" and read it aloud before I call out the next word—just to reinforce the rangier thinking this exercise is meant to encourage.

Note: In ten minutes, I can get through about thirty words from this list, more than enough for the purposes of this exercise.

VI. When students have written responses to about thirty words, they look over them and choose one to share. Then, each student reads what he or she wrote for one of the words—two if the class is small.

VII. The last part of the exercise—which can be saved for the next class session, if time is tight—is to use these definitions, which are usually only a line or so, as the impetus for a longer poem. I explain that association works in chains. One impression leads naturally and quickly to another, as long as we don't let the automatic editor get in the way. (This is a great moment to teach Charles Olson's essay "Projective Verse," if you have the time.)

I ask students to continue in that pre-editorial mode, beginning with a definition, and following it further, letting it take them where it will, using the same kind of time-limited, non-reflective writing.

Summing Up

I've had great success with this exercise—with students as young as nine as well as with adults, even fairly experienced writers. I owe the exercise to the extraordinary writer and teacher, Frances Mayes, who gave it to an M.F.A. class I took years ago, when I was her student at San Francisco State University. I loved it the day she gave it to us, and I have loved giving it ever since.

Examples

Knife

Waterfall of life, smooth is the
shine. The falling doesn't feel

The time is remembered perfectly
The steel is immune to everything

The water reflects my face eternally
It's my face that is crying, not I

~ *Joan Liven*

Rose

Heart shaped like a maze.
Code coiling in silence.
I pick the rose that I have grown
and watch it get redder and
redder as I hold it, admiring
its color. There are things
inside me just like this.
Intricate things that will not
be explained. I sent her
several roses because there are
too few words in the world.

~ *David Beale*

Cole Swensen is the author of more than ten volumes of poetry, most recently *Gravesend* (University of California Press, 2012), a finalist for the LA Times Book Prize in Poetry; *Greensward* (Ugly Duckling Press, 2010); and *Ours* (University of California Press, 2008), as well as a volume of essays, *Noise That Stays Noise* (University of Michigan Press, 2011). Swensen is the co-editor of *American Hybrid: A Norton Anthology of New Poetry* (Norton, 2009), the founding editor of La Presse Books, which specializes in contemporary French writing translated by English-language poets, and a translator of contemporary French poetry, prose, and art criticism. Her awards include a Guggenheim Fellowship, a PEN USA Award for Literary Translation, the Iowa Poetry Prize, and the San Francisco State Poetry Center Book Award. Department Chair and Professor of Literary Arts at Brown University, Swensen has taught at the University of Denver and the Iowa Writers' Workshop.

Nouns at Work, Verbs at Play

Beginning poets often don't pay attention to the role nouns play in creating place or how verbs can accelerate or slow the pace of a poem. This exercise illustrates the crucial role of nouns and verbs.

Procedure

I. Choose a poem you admire and then remove all the nouns in the poem. You can decide whether you want to include pronouns in this removal or not. Next, replace those nouns you removed with new ones. Choose carefully because every noun you choose affects every other noun in the rest of the poem. Nouns are always tightly woven together to create the physical world of a poem.

II. Go back through the new-noun version of the poem and switch out the verbs. Verbs are the engines of our language. Changing verbs allows you to quicken or slow the pace of the writing depending on how fast you want the information of your poem delivered to your reader.

III. You can also change the adjectives, which would alter the tone or mood of a poem. Or change all the nouns, verbs, and adjectives in succession to lead to new discoveries!

Tips

Have fun with this exercise. The point is to get a better understanding of how important each of the parts of speech is in writing well. Once you've had a chance to play with your favorite poems in this way, apply the technique to your own poems, especially those poems where you feel stuck and don't know what to revise next. You might find out that your poem moves too fast or that the setting is all wrong.

An Example

Here is a traditional poem you could use for this exercise:

Young Lambs

The spring is coming by a many signs;
The trays are up, the hedges broken down,

That fenced the haystack, and the remnant shines
Like some old antique fragment weathered brown.
And where suns peep, in every sheltered place,
The little early buttercups unfold
A glittering star or two—till many trace
The edges of the blackthorn clumps in gold.
And then a little lamb bolts up behind
The hill and wags his tail to meet the yoe,
And then another, sheltered from the wind,
Lies all his length as dead—and lets me go
Close bye and never stirs but baking lies,
With legs stretched out as though he could not rise.

~ *John Clare*

Now look at the poem with the nouns removed:

The _____ is coming by a many _____;
The _____ are up, the _____ broken down,
That fenced the _____, and the _____ shines
Like some old antique _____ weathered brown.
And where _____ peep, in every sheltered _____,
The little early _____ unfold
A glittering _____ or two—till many trace
The _____ of the _____ in _____.
And then a little _____ bolts up behind
The _____ and wags his _____ to meet the _____,
And then another, sheltered from the _____,
Lies all his _____ as dead—and lets me go
Close bye and never stirs but baking lies,
With _____ stretched out as though he could not rise.

Altered Version I: Most of the nouns have been replaced.

The **winter** is coming by a many **sounds**;
The **geese** are up, the **trees** broken down,
That fenced the **field**, and the **pond** shines
Like some old antique **mirror** weathered brown.
And where **wolves** peep, in every sheltered **turn**,

The little early **frosts** unfold
A glittering **paw** or two—till many trace
The **remnants** of the **haystacks** in gold.
And then a little lamb bolts up behind
The **fence** and wags his tail to meet the **sun**,
And then another, sheltered from the **snows**,
Lies all his length as dead—and lets me go
Close bye and never stirs but baking lies,
With legs stretched out as though he could not rise.

Altered Version II: Nouns and Verbs Replaced
This example shows what might happen if you start with the new-nouns version of the poem and then replace as many verbs as possible. Notice that when the writer changed "trace" to "dim," he changed "gold" to "faded gold." And when he changed "wags," he changed the entire phrase, from "wags his tail" to "hugs himself." Finally, when he changed "rise" in the closing line, he rewrote the entire clause. This is what happens as the poem moves further from the original and begins to feel more like your own poem.

The **winter** is *retreating* by a many **sounds**;
The **geese** *flare* up, the **trees** *bend* down,
That *greened* the **field**, and the **pond** *flickers*
Like some old antique **mirror** *tarnished* brown.
And where **wolves** *dream*, in every sheltered **turn**,
The little early **frosts** *embrace*
A glittering **paw** or two—till many *dim*
The **remnants** of the **haystacks** in *faded* gold.
And then a little lamb *lies down* behind
The **fence** and *hugs himself* to *absorb* the **sun**,
And then another, *blanketed by* the **snows**,
Lies all his length as dead—and lets me go
Close bye and never *breathes* but *freezing dies*,
With legs stretched out *as if he dreams of running*.

Note from David Meischen: The verb changes in Altered Version II are mine. By the time I got to the final alteration, "as if he dreams of running," the simple fact of new nouns and verbs had freed me from "Young Lambs." I could see a new poem, one of my own, finding its way out of the exercise. Excited by this possibility, I harvested what I could from Altered Version II, changing order as needed, deleting some words and phrases, trying to forge something new. Here is the result:

Winter in Retreat

with thanks to John Clare

The geese flare up, the trees that greened
the field bend down, the pond nearby
an antique mirror tarnished brown.
The morning dreams of wolves. The frost
embraces a glittering paw or two,
its remnants on the haystacks faded gold.
Beyond the fence a lamb lies down to warm
herself beneath the sun—and farther still
her brother blanketed by snow, his legs
stretched out as if he dreams of running.

~ David Meischen

This kind of work does not replace the arduous challenge of creating entirely new work to fill the blank page. But it can demonstrate the generative powers of nouns and verbs—and the crucial role tinkering with them plays in the creative process.

Tomás Q. Morín is the winner of the 2012 APR/Honickman First Book Prize for his collection *A Larger Country* (American Poetry Review)—also a runner-up for the PEN Joyce/Osterweil Award. Morín is co-editor with Mari L'Esperance of the anthology *Coming Close: 40 Essays on Philip Levine* (Prairie Lights Books, 2013). His poems have appeared in *Slate, Threepenny Review, Boulevard, New England Review,* and *Narrative.*

Definition by Opposition

We've all felt different from the people around us at some point—our parents, our peers, our idols. How we define ourselves in relation and opposition to these people shifts and shimmies as we grow, but in poetry we can fix a moment in time and explore who we were in that moment.

Preparation

Read Patricia Smith's poem "A Colored Girl Will Slice You If You Talk Wrong about Motown." Pay particular attention to how she uses alliteration and repetition in the poem. Think about who and what gets named in the poem, versus who the we and you are.

A Colored Girl Will Slice You
If You Talk Wrong about Motown

The men and women who coupled, causing us, first
arrived confounded. Surrounded by teetering towers
of *no, not now,* and *you shoulda known better,* they
cowered and built little boxes of Northern home,
crammed themselves inside, feasted on the familiar
of fat skin and the unskimmed, made gods of doors.
When we came—the same insistent bloody and question
we would have been down South—they clutched us,
plumped us on government cereal drenched in Carnation,
slathered our hair, faces, our fat wiggling arms and legs
with Vaseline. We shined like the new things we were.
The city squared its teeth, smiled oil, smelled the sour
each hour left at the corner of our mouths. Our parents
threw darts at the day. They romanced shut factories,
waged hot battle with skittering roaches and vermin,
lumbered after hunches. Their newborn children grew
like streetlights. We grew like insurance payments.
We grew like resentment. And since no tall sweet gum
thrived to offer its shouldered shade, no front porch
lesson spun wide to craft our wrong or righteous,

our parents loosed us into the crumble, into the glass,
into the hips of a new city. They trusted exploded
summer hydrants, scarlet licorice whips, and crumbling
rocks of government cheese to conjure a sort of joy,
trusted joy to school us in the woeful limits of jukeboxes
and moonwash. Freshly dunked in church water, slapped
away from double negatives and country ways, we were
orphans of the North Star, dutifully sacrificed, our young
bodies arranged on sharp slabs of boulevard. We learned
what we needed, not from our parents and their rumored
South, but from the gospel seeping through the sad gap
in Mary Wells's grin. Smokey slow-sketched pictures
of our husbands, their future skins flooded with white light,
their voices all remorse and atmospheric coo. Little Stevie
squeezed his eyes shut on the soul notes, replacing his
dark with ours. Diana was the bone our mamas coveted,
the flow of slip silver they knew was buried deep beneath
their rollicking heft. Every lyric, growled or sweet from
perfect brown throats, was instruction: *Sit pert, pout, and
seamed silk. Then watch him beg.* Every spun line was
consolation: *You're such a good girl. If he has not arrived,
he will.* Every wall of horn, every slick choreographed
swivel, threaded us with the rhythm of the mildly wild.
We slept with transistor radios, worked the two silver knobs,
one tiny earbud blocking out the roar of our parents' tardy
attempts to retrieve us. Instead, we snuggled with the Temps,
lined up five pretty men across. And damned if they didn't
begin every one of their songs with the same word: *Girl.*

~ *Patricia Smith*

Procedure

I. Think of a time you felt different from the people around you. What physical space are you in? Who else is there? Write down five concrete details about the physical space, and who else is in the space with you.

II. Who are you in relation or opposition to these people? What defines you in this space? Think race, gender, class, age, clothing style, appetite, etc.

III. Complete the wordplay bank chart (see below) to create a series of potentially nonsensical word groupings. In the first column, write any noun or adjective that comes to mind. In the second column, write a word that starts with the same letter or sound as the word in the first column—any part of speech (noun, verb, adjective . . .). In the third column, write a word that repeats a vowel sound from the word in the second column—also any part of speech. You may produce word groupings such as "jungle gym hymn" and "spiky spurious hug." Try to create five to ten (or more) of these groupings.

Random Noun / Adjective	Alliterative Word	Word with Repeat Vowel Sound
jungle	gym	hymn
spiky	spurious	hug
carrot	kick	pistol

IV. As a starting place, title your poem using the format of the Patricia Smith poem:

A _____ (defining characteristic) will _____
(verb/action) if you _____ (verb/action.)

V. You're ready to write! Using your title as a springboard, freewrite using concrete details on the physical space and the people sharing that space with you—and at least three of the phrases from the wordplay bank.

An Example

**a tattooed lesbian will even sing Katy Perry
if you give her enough pinot**

The flaming floral chorus uses both hands
on the cordless microphone. Belts Rihanna
as the anime dancers on each wall's screen
twitch their digital hips in synchronized time.
The answer to whether one will attend
one's girlfriend's straight friend's bachelorette
karaoke party is necessarily Yes
unless one plans to spend the weekend
processing triggers related to the time
the third grade field trip group forgot her
at the aquarium and the bus pulled away
with her still watching the nurse sharks
pace the tank. The bartender in the hallway
is drunker than any of the perfume-girdled girls
passing the mic and foaming pitcher manicure
to manicure around the large closet
lined with couches bolted to the walls
and the floor, and tells you so via a rundown
of shots he's downed with names that sound like
wasted whip distance and *truck tail sailor.* Your girl
can dance. Your girl sings Fleetwood Mac
in the shower and the faucets applaud.
Your girl rocks a button-down and haircut
so asymmetrical that no one
in her hometown recognizes her
at the Whole Foods. The bartender
sloshes an overdose of something white
into your waiting glass and the look
on your girl's face says *Who's driving* and
Let's blow this pop stand and you don't hate
the music or these strangers
though you could do without the penis straw
in your pinot grigio and despite the text

and the owl and the porcupine and the three
women's faces blooming on your body you know
you could pass if you'd have entered the room
not holding her hand or if you could bring
yourself to let it go. On the high school
newspaper staff one year there was a girl
somebody decided was a lesbian. A year
ahead of me, and new, she was not
my friend but when she'd enter
the newspaper room I'd look at her
with what I hoped would read
as quiet solidarity or at least the absence
of blame. Whatever she was, with her unpermed
hair and mascaraless, melancholy milk dish
face, I knew no songs about in 1989. Somebody
puts on *Teenage Dream.* Outside, the moon's
a mayonnaise jar about to tip. At home
our unmade bed, the patient
tea kettle, all the books we haven't read.

~ *Marty McConnell*

Marty McConnell is the author of the poetry collection *wine for a shotgun* (EM Press, 2012). McConnell's work has recently appeared in *A Face to Meet the Faces: An Anthology of Contemporary Persona Poetry* (University of Akron Press, 2012); *City of the Big Shoulders: An Anthology of Chicago Poetry* (University of Iowa Press, 2012); *Gulf Coast, Indiana Review, Crab Orchard Review, Salt Hill Review, Beloit Poetry Journal,* and elsewhere. Co-founder of the louderARTS Project in New York City, she returned to Chicago to create Vox Ferus in 2009. McConnell has an M.F.A. from Sarah Lawrence College.

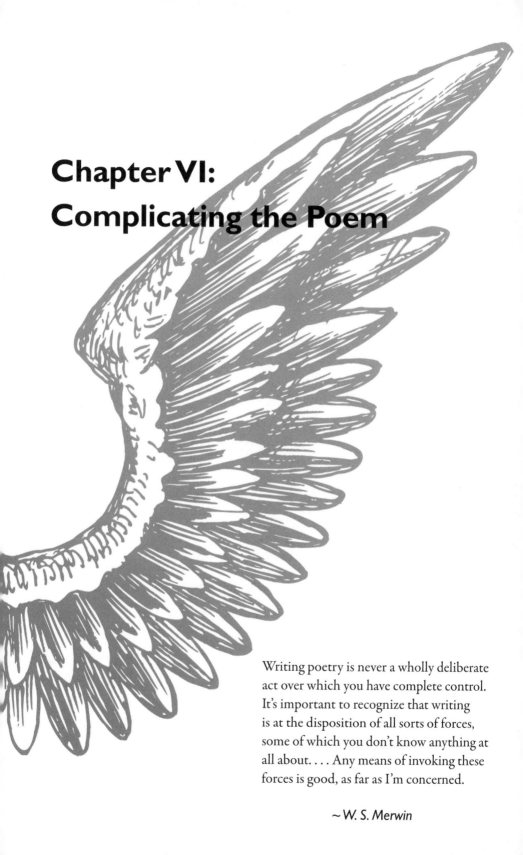

Chapter VI:
Complicating the Poem

Writing poetry is never a wholly deliberate
act over which you have complete control.
It's important to recognize that writing
is at the disposition of all sorts of forces,
some of which you don't know anything at
all about. . . . Any means of invoking these
forces is good, as far as I'm concerned.

~ W. S. Merwin

Right Turn, Clyde:
Ten Variations on a Broken Poem

Question: What's the best Clint Eastwood film?
I'll give you a minute.

. . .

. . .

Did you come up with one? What is it?
Million Dollar Baby? Meh.
Unforgiven? Yawn City.
Gran Torino? Whatevs.
Dirty Harry? Okay, that one was pretty freaking awesome, I give you that, but that's not where I'm going.

I'll tell you the answer. There's only one right answer.

It's *Every Which Way but Loose.*

No, I am NOT joking thankyouverymuch.

You remember it, yes? Clint Eastwood stars with Geoffrey Lewis (who I've always and inexplicably found sort of attractive), Sondra Locke (Clint's real-life lover at the time), and Clyde (Clint's character's orangutan companion!) as a trucker who bare-knuckle boxes in bars for side cash and causes general mayhem wherever he goes.

Go watch it, right now.

. . .

. . .

Did you watch it? Good. Now, do this exercise.

Preparation

I want you to take a broken poem—or a sub-par poem, a poem that isn't quite poem enough, something new but yet unformed, a bratty or malfeasant poem, a poem you're pissed at, a poem you've given yourself only five minutes to draft (try that for an added challenge)—and then paste it onto ten different blank documents (assuming we're working electronically—and if not, then do it however you please).

It's key that you work from ten different blank documents or pieces of paper. It makes a difference in being able to view each drafting as independent from all the other ones. And memory is cheap. Your hard drive can afford it. Ten documents.

Now take your poem, your shifty or silly or sub-spectacular poem and turn it—wait, how will you turn it?—*every which way but loose.*

I'm pretty convinced that sometimes we think things out of order. Or we think around things. Or under them. Or clockwise when we should be considering the counter-clockwise spin of the dial. We talk prepositional phrases when we should be speaking post-positional phrases. We rationalize in past tense when we ought to concede in present subjunctive.

Given that, it's likely that the problem at the center of one's problematic poem is an issue of direction. A spatial, dimensional quandary. The only solution is actually quite direct: you have to re-see the poem.

Don't throw it out. The poem you want is probably inside the one you have. You just have to find it.

And you may think you have already tried all the ways there are to find it, the poem you want. But you haven't.

I will walk you through ten steps. If you don't find something in these ten steps, then perhaps there was nothing there to begin with. But you'll find something. You may even find more than one something.

Procedure

1. The As-Is Draft

Now, Kids, don't judge a poet too harshly. I set the timer for a single minute and came up with these six lines. And they're bad. And not "bad" in a Michael-Jackson-is-singing-about-them way:

> The sun was round and on fire
> I loved you the entire summer
> I fed you peaches plucked from air
> And called you an unmentionable name
> Only the cicadas knew
> You were my secret husband

As you can plainly see—they're rubbish. That's okay. Maybe your lines are terrible too. Do you know what's good about that? What's good is that it only gets better from here.

2. The Gospel Draft

(The last shall be first and the first shall be last—get it?)
In this draft, you reverse the line order. That's all.

> You were my secret husband
> Only the cicadas knew
> And called you the unmentionable name
> I fed you peaches plucked from air
> And I loved you the entire summer
> The sun was round and on fire

3. Even-Stevens

Starting at line two, list every other line until you reach the end, then go back and finish with the odd lines.

> I loved you the entire summer
> And called you an unmentionable name
> You were my secret husband
> The sun was round and on fire
> I fed you peaches plucked from air
> Only the cicadas knew

Now we're getting somewhere. At this point my head is starting to thrum with potentialities.

I want to stop, however, before going on and remind you that what we're calling these at this point is *drafts*. Which means they're drafty. Like a house with holes in its walls. You may well get to the end of this exercise and have a perfect poem fall into your lap, but what's more likely to happen is that you'll go back to whatever drafts (one or two of them) resonate with the most energy or possibilities. From there you'll flesh them out, maybe delete the lines you started with and introduce new ones altogether. That's not only fine, it's fantastic. Let this and all other exercises in this book serve as a means to the end of a kick-ass poem. Which is to say: you put the drill down when you're ready to twist in the screw.

4. Odds Bodkins

You are to do the same thing you just did in the third document, only this time start with the odd lines.

The sun was round and on fire
I fed you peaches plucked from air
Only the cicadas knew
I loved you the entire summer
And called you an unmentionable name
You were my secret husband

5. Opposite Day

Pretend it's opposite day. Take the whole poem—as *much* of it as possible and in all ways—and make it a mirror of itself. This can get complicated. That's part of the fun.

Every moon is square or wet
But they hate me for a small part of the fall
You crap apples pressed into the earth
But silence my bidden namelessness
Lest every tiger forget
I will not be your well-known wife

Um, yeah. But—do you see what just happened here? The text might be muddled and it might be ornery and how is a tiger the opposite of a cicada (and really, Essbaum? "Crap apples?")—but you know what? Stuff just got way more surprising and interesting and unexpected. Too often, we fall into the same old tropes and images and dull, dumb defenses. Shaking things up is the exact right thing to do.

For a truly opposite poem, complete this exercise, followed by exercise 6. Then take that draft and go back to exercise 2. (See also James Harms' "Minor Lies," page 303.)

6. Axis of Evil

Fold the poem down its middle into imaginary, vertical halves and then rotate it syntactically on that axis, as best you can. This exercise is extremely mutable. Try it in two steps.

Round and on fire the sun was
The entire summer I loved you
Plucked from air I fed you peaches
An unmentionable name I called you
The cicadas knew only
Husband you were my secret

Now, to avoid sounding very, very silly, you would do well to practice inter-changing parts of speech, moving ideas, images, connectives around, and maybe here even starting to clip and curtail, to experiment with new line breaks....

> it was the fire, the entire
> sunned summer; round,
> loved, plucked from air,
> well-fed, I was a peach;
> you, an unmentionable
> name—cicada, the only
> husband, you, my secret

Now that's a changed text indeed. Something I will definitely have to consider. I'm also very piqued by this new shape. Leaps made? Of course! But that's part of the game.

7. Swap Meet

Swap the verbs with the other verbs in the poem. Swap the adjectives with other adjectives in the poem. A snip here or there is permissible. Again, this is highly mutable.

> The sun was unmentionable
> And I fed you the summer
> I knew peaches on fire
> And loved the secret
> Only the cicadas called your name
> You were my entire husband

To take it a step further, move around the nouns:

> The summer was unmentionable
> I fed you the sun.
> I knew the secret peaches
> And loved the cicadas
> Only the fire called you my husband
> You were my entire name

Whoa! You see what just happened?

8. Tense People!
Fiddle with both person and tense. Play, too, with verb modalities, moods.

> The sun will be round and on fire
> And he will love her the entire summer
> And feed her peaches plucked from air
> And call her an unmentionable name
> That only the cicadas will know
> And she will be his secret, his wife

Or:

> Sun, be round
> Sun, be on fire
> I will love you
> The entire summer
> Feed you peaches
> plucked from air
> I will call you
> The unmentionable name
> Only the cicadas know
> Sun, be my secret husband

This is very interesting. By simply re-writing the first line as an imperative, we reset the tone, thereby shifting the poem toward the suggestion that it's a love poem intended for the sun. That's *huge*. Would you have seen this possibility? I wouldn't have, not without this step.

9. Question Everything

> Is the sun round?
> Is the sun on fire?
> Is the sun on?
>
> Do I love you?
> An entire summer?
> Is any summer entire?
>
> Can a peach be plucked
> From air? How can a name
> Be unmentionable?

Who would ever answer?
Who would ever?
Would you ever?

What is a cicada?
Why is it so sad?
Do I love you?

10. Assimilate

You're on your own here. But let me offer a few words of counsel. At this point, there's an extreme likelihood that however crappy your poem was to begin with, you've stumbled upon something that's probably really good. I can practically guarantee it. What I can also assure you, as I intimate above, is that whatever you've stumbled on still needs a lot of work. That's okay. Work is what gives us our credibility.

So take your draft, that daft, dusty draft and wrench it and wring it and warp it but don't—*do not!*—let it go.

Oh, and why is *Every Which Way but Loose* the best Clint Eastwood film? Um, that's a no-brainer, Kids.

It has an orangutan in it.

Jill Alexander Essbaum is the author of several collections of poetry including *Harlot* (No Tell Books, 2007), *Necropolis* (NeoNuma Arts, 2008), and most recently the single poem chapbook, *The Devastation* (Cooper Dillon, 2009). A two-time National Endowment of the Arts Literature Fellow, Essbaum is currently on the faculty of the University of California–Riverside's low-residency M.F.A. program. Her first novel, *Hausfrau,* is scheduled to be published by Random House in spring 2015. She lives in Austin, Texas, with her husband, Alvin.

Between Sentiment & Language: Creating Tension

During my many years of teaching beginning and intermediate creative writing students, I have found that one of the most difficult skills for student poets to master is creating tension through complexity of tone. Most of my students can easily write love poems or hate poems, happy poems or angry poems. The trick is to encourage them to introduce additional layers so that they produce more compelling and sophisticated work.

I start with an assignment, usually early in the semester, to write a love poem with harsh sounds or a hate poem with soft sounds. This exercise challenges students to seek language that does not lend itself to their original message.

Preparation

To prepare students for the assignment, discuss **euphony**—a sequence of pleasant, harmonious words or sounds—and **cacophony**—a sequence of harsh, discordant sounds or words. The following chart is useful:`

liquids:	**r, l**
glides:	**w, y**
plosives:	**g, k, b, j, p, d, t**
fricatives:	**zh, th, ch, v, f, sh, z, s, h**
nasals:	**m, n, ng**

Note: Liquids and glides are frequently euphonious while plosives and fricatives are more often cacophonous. A nasal can go both ways. The *m* sound, for example, when it produces a humming sound, as in the word *hum,* is generally considered euphonious. But in a word such as *mangle,* both nasals—*m* and *ng*—contribute to the word's harsh sound.

Remind students that connotative language can reinforce what they're trying to accomplish in this exercise. If they're seeking harsh sounds for a love poem, they might also want to think about words with harsh, jarring, or negative connotations. Conversely, if they want soft sounds for a hate poem, they should consider words with un-hateful connotations.

Many wonderful poems exemplify this kind of tension, and I like to share a few of these with my students before they start writing. Bruce Covey's "Body & Isn't" is an excellent starting point.

Body & Isn't

I have a hard time making my mind take place.
Every input adjusts the chemistry—water, peppermint stick, analogue.
Kisses are circles. With eyes closed, every taste buds almond orange.

Ceiling defines the segment; door, the vector. Exits & entrances.
My location's ribcage is beneath the changing spectrum's breast.
Heft of a wet peony, white & pink, drips its honey south.

Conducted back, your body accelerates—biology of a taxi ride.
Kept kempt, migraines at bay, tidy nails, & sneezes away.
Sex through collisions—bridges jumped & limbs tangled.

Or the chromatic staff arranging the spheres' accidental spills.
Frets & intonations strung across a tempered series of knots,
Strung through the loops of our virtual displacement.

But it isn't wings or hooks or hooves or horns or see-through or white.
Whether afloat in a boat or aloft in a plane. The way maps affect time.
For a second I think I feel the fleeting texture of your skin.

Lumbar & sacral nerves descend to exits beyond the end of the cord.
Keep the blood in at all costs, even when the wind crackles its cells.
The coming of electricity, half next time & half this:
My five. My unending ache at the absence of you.

~ *Bruce Covey*

Covey's poem has two clearly affectionate gestures: "For a second I think I feel the fleeting texture of your skin" and "My unending ache at the absence of you." If the poem sustained that emotional note for nineteen lines instead of two, it would risk sentimentality. But the poem excels at cacophony—the harsh sounds in *peppermint stick, taxi ride, chromatic, accidental, vector, ribcage, spectrum, kept kempt, crackles,* and elsewhere. These words create an unsettling sound in the poem that runs at odds with the message of love.

And consider this line: "My location's ribcage is beneath the changing spectrum's breast." In a traditional love poem, *ribcage* and *breast* might ache with love, with being out of breath. But Covey sets them against words such as *location* and *spectrum* that would feel more at home in a geometry textbook. They're not love poem words.

Many other fine poems use this technique. In Dean Young's "Easy as Falling down Stairs," the love notes are tempered with language that creates a balance and tension. These words work to temper the poem's romantic tone: *frigid, seethe, fizz, sunken, crank, leaks.* How about this as a way to tell someone you love her or him: "some crank in me / tightens the whirly-sprig each time I see / your face so thank you for aiming It / my way"? Instead of the flowery language we might expect, the poem creates layers; it looks at romantic attachment in an unexpected way.

Carolyn Kizer's "Food of Love" begins with an unexpected tension: "I'm going to murder you with love." The reader is intrigued to know what kind of love poem this will be. Throughout, Kizer uses harsh sounds—and words with connotations that run counter to traditional notions of love—to complicate the message. Consider these: *suffocate, dead, delectable, brackish, chop, dripping, undulating,* and *devour.* Although the message of the poem is clear, the mystery is in the tone, in the tension between the language and the sentiment.

Procedure

I. Decide on a relationship (love or hate) you wish to represent in the poem and freewrite about it for ten minutes. Don't try to be "poetic." Simply explore your feelings.

Note: If the love/hate dichotomy does not suit you, try another one: joy/pain, death/birth, sickness/health. There are many ways to access the power of tension in a poem.

II. Make a list of words that are the opposite in sound and connotation of the primary emotion you wrote about in step I. If you're writing a love poem, list words with harsh sounds/connotations. If you're writing a hate poem, list words with pleasing sounds/connotations.

III. Draft the poem using the words from your list.

IV. Read the draft aloud, paying close attention to the sounds. Revise by sharpening the tension between the poem's emotional content and its language.

Examples

Body Murmur

What luck to live
next to a harpist,
to learn through symbiosis

the callus behind the nail
and the trail of the fingers,
brush of nylon or wire.
I was so busy counting the specks
of dust in the atmosphere
which attach to a droplet
and freeze in their descent
that I forgot to call it snow
and lost the concept of any name,
of any drifting through my window,
no matter the octave or frequency
or pure melodic scope.
Yet even after the release of winter,
I begged for a moment
whose atoms could not materialize,
and when I realized you were gone
I got going on myself, yet sensed
this hereditary pathogen;
some incalculable integer
that pulses forth a blood-born
murmur, rushes
from your chest toward a stethoscope,
through my window,
through my chest.

~ *Alex Linden*

Note from Alex Linden: "Body Murmur" attempts to create discord be-
tween tone and message through various shifts, starting with the first two lines
and a deliberate line break—"What luck to live / next to a harpist"—launching
the poem with a declaration of gratitude and the soft sonic pull of *harpist*. The
language tends toward euphony accented by slant rhymes: *symbiosis, callus,
droplets, descent, snow.* However, a change occurs as the poem moves forward.
Notice the cold, medical words: *materialize, ribcage, hereditary, pathogen, in-
calculable, integer, stethoscope.* This shift raises a question about which sounds
work best for a poem that renders longing as a biological and environmen-
tal force. How might the poem be received if it only employed euphony?
Cacophony? Which words leave a deeper imprint in presenting a theme of
longing—those which soothe the ear or cut into the lines with sharper edges?

What They'll Say about Us

The rumor is that forgiveness falls to another dimension.
Your fatherhowl etches the earth; I come behind and crack it

open with the rattle of your supposed last breath. You love
the tenderness, the announcement like a gunshot, of possible

extinction. We will always have this strange stew, our shared
injury gleaming like a trophy: *Longest Distance Between Blood.*

And I think we are born with a torch in each ignorant hand.
And the fire that breathes because you breathe—blasted out

long before your body. Will I regret this last withheld consolation?
That I didn't search the ether? I did not take the apology, your

fleshchild; it was more than this world could expect: some shades
of yellow cannot be named. Your sick skin, all I will carry on.

~ Sarah Pape

Note from Sarah Pape: In my freewrite, I wrote about a conflicted relation-
ship in a loving way, consciously attempting to include euphonious words, but
the language kept veering toward cacophony. From that writing, the words I
chose to build my poem around were *extinction, blasted, rattle,* and *trophy*—
all words with a plosive *t* sound. Once I relented to the language and its pull
toward conflict, I considered the central inquiry these words were attempting
to explore—separation from a parent, forgiveness before death, what is left
after loss—and looked for available metaphors, such as the gun, the award,
and the torch.

Patricia Colleen Murphy teaches creative writing at Arizona State University,
where she is the founding editor of *Superstition Review.* Murphy's writing has
appeared in *Calyx, The Massachusetts Review, Clackamas Literary Review, New
Orleans Review, Notre Dame Review, Seattle Review, Cimarron Review, Kalliope,
Quarterly West, American Poetry Review, Green Mountains Review, Indiana Re-
view,* and *The Iowa Review,* among others. Her poems have received awards
from *The Madison Review, The Bellevue Literary Review, The GSU Review, Glim-
mer Train Press,* and *Gulf Coast.* She has been the recipient of a project grant
from the Arizona Commission on the Arts, an Artist's Grant from the Vermont
Studio Center, and a fellowship from Mesa Refuge in Point Reyes, California.

Dip, Rise, Dive: Personal Questions & the Leap into Poetry

Through a process that employs the rational and irrational—invoking association and reflection—this exercise provides the spark for poems.

Procedure

I. Hand out the questionnaire—on the following spread—and ask writers to respond to the items without over-thinking, skipping questions they don't want to answer, moving forward and backward as they wish. Responses need not be "right" or "perfect." Writers will not share their responses unless they want to.

II. When most of the writers are halfway through the second page, tell them you'll stop them in five minutes and that finishing the questions isn't important.

III. At the five-minute point, ask writers to stop, look over their responses, and identify the three that most interest or surprise them. Then ask them to choose the one they like best and copy both the prompt and their response at the top of a sheet of writing paper.

IV. Ask everyone to write by leaping from the prompt and response. Grammar, spelling, staying on the point, even making sense are not important. The goal is to dive in. If students get stuck, suggest they write the same word or phrase over again until the next words come. Time the writing: five minutes.

V. Stop the freewrite. Ask writers to read what they wrote and underline a phrase, a sentence, a string of words that strikes them as the strongest writing/thought/truth.

Ask writers to skip down to the bottom of the free writing, leave a blank line, then write the underlined phrase, verbatim, there.

VI. Have writers start the process again, this time leaping from the new prompt—the passage they selected and copied. Time: four minutes.

VII. Repeat Steps 5 and 6, writing for three minutes instead of four. Repeat again, this time writing for two minutes instead of three. Have writers read this last entry and underline the strongest passage.

VIII. Ask volunteers to discuss the questions they found most interesting, a passage they underlined, what they discovered as they wrote.

Dip, Rise, Dive

Write quick responses to the following questions. Try not to think too hard: first thought, best thought. You will not share your answers with anyone unless you're willing.

1. My favorite creature is _____

2. My earliest memory is _____
   Briefly describe it: who, what, where, when.

   _____

   _____

   _____

3. I have recurring dreams about _____. One thing that always happens in these dreams is _____

   _____

4. Crazy opposites: silver and sliver, lollipops and pussy willows, overalls and _____.

5. Secretly, I've always wanted to be a/an _____

6. I like to collect _____ because _____

   _____

7. What outside place or spot resonates with you on a deep level? Why?

   _____

   _____

   _____

8. Which of these colors makes you *feel* the most: Indigo. Ruby Red. Deep Green. Cinnamon-Brown. Neon-Yellow. Why?

   _____

   _____

   _____

9. What part of your body do you love? Why? _____

   _____

   _____

10. This part of my body causes me the most grief: _____

11. My lucky charm is _____

12. I have an obsession with _____

13. These are three pivotal moments (positive or negative) in my life:

   _____

   _____

   _____

14. My favorite movie or book or song is _____ because

   _____

15. I have never told anybody that _____

16. For what cause or which person would you give up your life? Why?

     _____

     _____

     _____

17. Honestly, I know more about _____ than most people.

18. When I don't care what anyone thinks, I _____

     _____

19. Finish the sequence: *blubber, rebel, lobotomy, mobility, tenebrous,*
     _____. (It doesn't matter what the words mean.)

20. My favorite place in my house is the _____
     because_____

21. I use my sense of sight, smell, hearing, taste, touch the *least* (circle one).

22. The worst mistake a parent could make is to _____

     _____

23. My favorite relative/person is _____ because _____

     _____

24. My travel(s) to _____ have made a significant impact on my
     life. My travel(s) to _____ have made no impact on my life.

25. The greatest instance of injustice I have ever seen/experienced was

     _____

26. I am fascinated by this work of art: _____

27. This item of my clothing tells people a lot about who I am/want to be:

     _____.

28. When I smell _____ I think of _____

29. The biggest mistake I have made in my life is _____

     _____

30. I will stand up and *run* if you _____

31. Which of these would you eat? Circle the *wrong* answer: bullets,
     blackberries, plastic grapes, marginalia, oxygen, meteor.

32. What worries me the most is _____

     _____

33. I know this person/event has definitely changed the world: _____

     _____

34. Respond to this statement: "To lie means my truth isn't good enough."

     _____

     _____

     _____

IX. Engage writers in a discussion of how the prompts might lead to poems. Ask writers to come to the next class with a poem inspired by the exercise or any of the prompts.

Variations

There are endless ways to vary or adapt the "Dip, Rise, Dive" responses. Certain items (4, 19, 31) might generate poems that emphasize language play. Others (15, 17, 30) might lead to poems exploring secrets, hubris, humility, aversions. Items 11 and 16 might prompt a discussion of how abstraction and imagery work differently in poetry. There are also many ways to use the freewriting. Underlined passages could be reworked into lines of poems; the prose could be edited and line breaks added to create a poem, and so forth.

Tips

Usually, this exercise engages everyone—from the most fidgety to the most focused. Something about the quickness of the questionnaire, paired with the intensity of the timed writing, seems to satisfy diverse needs. Occasionally, though, a student will rush through the questionnaire with time to spare. Have sample poems available for them. Finally, if you have writers who work only by computer, make the questionnaire available in electronic form.

Examples

I. Sara Ryan, my student at the University of Miami, wrote from item 11 on the questionnaire, "My lucky charm is _____." Here are the three stages of Sara's freewriting:

> I have recurring dreams about falling. It feels like I'm jumping out of my dreams, I fall from stairs, buildings, down thrashing waterfalls. I always wake up swimming in my own sweat, my heart escaping my chest like a caged bear. I claw at the night, grasping for edge or sheets. Once someone told me that jolting out of sleep causes heart attacks, so now <u>every time I wake up I think I'm going to die.</u> I'm waiting for my chest to split, for my heart to crack in on itself. And when I was young, the fall was always spinning. I'd wake up dizzy and frighteningly alive—plummeting from monkey bars or two glassy skyscrapers while I tried to tightrope. I still wake like this once a week at least, I wake my own head up.
>
> <u>Every time I wake up I think I'm going to die.</u> Every day is an end, a sweet death, and I worry about dying every breath I pull into me, like maybe someday it won't be enough and I'll suffocate right there on the spot, <u>drop like a stiff broom, my hair all wild, my limbs wooden.</u> I run by a stop sign and almost get hit by a car that doesn't see me; this has happened so many times but each is

still as terrifying. When does my leg splinter, when does my body become an insect, when do I paint the Mercedes red? I've killed myself in my mind more times than I can count. I'm

<u>I drop like a stiff broom, my hair all wind, my limbs wooden.</u> My heart is a cold doorknob, a ringing, gold ball. I become inanimate with how green you are your soft, your mouth smoke, your willing body. I draw myself standing still, I crack myself into equal, packable, parts and fold myself shut. I twist my hair into a tidy knot and put it in your pocket, you are my keeper, locked chest, cabinet of hearts and wind and mirrors. You make me a portable mess.

Note: There is plenty of material for poetry in Sara's freewriting—in the first paragraph, images of heart attack, dizziness, falling; in the second, the leaps of imagination in this series: "When does my leg splinter, when does my body become an insect, when do I paint the Mercedes red?" And consider the dream-like images in the third paragraph, the material Sara drew on for her poem.

Love, You Sweet Dream

after Ross Gay

Babe, for you, I eat up the sun like a runny egg.
You make my heart a cold doorknob,
a ringing, blue bell.
Love, for your smoke mouth,
your willing body,
I stand so still,
piece myself into equal, packable parts
and fold myself into a two-dollar bill.
Boy, I twist my hair into a tidy knot
and put it in your pocket.
I tear you a fresh rabbit's foot;
I paint a horse on your neck.
I give you curtain ties, my hollow bodies
of wine, my wet, open throat.
I give you the flower of my shoulder,
my body bloom.
For you, sugar, I can't put anything down.
I can't keep hummingbirds out of my mouth.
I just need to lick every bone.
Love, you got me wishing on clouds and

for you, dear, I always smell like
cracked pepper.
You, my whistle, my lightning siren,
I'm a tangle of thread for you,
Love.

~ *Sara Ryan*

II. For the prose poem that follows, Jen Mehan, another of my university students, wrote from item 22, "the worst mistake a parent could make."

Nightlight

I.

The worst a parent could do is to smoke too many cigarettes, to leave bottle caps on the counters, and to have pin-up posters on the wall. To memorize every route out of town—85 on Wednesdays, 54 on a Thursday, 29 on the weekends, and otherwise, backroads. Five gas stations, two roadblocks, thirteen churches on the way. The worst is to have your gas tank always full and so many stacks of cash, you can't remember them all. To name the children Memphis and Dallas and Savannah and Charlotte and all the cities you've never been to. The worst is to play Sammy Kershaw in the kitchen every night, sketching business plan after business plan. The worst is to stay when you don't want to.

II.

Think of my fifth grade dance and picking out the corsage. Or the day I won game ball—my knees were swollen and hard, hand reddened to every stitch. Or all the checks I folded into my notebook to deliver. Think of my first car and how I drove ten under for months. Think of my spelling bees, my mathletes, my Hawaiian pudding project. Think of my brother, teaching me to skate and bike, to basketball, to clean and scare and be thoughtful. Think of me, four years old, cooking biscuits and washing dishes and ironing wrinkles in mom's clothes.

III.

You could always call me a failure. A try-for-nothing, why-don't-you-just-give-up failure? Don't break my models, don't spill the candle, learn to swim and sweep and launder. Learn to pour the milk, make the bed, wake your sister up. Learn again. That house—blue, birded, wooden, trampled, dogged, watergun, baseball diamond, cow pattied, biked, fundraisers, go-cart crash, dog pen stink, over-crowded stepfamily, and granny singing in the kitchen.

Stars on the ceiling—I peeled them off when she was sleeping, curled the glow-in-the-dark shape in my palm. Was the room big, or I just that small? I think of this nightlight, two inches from my eye and how with it, I could see everyone.

~ *Jen Mehan*

III. Lex Bobrow, also one of my university students, wrote from item 10: "This part of my body causes me the most grief:_____." Here is his three-part freewriting, followed by the poem he developed from it.

Skin grief: sad-luft epidermis ich habe todes this same day lad largest organ by which our insides are separate from the rest of everything touching the luft all quiet all, all the time away from internal organs. Sad skin is a seam between everything everywhere, everyone. Alone. But physically does it really mean we're alone? Breathing brings in the luft, touching the inside of our lungs taking away the alone the skin causes—you are breathing the same air as dinosaurs did millions of years ago, eating comets and bits of the big bad asteroid that now instead of annihilating sits in those torso-sacks, less harmless than even a single drag of a cigarette.

Sad-luft epidermis ich habe todes this same day. Deathfugue, German, is the only piece of poetry or spoken bit that has ever brought me to tears. I am the bulky bits of Paul Celan's voice. I am easy and he is dead but moving still on through pages and codices in which Dein aschenes Haar Sulamith sings death and lives on. Black milk wir drinken und drinken, even though America won that war. We have new black milk new todesfuge to repeat and sing out to the march of post-modernity.

We have new black milk new todesfuge to repeat and sing out to the march of post-modernity. It is not my hand that is tired, but my heart, my torso, my non-apathy. I don't care—I'm too tired. I wish I could speak German, that most tear-rendering of languages. Ach du lieber. O mein Gott. Where, when is anything, When, how, why, what, now? This sucks Muck chuck luck, tuck suck ruck buck luck nuck Chuck cuck duck euck fuck guck huck iuck juck kuck luck muck nuck ouck puck quck ruck such tuck uuck vuck wuck xuck yuck zuck-------------- just to keep my pen moving during this free write.

Todeshaut

after Paul Celan

Press all you want.
Ich habe den Tod in meiner Haut,
which is to say, the death in the atmosphere,
the corpse-dust of every living thing never buried
has settled on one side of the seam,
and disturbing it
does not change the fact
that it will settle again.

Kiss me all you want.
The seam does not fade
just because our insides meet.
When we kiss, we drink
the *Leichestaub* caking the inside of our mouths—
wir trinken und trinken.
To you, it is poison. To me, it is water.

And yet,
meine Haut brennt immer noch
where you touched. *Meine Haut*
brennt immer noch.

~ Lex Bobrow

Valerie Martínez is a poet, translator, teacher, playwright, librettist, and collaborative artist. Her award-winning books of poetry include *Absence, Luminescent* (Four Way Books, 1999), *World to World* (University of Arizona Press, 2005) and *Each and Her* (University of Arizona Press, 2010). Her poems, essays, and translations have appeared in *American Poetry Review, AGNI, Parnassus, Best American Poetry,* and *Touching the Fire: Fifteen Poets of Today's Latino Renaissance,* among others. Martínez is a Director and Core Artist with Littleglobe, an artist-run non-profit that collaborates with diverse and underserved communities in the creation of significant works of art. She has taught at the University of Arizona, Ursinus College, New Mexico Highlands University, University of New Mexico, College of Santa Fe, and elsewhere. She was the Poet Laureate for the City of Santa Fe, New Mexico, 2008–2010.

Lying: A Series of Exercises

Here are five separate but related exercises designed to take us further and further into the realm of poetic lying. Since so much of poetry is about invention, it is worth considering how we use the imagination in the service of autobiography.

Procedure

1. Always and Never

Write a simple litany that follows the pattern: *You always/You never.* The *never* isn't necessarily a lie (though it can be), but it is an absence of reality that makes what is real clearer, more poignant.

An Example

To My First Friend

You always were my age (before you died).
You will never remember our memories—
         the time I asked if you ever made a scrunched-nose face,
the earring we always passed back and forth
         like the animal crackers at school.
You never made me feel bad about the one time I kept an animal cracker
         in my pocket, my palms sweaty about getting caught. You just
         laughed.
You always laughed.
You never missed a word in the Pledge of Allegiance.
You always let me pretend your whistle was mine
         because I couldn't whistle,
like I could never go into work after your viewing
because your life always meant something great to lose.
Your life never meant this absence.

~ *Christina Seymour*

II. Two Truths and a Lie

Write down two truths and a lie about yourself. The lie is intentional and meant to be believed, but the context is autobiographical and playful. Take these three statements further in a poem that in some way reconciles them.

An Example

Truth 1: Every Saturday night as a child, I ate cotton candy.

Truth 2: Our dog got a kitten from the next yard over, and I picked it up to hand it to our neighbor; it had green ooze on it.

A Lie: At preschool, my favorite teacher shook a mixture of baby powder and glitter on my head to make me fall asleep.

Wonder and Restraint

Every Saturday night as a child, I ate cotton candy.
It was a kind of reward from my parents for the way I was put to sleep
       at preschool:
my favorite teacher, the one with the perfectly curved hair,
shook a mixture of baby powder and glitter on my head.
I can only think of the same twilight feeling
when my brother taught me how to spit
while killing fireflies with a baseball bat—golden spots stopped, shot
       to the ground.
A similar night, our dog got a kitten from next door's litter,
and I was the child brave enough to lift the white lump,
still heaving, a green ooze coating its matted fur,
and hand it over the fence to my neighbor's dirty hand.

Now, without a perfectly mixed someone to sing me off to sleep,
I am brave enough to put myself to bed with only a cup of tea.
I gave up the cotton candy but keep a few fireflies on the sill,
fixed in a jar like glitter on a Christmas tree. Once the covers are right,
I shut my eyes because it seems like the right thing to do,
crickets sounding even in the depth of the room,
neighborhood cats padding the sidewalk just beyond the window.

~ Christina Seymour

III. Minor Lies

Replace all the autobiographical facts in an existing poem with minor lies. Red is blue, snow is rain, the five-year-old is six, etc.

An Example

Note: Even the titles have changed between the original version ("Weekend Jog") and the revised version ("Weekday Walk"). Study both poems line by line. (See also Jill Alexander Essbaum's "Opposite Day," page 284.)

Weekend Jog   (original)

The floral air is heavy in my chest
as I run the wooded path.

I know enough to know I must work up to beauty
like the orange decaying in the grass, pitched, now flecked with brown,
and halving itself.
Quickly, I know
the fat robin bending a branch
is something I wish I brought my camera to show you—
(I am homesick).

When I return to my car and sit,
a distant goose call is not a happening
but the mood of midday
as my friend calls again to ask for relationship advice.
I can't say that I have any,
and I am quiet enough to listen,
which is a kind of advice:
I am quiet enough that lonely makes sense,
is all okay.

Weekday Walk   (revised—with minor lies)

The smog is heavy in my legs
as I walk the busy street.

I know enough to know I must fall into ugliness
like the kiwi decaying on the church step, pitched, now flecked with black,
and quartering itself.

Slowly, I know
the skinny squirrel smoothing wet cement
is nothing I wish I brought my camera to show you—
(I am content).

When I stop by the fence and kneel,
a close cheeseburger smell is a happening,
the mood of the evening
as an acquaintance passes me without waving.
I can say that I would have waved,
and I am loud enough to speak,
which is a kind of waving:
I am loud enough that lonely doesn't make sense,
is all unsettled.

~ *Christina Seymour*

IV. Major Lies

Replace all the autobiographical facts of a poem with major lies—e.g., the cousin commits suicide when she actually died in a car crash. Study both poems side by side.

An Example

Being Here to Be There   (original)

Because I didn't know my cousin very well
and can't make it to the funeral,
I need to mourn in my own way:
I listen to the windchime's bell make its way to each of the four bars
until it's hardly a sound.

Being There to Be Here   (revised—with major lies)

Because I knew my cousin very well
and rushed home to make it to the funeral,
I am mourning in everyone else's way:
we look at his hardened face and say, *such a good man, such a sweet man,*
until he fills the room.

~ *Christina Seymour*

V. Mixing Truth and Lies

Mix truth with lies in the fashion of Robert Lowell—what Elizabeth Bishop described as "infinite mischief." You invent a phone conversation with the cousin who died in a car crash where she talks about how she feels unwanted and ugly, and how her parents have refused to let her move back in with them. So now the car crash looks suspicious. You use her real name.

An Example

Note from Christina Seymour: First, I mixed truth with lies in this poem by creating the premise "Letter from my Grandfather," which is an inherent lie because my grandfather is dead. Writing from his perspective, though, I was able to write things I felt I needed to hear him say. Many of the details are also a mix of truth and lie. For instance, my grandfather was depressed and died of a heart attack, but I really don't know where or when, whether he was cutting a radish or reaching for cereal, or whether my grandmother was there to comfort him. Similarly, while my grandmother did keep cereal boxes in the oven (for no known reason), she did not bury a grape in the yard for every night my grandfather didn't speak, though the idea came from a common wives' tale of burying a potato in the yard to get rid of warts.

Inadvertently, this poem helped me discover my admiration for my grandmother as a strong central figure of my father's homestead, her "sweet fight" and her cantankerous behavior, and the trueness of walking me around the block to air out a cut I got on her porch stairs as a child (on my hand, not my head). Perhaps the most important lesson I gained from this exercise is that, even though the memories are not necessarily all factual, they are true symbolically and emotionally. They help me create closure—or at least some sense of my grandfather's death and depression.

Letter from my Grandfather

The day your grandmother walked you hand in hand
around the block to air out a fresh cut on your forehead—
this was how she eased me into death during my heart attack.
Reaching for my morning cereal,
I fell on a knife I'd used to cut a fresh radish—
you know, one from her garden under the clothesline you used to chase
      strings around,
chase your brother around, chase your cousin around,

while we grown-ups sat in our chairs and talked and were silent
and did whatever we did. Maybe I retreated to my room,
which is what your dad told you
depression was mostly about. That is my fault.
It is much more than that, and I tried to tell him
by singing, *once, twice, three times a lady*
while sweeping the garage clean,
by forcing him to shovel coal,
and by being too tired to teach him a useful thing, like fixing a leak—
I tried to tell him. But depression is not the thing that got me (and it
        will not get your dad);
it was the hardening in my chest beside your grandmother's wives' tale
of keeping cereal in the oven,
of burying a grape in the yard for every night I didn't speak,
a slow breathing beside her sweet fight that made her the one for me—
the sweet fight that yelled "hey shorts!" at your dad across a crowded
        church.
Just as she led you purposefully into the pain of the scrape on your head,
pointing out your father's schools, gravestones of our neighbors,
she knew it was my time, and led me steadily into it.

~ *Christina Seymour*

James Harms is the author of eight books of poetry, including *Comet Scar* (Carnegie Mellon University Press, 2012), *What to Borrow, What to Steal* (Marick Press, 2012), and *The Joy Addict* (Carnegie Mellon University Press, 2009). Winner of three Pushcart prizes, Harms teaches in the M.F.A. Program at West Virginia University, where he also chairs the Department of English.

Memory, Periphery, & Then Some

I often do this exercise with students on the first day of class. I don't give it any introduction or explanation and, in the interest of creating a similar possibility in a book of exercises, I'm going to hold the rationale until later. The exercise proceeds through a series of steps that I call out one at a time, waiting for students to finish each step before proceeding. I ask them to number each step on the page.

Note: I include with each step an example by a student, a wonderful (and well-published) poet, Jonathan Weinert.

Phase I: The Steps

I. Make a list of the scars on your body and how you got them. Maintain the format of a list, but be as exhaustive as possible. Physical scars only—no emotional scars and no feelings about the actual scars.

> Scar at the base of my right thumb—pushed down trash containing dog food can lid, which sliced the muscle to the bone
> Scar at the top of my right index finger—ex-girlfriend's American Eskimo dog bit me
> Long thin scar on my right forearm—Younger brother stabbed me with a fork at dinner because I wouldn't stop harassing him, I pulled back my arm, and a tine made a long shallow gash
> Scar between first and second joint of left thumb—Bronze ibis, black wax stain, metal chisel, in my friend's antique store
> Right knee—Repeated falls from the childhood bike

II. Take one scar and describe how you got it in no more than ten sentences.

> My wife and son were off somewhere. It was summer, and I had fed Loretta (the dog), preparatory to a walk in the woods, perhaps. I threw the can of dog food in the trash, then shoved the trash down with my right hand to make more room in the trashcan. The dog food can sliced the muscle to the bone. There was no pain, but there was blood all over the kitchen. I had to write my wife and son a note with my left hand while attempting to stanch the wound, then drove myself to the emergency room.

III. Write one sentence that focuses on at least one of your senses—something on the periphery of the moment that you have not yet mentioned. Think weather, light, birds in the trees, and so forth.

The sun was pouring into the back yard, and the hedges probably needed cutting.

IV. Write one sentence from another point of view. It could be a sentence from a neighbor looking out her window; it could be a shift from a child's perspective to the parent's point of view. The person speaking might not have actually seen the moment described. In the example below, Jonathan Weinert wrote a sentence from the dog's point of view.

What's that smell of metal, human, and when do we get to go outside?

V. Complete a sentence that begins "That was the year. . . ." You could refer to something familial (e.g., "That was the year my brother left home"); historical (e.g., "That was the year men walked on the moon"); cultural (e.g., "That was the year I dreamed I married Kurt Cobain."). Here's Weinert's:

That was the year that I had started playing guitar again.

VI. Add one more sentence of something else on the periphery.

The Ipswich Shellfish trucks were idling behind the refrigerated warehouse in the business park.

VII. In a single sentence, reverse or say the opposite of something you've said. For example, if you've earlier noted the sun pouring in the window you could write, "I heard rain hitting the gutter." Here's Weinert's:

I pulled my wounded hand out of the wastebasket, and look—it was healed.

VIII. Take three words from different sentences you've written in steps 3–7 and use them in a new sentence. Weinert used *pouring, idling,* and *wounded.*

The idling concrete trucks were pouring cement over the wounded.

IX. Write a sentence that the person you are today would say to the person you were in the moment you are writing about. It could be a wish, a warning, an encouragement, a glimpse of what will unfold.

I'd like to depend on you in an emergency.

X. Ask a question. To anyone or anything. About anything.

Where did Loretta's quizzical expression go when she died?

XI. Go back to step 2, and cross out all but two sentences. They don't have to be consecutive sentences. They don't have to "make sense" regarding the management of the incident's narrative.

Now you're done with this part of the exercise.

Phase II: Sharing

We go around the room, and each student reads the exercise as a whole, like a draft of a poem. I usually ask the students to include the list—because lists are amazing and because it's the first day and we learn a lot about one another from the list. With a good title, the list itself can turn into a poem.

Exempting the list and using only the two saved sentences from step 2, Jonathan Weinert read the following:

> My wife and son were off somewhere.
> The dog food can sliced the muscle to the bone.
> The sun was pouring into the back yard, and the hedges probably needed cutting.
> What's that smell of metal, human, and when do we get to go outside?
> That was the year that I had started playing guitar again.
> The Ipswich Shellfish trucks were idling behind the refrigerated warehouse in the business park.
> I pulled my wounded hand out of the wastebasket, and look—it was healed.
> The idling concrete trucks were pouring cement over the wounded.
> I'd like to depend on you in an emergency.
> Where did Loretta's quizzical expression go when she died?

Aside from aspects of memory and the physical, there's no shortage of things to observe in the exercise thus far:

- How quickly narrative unfolds.

- How what happened is often best managed by what's not looked at directly but at odd angles and from multiple perspectives.

- How using your senses and veering away from explanation and elaboration of feelings often evokes the feeling more profoundly.

Students often are surprised by having visited a memory/moment that they have not considered in many years.

Phase III: A Poem

After the sharing session, I send students home with the assignment to draft a poem using this material. The poet can use, bend, shift, and discard any of what surfaced in class, perhaps letting the draft take an entirely different direction. I do ask that the draft keep away from explication of feelings. (For another approach to poems that focus on scars, see Sheryl Luna's "Scars: Getting Under the Skin," page 42.)

An Example

Black Sutures

That was the year that I pushed my hand back down
into the trashcan of marriage. Trucks
were idling behind the refrigerated warehouses
in the office park. What's that smell of metal,
human, and when do we get to go outside?

I pulled my wounded hand from the trashcan.
The sun poured fire into the back yard where the hedges
waited to be cut. I wish I could depend on you
in an emergency. The idling concrete trucks
were pouring cement over the wounded.

My wife and son were off somewhere.
Where does your expression go when you die?
The dog food can lid sliced muscle to the bone.

~ Jonathan Weinert

Victoria Redel is the author of three books of poetry—*Woman Without Umbrella* (Four Way Books, 2012), *Swoon* (University of Chicago Press, 2003), and *Already the World* (Kent State University Press, 1995). Redel is also the author of four works of fiction, one of which, her novel *Loverboy,* was adapted for a feature-length film. Her work has been widely anthologized and translated into six languages. Redel has been the recipient of fellowships, including a fellowship in poetry from the National Endowment for the Arts. She teaches at Sarah Lawrence College in the undergraduate and graduate writing program.

Braided Narrative

One of the great original functions of poetry was story telling. In early, oral poetic traditions, narrative poems preserved the cultural histories of nations and peoples and, in doing so, encoded systems of moral and social identities. The point of Homer's *Odyssey,* for instance, is not merely to tell an engaging story—though of course it succeeds at that—but to articulate for listeners a set of cultural values. What, the poem asks—and answers—does it mean to be civilized? What are the duties of a leader? How should you behave when on a journey? What is your responsibility to the dead?

One of the intriguing ways Homer accomplishes what he does is through very deft, not-exactly-linear narration. The story begins *in medias res,* with Telemachos' story of insult and action. It slips briefly into a time years before, in a tale Menelaos recounts of Odysseus' adventures after the fall of Troy. Much of the middle part of the poem is told in first person, by Odysseus himself, who recounts his adventures to Alkinoos—a tale which may, given Odysseus' reputation for trickery, be wildly embellished. The rest Homer narrates in a more trustworthy third person, as Odysseus makes his dramatic return to Ithaca. Throughout these narratives, Homer braids the stories of the doings of the gods, particularly Athena.

Rationale

My students generally shy away from narrative, suspecting, I think, that it is a too-simple, too-linear approach to poetry, or that it contains within it a germ of sentimentality or dogmatism. Narrative, they have implied to me, is the domain of the novelist or memoirist. Poetry exists in a more reduced sphere, bringing together rarefied images, asking the reader to make deft mental leaps as she navigates the delicacies and nuances of the lyric poem. And to be sure, we're living in a time when lyric poetry is ascendant and poets of all kinds are mining the tradition for new and interesting ways in which poems might enact lyric meditation and thought.

But narrative, as Homer—and many others—suggest, is complicated. The options available to narrative poets are numerous; they are as open to experimentation as those offered to lyric poets. And in the same way that the lyric poet might make two unlike images work together in surprising ways, a narrative poet can do the same with two seemingly dissimilar narrative modes.

Procedure

For this exercise, I'm asking that students write a **braided narrative**—that is, a narrative poem which brings together two distinct stories or styles of storytelling and makes them work together. Is it possible to write a poem that takes place in two vastly different times? That is narrated by two quite different voices? Perhaps a poem in which one narration is "true" and the other is "fiction"? How can these disparate narrative modes be brought together in one poem? To begin, most any compelling narratives will do. There's no reason to stick to true stories. The world of the not-true is, after all, so much larger than the world of verifiable fact. And it may be that the more unlike the stories are, the more interestingly they will resonate against each other.

I. Choosing the First Narrative

On the facing page is my own attempt at this exercise, a poem called "Churches." I began with two remembered narratives, both of which I felt free to manipulate and adorn. The first was the memory of encountering an eerily striking young girl in a hotel gift shop in Arizona more than thirty years ago, when I was just ten years old. I remembered watching her from across the store as she turned the postcard rack around and around and, from that memory, constructed the story of her spinning it faster and faster until it falls through the plate glass window. No such thing ever happened, of course. But it seemed to work for the poem.

II. Choosing a Second Narrative

The second narrative was more immediate, a memory of my father dying in a hospital bed in Cleveland, Ohio. He had a large window in his room, and now and then nurses would check in on him, patting his head as though he were a little boy. In the very end, he grew delusional and my sister told me she'd seen him gesturing with his hands. "What are you doing?" she'd asked him. "I'm building a church," he answered from far beyond (I imagined) a curtain of sickness and medication.

III. Braiding the Narratives

These two narratives seemed, at first, to have little to do with each other, though as I twisted them together, I found that they had much in common, one commenting easily on the other. When, after a few drafts, I stopped to ask myself who that little girl had become in the poem, I realized that she was functioning either as Death itself, or as a kind of Greek chorus that announces truths about death and the irretrievability of the past that the narrator of the poem is too afraid to say himself.

IV. Revising, Re-Braiding

I've written several narrative poems that work in more-or-less this way and have always found it best not to worry too much at first about what the narratives have to do with each other. I can grope through early drafts on intuition alone. At some point, though, I have to ask myself how the narratives are living together and, once I've figured that out, I must go back into the poem and make them do it even more.

An Example

Churches

In 1981
       in a hotel gift shop outside Phoenix, AZ,
a little girl stood by the postcard rack, turning it gently.
It creaked.
      She considered a picture of the desert, then
looked around for her mother,
          who was elsewhere.
She gave the rack a firm push so it spun
gently on its axle,
      smiled, pushed it again,
and the postcard rack wobbled on spindly legs.

And soon she had it spinning
        so quickly the cards
made long blurry streaks in their rotation, gasps of blue
for sky,
     yellow for sand, and then faster,
the girl slapping at it with her hand,
         grinning at me,
and then a single postcard rose from the rack, spun in the air
and landed at my feet,
      a picture of a yawning canyon,
and then another, handfuls of postcards
rising from the rack,
      turning in the air
while the girl laughed
      and her oblivious mother, at the other end
of the store, bought a map or a box of fudge,

and then the air was full of pictures
                                    all of them shouting
Phoenix, Phoenix, Phoenix,
                              twirling and falling
until the empty postcard rack
groaned once more, tipped,
and crashed through the window.

+

There ought to be a word
                              that suggests
how we're balanced at the very tip of history
and behind us
                    everything speeds irretrievably away.
"It's called *impermanence*,"
                              the little girl said,
looking at the mess of postcards on the floor.
"It's called *transience*," she said,
                              gently touching the broken window.
"It's called *dying*," she said.
                              It was 1981
and the clerk ran from behind the counter,
                                    stood before us.
The girl smiled sweetly.
The postcard rack glittered
                              in the sun and broken glass.
He turned to me and my face grew hot.
I couldn't help it. I was blushing.

+

In 2009, my father lay in a hospital bed
gesturing sweepingly with his hands.
                                    "What are you doing?"
I asked him. "I'm building a church," he said.
"You're making a church?" I said.
                              "Can't you see?" he said.
He seemed to be patting something
in the air, sculpting something—a roof?—that floated above him.

The hospital room was quiet and white.
"What kind of church is it?" "I'm not finished."
"Is it a church you remember?"
                        "Goddammit," he said. "Can't you see I'm busy?"

+

It was 1988 and I stood in line for my diploma
and my father took a picture
                        that I've lost now.
1984 and there we are
                        around a campfire I can't remember.
It was 2002
            and his cells began to divide wrongly, first one
deep in the wrist bone, then another
                            turned hot and strange,
deformed, humpbacked and fissured,
                        queer and off-kilter,
one after the other,
            though no one would know it for years.

+

"It's called *dying*," the girl said,
                        while the postcards suspended
in the air like a thousand days.
                    I reached out to touch one,
then another,
            and all at once they fell to the floor.

Then the clerk said
                I was paying for the window,
where were my parents,
                and who was going to pay
if I didn't know where my parents were?
                            And the girl
smiled from behind the key chains
                        and her mother
pursed her lips at the far end of the store.
                            The window

had a hole in it through which a dry breeze came.
The postcards shifted on the floor.

+

Years later,
              my father was still making a church
with his hands.
              "They do that," the nurse said,
patting his head like he was a little boy.
                              He was concentrating
on his church, though,
                              his hands shaping first what seemed to be
the apse, then fluttering gently down the transepts.
He sighed heavily, frustrated,
                    began again.
"Can I bring you anything else?" the nurse asked.
"No," I said. "Thanks."
                    "Are you sure?" She watched him
tile the roof, watched his finger shape another arch.
And then it was much later.
                         He'd fallen asleep.
Outside, snow covered up the cars.

+

"It's called *forgetting*," the girl said,
                              while the clerk
watched me and I blushed. "Until there's nothing left."
And a breeze entered
                    through the hole in the window.
"And then you're out of time," she said,
                              and shrugged.
Some of the cards were face up on the floor:
                              two burros
climbing a craggy slope,
                    the Grand Canyon like a mouth
carved in the earth, a night-lit tower like a needle.
                              I was sweating now,
but I couldn't speak.

And then I was running from the shop,
past the fountain and the check-in desk,
down the tiled hall to the hotel pool,
where my father lay on a plastic beach chair,

                                    reading a book about churches.
Sunlight flecked his chest.
                          His hair was wet from swimming.
"What's the trouble?" he asked.

+

First
        his cells were thick and soupy,
clotted and aghast.
                          Then they were spinning
through the air.
                    And it was 1986 and rain
drummed on the roof.
                          Or it was snowing, years later,
in Cleveland,
                    his hands working the air
while the nurse stood in the doorway and sighed.
                                          Wind and sun,
a bright day, a lovely day
                          to lie by the hotel pool and read
about how men spent lifetimes building them

and never saw them finished.

~ *Kevin Prufer*

Kevin Prufer is the author of *Churches* (Four Way Books, 2014) and five other books of poetry. *In a Beautiful Country* (Four Way Books) was a finalist for the Rilke Prize and the Poets' Prize in 2011; *National Anthem* (Four Way Books) was named one of the five best poetry books of 2008 by *Publishers Weekly*. Editor of several books including *New European Poets* (Graywolf Press, 2008) and *New Young American Poets* (Southern Illinois University Press, 2000), Prufer teaches in the Creative Writing Program at the University of Houston and the Lesley University Low-Residency M.F.A. Program.

Tessellation:
Obsessing over Patterns

Simply defined, a tessellation is a pattern of shapes that fit together without any gaps—but it can also be a frame of mind. The tessellation frame of mind explores a possibility for reading and thinking about poetry. It offers a way of approaching poetry that is obsessive, loves complex patterns, loves destruction, seeks other dimensions, and undermines and clarifies the old question of "making sense." This tessellation frame of mind focuses on process as much as—if not more than—on product.

Preparation
Before conducting this exercise, gather up and explore tessellations yourself, though I strongly recommend you not worry about understanding or explaining these patterns. Extend that lack of worry to your students.

I. Online, gather some basic information and comparisons of tessellation patterns or shape-ways; tessellation will likely lead you to phenomena such as fractals, spirals, mosaics, mandalas, and polychorons. Seek out complex patterns; seek out simple patterns. A Google image search will reveal multiple examples of most of the following types of tessellations (some of which you might actually have around your house):

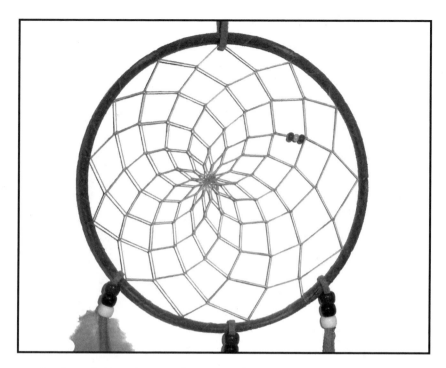

- brick work (See photo on facing page.)
- dream-catchers (See photo above.)
- mosaics (e.g., the floor in the Temple of Herakles or the Megiddo mosaic)
- tangram polygons (Better yet, have students cut out tangrams with poster board and make their own patterns with them.)
- mandalas (Better yet, have students make mandalas with colored pencils or pastels or whatever.)
- U.S. postal code lines
- henna tattoos
- Hopi flat baskets
- yin-yang symbols
- patchwork quilts
- tessellations in nature (e.g., a tortoiseshell, honeycomb, pineapple)
- fractals
- spirals (e.g., Spirograph creations)
- rose windows (also known as Catherine windows)

II. Look up images to illustrate reflection symmetry and rotational symmetry. Researching tessellation will move you into other patterns and ways of pattern making, and it will move you into the artistic traditions that both create and undermine the patterns. Saturate yourself so you can saturate your workshop. I'm not sure where you'll end up, but follow the rabbit.

Materials

- Check out a few art, math, and other books from the library that have images of tessellations—anything on Escher, Islamic mosaics, polychorons, fractals, mandalas, temple floor plans, and so on. Bring these books to the workshop, with any physical examples you have from around your house.
- Bring a ream of paper and some art supplies (e.g., colored pencils, rulers, markers, graph paper, etc.) Match sticks, scissors, and a power drill would come in handy, too.

Procedure

Phase I: Saturation

Bombard students with images and vocabulary around tessellation. Share images and information you found online. Chances are, several participants will have laptops, tablets, and/or smartphones, so the process of saturating will turn into group-scavenger-hunt-style saturation. Pass around the books you brought. Pass around physical manifestations (e.g., dream-catchers, Hopi flat baskets). Explore websites.

Phase II: Constructing Visual Tessellations

At some point in the saturation process, have students make their own tessellation or tangram or mandala or mosaic efforts with the paper and art supplies. Don't worry about poems yet; just hang out with the visual patterns. YouTube and WikiHow offer several videos on making tessellations.

As a group, consider how art is deeply intertwined with complex patterns, with interruption to those patterns, with undermining of those patterns.

Phase III: Segue

Look at the patterns on the facing page—four polychorons (5-cell, 16-cell, 24-cell, 600-cell), also called 4-polytopes.

To segue from visual patterns to verbal patterns, consider with your students questions such as the following:

- What is a 5-cell poem?

- How do you move a poem from a 5-cell to a 24-cell to a 600-cell poem? Is there any reason to do so?

- Is one more beautiful than another? (To me, these images and patterns are all beautiful.)

- What does beauty have to do with poetry or with art?

- What do you associate with these patterns? (Repetition, symmetry, balance, centers, spiral, etc.)

- How would we make these patterns ugly? Would that be more or less interesting to you?

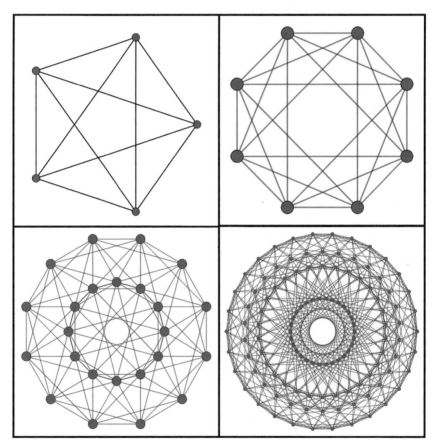

5-cell polychoron and 16-cell polychoron (top row, left to right).
24-cell polychoron and 600-cell polychoron (bottom row, left to right).

Phase IV: Destruction

Give students some time to make ugly one of the patterns they have made with the art supplies. Let them cut it up, put holes in it, set it afire, spit on it, drill holes in it, etc. Ask them to destroy the pattern, to undermine the pattern, to bury the pattern, to integrate the pattern with something that is pattern-less, if they can think of such a thing. Students should be surrounded, at this point, by intact and destroyed tessellations.

Ask—without expecting answers—questions such as these:

- What is the word/verbal/written equivalent of tessellation?

- If we took one of these tessellations and made its equivalent in poetry, what poem would that be?

- And then, if we "made it uglier" somehow—what poem would that be?

- If we integrated the tessellation-poem with something with "no pattern" or something "ugly"—what poem would that be?

Phase V: Poems, the Writing Part

I. Word and Problem Gathering: Prompt students, without writing anything down, to come up with a problem, a memory, an outrage (think M. NourbeSe Philip), a social injustice (think Juliana Spahr), a deformation of famous words from somewhere or someone else, a historical revision, a single object (think Gertrude Stein)—whatever grabs their interest at the moment.

Now prompt them to write down a couple of nouns, an adjective or a few adjectives, some phrases that they associate with the problem/memory/ outrage that they will be tessellating. It doesn't really matter how many words they've gathered, the effect will be important and distinct regardless.

II. Drafting: Ask students to choose a visual pattern (intact or made ugly), such as any they see around them in the room. Then—on another sheet of paper—they are to piece together a first draft. *The idea is to see if they can make a verbal equivalent of the visual pattern with the words and phrases they have just generated* (and, if they want, with the opposites or slant-opposites or slant-equivalents of those words and phrases).

Students can write concrete poetry (think Ruth Ellen Kocher's amazing Empire columns/baby girl poem in her collection *domina/Unblued,* where she has used the geometrical patterns of Greek architecture and filled them in with words). Or they can do something like Gertrude Stein does in *Tender Buttons* and tessellate objects/words. The possibilities are endless.

They will ask, "What do you mean?" I mean, if the pattern repeats four times around a center, do that with your words. If it disintegrates at the edges, do that with your words. If the center is a blank hole, do that with your words. I don't know what I mean exactly.

Students should play. They should not second-guess themselves; they should not over-think. They should absorb the pattern and the pattern's destruction; they should consider a subject and then see what happens.

Note: Make the exercise as loosey-goosey or as rules-bound as you want; both can be provoking.

Follow-Up

- Work toward a final draft of the poem.
- Give students time to do several rounds of visual and verbal tessellations based on the same or different patterns/words.
- Students can share tessellation poems and visual tessellations. As a group, they could think about things such as Gertrude Stein's quotation, "There is no such thing as repetition. Only insistence." What is each of these poems insisting upon? These poems might resist a traditional workshop discussion of *line* or *sense*. The group might consider, then, how these poems engage *sense* and *making sense* and *not making sense*. How are they engaging certain conventions, such as *line*? Ask the same questions about the visual tessellations. And so on.
- Have students "make ugly" their tessellation poem (or mosaic poem or spiral poem or . . .).
- Have them make the tessellation poem "even uglier."
- Have students try to use the same words to write a poem with "no pattern."

Tips

- You could use this basic process, or parts of it, with almost any group— children, graduate students, a long-term or one-time workshop. You could spend a year with tesselations.
- Resist over-explaining.
- Resist trying to connect too many dots between patterns and the poems they help generate. Still, I like to make sure a few are connected.

- Resist telling students at the beginning what might happen by the end. That said, it's usually helpful to let them know they will, over the next x amount of time, saturate, write, destroy, and repeat.
- Be as technical or un-technical as you want about these patterns, but be mindful that the mathematical language, the technical mind frame, can be intimidating or off-putting. When that happens, you might emphasize destroying: the patterns, the language—destroy everything.

An Example

Signatures

I. **Water stares back**

Here, a thicket
of Nootka rose,
salal clouding low.

Here, a stand of alders.
Each tree a moment.

The forest stories,
writing on the ground,
sound puddled.

The pond opens, a door.
Sudden gold surfaces.

A sunlight knife.

II. **The knife writes**

The hand signs its name.
Two cups for water.

Sunlight streaks the knuckles.

A palm, a psalm,
another dusk.
My kingdom for a thumb.

In the hand, a glass,
wine darker than blood.

Hands carve the soil,
plant calendula,
tomatoes, peppers, kale.

Sun on dirt.
Iron residue.

III. Far from Ypsilanti

Noise for the eyes,
the wind clapping,
slim shivers.

Each leaf shimmers its notes
without sound.

I write around the pool's verge,
stack my little words
like a city built of toothpicks,

empty matchbooks.
Without light.

I leave out
the hard parts,
but I do not leave.

Each silence glints, another knife.
Each cut mutes and opens,
a bad mouth gulping.

Syllables chuck
in my throat, in mud,
on brambles.

Empty pockets.
Raw.

I want to give you a white horse,
a slap on its rump,
a clear path out of here.

I want to give you a glass of wine,
fish and spinach.

I don't want to watch you
through that door.

~ Joannie Stangeland

Note from Joannie Stangeland: When writing "Signatures," I had several images and fragmented texts to work with, including pictures of sunlight slicing through a forest to a pool, a staircase, gravestones, and a franc note from the Banque Centrale.

In class, we began by numbering a section for each of our images and writing a few lines about it. Quickly, we switched to working off *The Book of a Hundred Hands* by Cole Swensen, writing a poem using the same word as many times as possible. We wrote in the margins of poems. We ripped a Sapphic fragment down the middle and filled in its other half. We wrote short prose poems in the style of Gertrude Stein's *Tender Buttons*.

The fast pace of the exercises left omissions, jumping-off spaces for future explorations. After the class, I had pages of writing—imagine each page as a node. With the initial numbered sections as a starting framework, I focused on how juxtapositions set up resolutions or collisions, as well as the tension between repetition and omission, adding, sorting, and paring—*much* paring—to leave only what was at stake in the poem.

Sarah Vap is the author of five collections of poetry, most recently *Arco Iris* (Saturnalia Books), which was named a *Library Journal* Best Book of 2012, and *End of the Sentimental Journey* (Noemi Press, 2013). Vap is recipient of a 2013 National Endowment of the Arts Grant for Literature. Her first collection, *Dummy Fire*, received the Saturnalia Poetry Prize. Her second collection, *American Spikenard*, received the Iowa Poetry Prize. Vap lives in Venice, California, where she is pursuing a Ph.D. at the University of Southern California.

On a Toehold, on Curious Rocks: The Poem as Collage

This exercise is for a collage poem, a self-portrait constructed of memory and historical detail. It has brought forth strange and daring poems from my students, more memorable than the confessional/autobiographical poems they otherwise lean toward.

Procedure

I. Make a fast list of your earliest memories—short phrases or images at first—but you should come up with 5–12 fragments. Don't edit, don't over-think; freewrite quickly.

II. Estimate your age for the images that most interest you, and decide what year is most likely the source of those first memories.

III. Do some research on that year. What major events, inventions, catastrophes, celebrations, wars, medical advancements (or challenges) were part of that time? Make a list of 5–12.

IV. Do some research on the events. Jot down snippets—details, facts, quotations, etc.—that grab your attention.

V. Select 15–20 images/memories/historical events. Start arranging them in lines—e.g., the first line, a personal memory; the second, a historical detail; the third, another memory; and so on.

Note: The result will likely be more surreal than narrative. Or the narrative will have the feel of a collage. What my students and I appreciate is the blend of the personal (but probably imperfectly remembered) and the larger social, historical elements.

Tips

- I've had students physically cut the lines apart with scissors and compose by taking them randomly from the pile, but one can be more deliberate—structuring, editing, etc., in whatever way works best.

- You can choose to stay local (Where did you live during those years?) and research a town, neighborhood, region, or state. Worldwide is often more interesting, but it involves more to sift through.

- The poem should involve some blend of the abstract and the specific, the personal and the collective.

An Example

Here is one of my own first poems from this exercise:

Crossings

Streetlamps in March, headlights turned
on the realization in '64

that apparently altruistic traits in species
could be versions of light on water. Motion

passing through New York City, its wounded
impaired for the rest of their lives. Long-reaching

steps from one to the next. Each of us
on a toehold, on curious rocks

in streams with our new blood
spent. Think of Verrazano Bridge. The longest

suspension bridge in the world opened
to traffic. A voice saying, *Careful. Don't fall in.*

So there's caution. Light.
Always arms being held straight up

in the air. Harry Harlow showing how monkeys
reared in isolation suffer

severe emotional impairment. We cross
on pebbles worn flat, try to stand

in the midst and above the rushing.
Like glittering ragged snow. The same

plasmid that carries resistance to penicillin
in staphylococci

permits the bacteria that possess the plasmid
to survive a mercury-based variety

of normally toxic metals. Venus and Saturn
cross streams with their arms up. Artemis

falling in brilliance. A raindrop, a tin flame,
headlights on ice. We learn the mathematics

of Mendelian heredity (peas in the monastery
garden), but don't yet understand impairment.

How a great earthquake shook Alaska, how
the International Year of the Quiet Sun begins.

~ *Rebecca Wee*

It's clear which segments are factual or historical, I think. Then there are my earliest memories—of crossing a river or stream on stepping stones, with someone holding my hands, my arms raised over my head. The remembered images involve shine, sparkle, motion, ice, reflection; the emotional associations I have are fear and excitement. I would have been two or three at the time (my parents say we took stepping stones to cross a stream near the place we lived in England), which makes the year 1964 or 1965, so those are the years I researched for world events and scientific discoveries. It's interesting that when I read the poem now, there's no way not to read 9-11-01 in the references to New York City and the wounded, but I wrote the poem in 1990–91.

Rebecca Wee is a professor of English and creative writing at Augustana College in Rock Island, Illinois. She moved to Illinois after completing her M.F.A. in poetry at George Mason University, where she studied with Carolyn Forché, serving as an assistant on Forché's anthology *Against Forgetting: Twentieth-Century Poetry of Witness* (W. W. Norton, 1993). Wee received the Hayden Carruth Award for New and Emerging Poetry for her first book, *Uncertain Grace* (Copper Canyon Press, 2001). She was awarded a 2002 Witter Bynner fellowship by U.S. Poet Laureate Billy Collins and the Library of Congress. She plans one day to finish her long-stalled second book, *Instead.* Meanwhile, she lives in Iowa with her two best poems, Rohan Auden (10) and Maren Elena (5).

Syllabus for a Seminar on Silence

Week 1: Sculptural Space

- Silent meditation: five minutes.

- Look at paintings by Agnes Martin; look at a dance by Kazuo Ohno (You-Tube has several).

- Look at the following books for examples of how different writers have used the space of the page: *Cascadia,* Brenda Hillman; *Commons,* Myung Mi Kim; *The View They Arrange,* Dale Going; *Afterrimages,* Joan Retallack.

Write a poem using physical silence on the page. The poem can only use up to twenty words (repeated words will count twice) but should occupy the entire space of the page. Explore how empty space can be sculptural.

Note: For a stunning use of empty space as sculptural, see Blas Falconer's poem at the end of this exercise (page 337).

Week 2: Musical Intent

- Silent meditation: seven minutes.

- Listen to Sheila Chandra's *ABoneCroneDrone* sequence.

Write a poem using limited vocabulary—twenty words maximum—which can be of any length or combination. Distribute the words carefully among nouns, verbs, and other parts of speech. The goal of your poem is to repeat and recombine phrases with musical intent. Your strategies can include puns, homonyms (multiple homonyms can be used as a single word), and words that double in multiple parts of speech.

Week 3: Language that Disappears

- Silent meditation: ten minutes.

- Listen to Alice Coltrane, *Universal Consciousness.*

- Read Jean Valentine's *Home Deep Blue.*

Write a poem in which language stutters and disappears at the end. Say something with your silence.

An Example

Poem that Disappears at the End

I lit a cigarette
      and shot a bullet
      of smoke
that went right through you.
            It was so easy then.

        The flame
      of the lighter
      pulled the shadows
         around us like a net.

You peeled
      my eyelids back
      and said "look at me,
      look at me goddamn it,"
        and I did.

Your body was the darkest
      thing on me, full of panic
      and thirst.

        Neither of us knew
        what we wanted.

        And the bow resting
            on the string,
        has it just
        or will it barely.

~ Marcelo Hernandez Castillo

Note from Marcelo Hernandez Castillo: I had always been uncomfortable with silence in my poems, so initially I resisted. I remembered the silent spaces of the body and how sound reverberates within these spaces to create meaning not through syntax but through vibration. I felt the weight of that silence but was still afraid of nothing being spoken. I wanted a poem where the silence was on the periphery, orbiting around a single phrase. But more than anything, I wanted it to vanish, to disappear at the end as the title goes. The silence between notes, the uncertainty of whether a song has just started or has already finished came directly from a quote in Ali's lecture when he spoke about Jean Valentine.

This is very much a poem that stutters and disappears at the end. Somehow, the noise and violence needed to disappear with the poem, so I ended it with an interstitial uncertainty, the moments between song when sound is both present and absent.

Week 4: Chanting and Vowel Sounds

- Silent meditation: fifteen minutes.
- Chant A, U, M—A with hand on chest, U with hand on throat, and M with hand on top of the head. Feel the body's resonances. Chant AUM three times with hands alternating on chest, throat, and top of head in order to tune the body's resonances.

Take a poem you have completed on any subject of your choosing. Remove all the consonants in the poem. Perform the poem using only the vowel sounds.

Week 5: The Suppressed Narrative

- Silent meditation: fifteen minutes.
- Chant A, U, M and AUM to tune resonances inside the body.
- Read the final section of *Zong!* by M. NourbeSe Philip, "Silence Wager Stories" by Susan Howe, and *River Antes* by Myung Mi Kim.

Write a poem on a personal experience you have always avoided in which the suppressed or silenced part of your story or narrative appears in half tone either in the margins or beneath/within the text of your poem. You may also use strike-through text or another strategy to indicate a suppressed or silenced voice.

An Example

Aubade for One Still Uncertain of Being Born

Lie still. Make their desperate hunt for your heart
beat them frenzied & let them second-guess
your muted tempo as counterfeit for their own.
Press your palm, still learning to unfurl,

to your den's wet beams & steady yourself
against the doorjamb of your lair; it will be time
when it is time. If your mother is a horse—& I am,
I am—let her approach Troy with you still hidden
within. Let her carry you like a bouquet of splinters
in her belly of timber still hot from hatching
at the future for firewood like it was a family tree.
All your life they will surround you, will stalk & strain
to hear that ballad from your canary pipes, will tempt
your quiet cover, will kick the keg of your desire
until it is dented nameless; all your life they will try
to say you are built for something else. It begins now—
so hush, hush: be nothing, just this once.

~ Meg Day

Note from Meg Day: This approach asks that the poem center itself on a subject about which the poet has consistently avoided writing, and asks that the suppressed or silenced part of the narrative appear as marginalia or otherwise isolated via formatting. This poem, despite its intact appearance, is the entirety of the margin-notes for a poem that, in the end, I could not write; the original and intended poem appears next to and above and below this margin-poem as blank, enduring silence.

I am a poet writing and living as part of a larger queer community that, because I am frequently read as masculine-of-center, often expects me to reject hetero- and homo-normative desires like participating in a long-term monogamous relationship or giving birth to a child with my partner. In the end, the subject that feels perpetually suppressed (by public opinion? by my own insecurity? by my rage at having to justify my desires to a community that fights to protect the right for people to do what they want with their lives and bodies, except when it is within a "straight" trajectory?) allowed me to revel in its silence and provided an avenue for re-focusing my energy.

These margin-notes capture, instead, the real conversation I am interested in having: one that not only addresses my desire to have a child—in spite of how the world reads my body or my relationships and what either is capable of—but also contains the very real, very private hesitations and apprehensions of becoming a parent.

Week 6: The Body

- Silent meditation: fifteen minutes.
- Chant A, U, M and AUM to tune resonances inside the body.
- Participate in a group chanting of AUM. The group will chant AUM together. As each person ends and begins again, the sound of AUM will go on, passed among group members and unending.
- Read *Sappho's Gymnasium* by Olga Broumas.

Write poems on your own body. Prepare your portfolio by revising each poem with your hands on your own body: recite each poem with your hands on your lower belly, solar plexus, heart center, throat, third eye and crown of the head. Revise vowels and consonants to the tune of the body and its silences.

An Example

Meditations on Silence

I.
Around the edges of silence,
        another kindPoem of silence.

The after Om of
           in-breath, pause, then
           silence
after
the out-breath.

Pockets of empty space
        like windows with no screens.

2.
Around the edge of the alpine pond, a beaver glides
        with silent strokes, his wake erased

by motion.

We watch in awe.   Mostly his swimming
is silent, then

THWACK!

Like memories we cannot erase, the sudden impact
        stuns us into silence.

The aspen shiver, though their roots
hold steady.

3.

There are silences from which
I refused to speak,

silences I could not penetrate.

I remember my mother tap-tap-tapped
the steering wheel,

      a rhythm of her own making, distraction from truths
she practiced un-saying.

And the silences from others I couldn't bear—
A grandmother's past of madness, her Judaism,

a veil of silence around her death
like the quiet vibrations of lives
inside my own—hunter, pirate, slave.

And the others I've loved
        continued their hauntings
silently in dreams.

      I loved them through memories of unspoken love
        in bookstores and bars.

And in silent stories I told myself
   I cannot love them
   or
       Because I love them—
They became primary characters in handsome coats.

    For years I endured the dreadful silence
    around my will to forget

how our knees touched under the table,
how our hands lay
painfully still in our laps

like helpless fish, unhooked on the shore,
lay mute after their terrible thrashing.

    ~ Amy Antongiovanni

Note from Amy Antongiovanni: During Ali's talk, he asked us to stand and say the three part "Om" together and pronounce each of the vowel sounds as "Ah-Oh-Um" more distinctly, and then to place our hands over our hearts and throats to feel the vibrational silence thereafter. My poem began to take shape in that moment.

I decided to write a three-part poem on silence in which I explored the experience of being silent in different ways. The first part explores being silent in meditation, the quiet around meditation for me is a circular experience, always returning to the breath and the ways in which we cycle and recycle the prana in our bodies—also the symbol of "om" being a circular, everything being connected.

The second part of the piece is about just what the image describes: a beaver/marmot (I'm not sure which it actually was) swimming in circles around a pond and the quiet of his swimming interrupted by his commanding thwack of a tail when he felt threatened or was just feeling alive. We can't know which. But I stood silently watching this creature in awe.

The third part is about the silence in relationships: what we don't talk about because we fear hurting the other, or what we can't say to our loved ones out loud. The silence on the page is also there, around and between the lines. It's a quiet poem, visually. There's a lot of breath implied in the spaces.

Week 7 and Onward: Beyond the Syllabus

Using space on the page to embody silence, writing with musical intent, allowing language to move toward silence, arranging words to suggest a suppressed narrative, cultivating the awareness, the presence, that goes with chanting—these are practices that move beyond this syllabus. They can shape poems in wonderful and intriguing ways, as Blas Falconer demonstrates here.

Note from Blas Falconer: I began by following Ali's prompts, but as I continued to revise, the poem moved in its own direction. Several of the devices are still prominent, however—repetition, exploring "how empty space can be sculptural," and especially the challenge to incorporate a "suppressed voice" (Week 5). While the numbered sections reflect upon the image of a storm's aftermath, the footnotes create a personal letter to someone who is very sick.

This direct address reveals the subtext in the study of the landscape and explains the associative leaps made by the speaker, whose figurative storm, of course, is the terminal diagnosis of a loved one. The exercise helped bring together a distant or public tone and a personal or intimate one, which seemed true to the experience of grief, how one often moves in the larger world with his or her private joy and hope and pain and dread.

A Study of *Tras la Tormenta*

by Jose Melendez Contreras, 1963. Oil/Masonite.

I.

A wooden chair fallen on its side,

the back's broken spindles, broken legs—

like broken bars

on a window

through which the ocean can be seen

each darker shade of blue

making the seafloor's steady decline,

how far down the light

can reach. You can look

and wonder. You can look forever

almost, waiting for

something to happen, a body to break

the surface.[i]

---

i.
You'll visit, won't you? We'll toast you're still
alive? I'm sorry summer kept you
inside. The garden full of jasmine,
soaked confetti blooms, and mornings,
the fragrance inhabits our small yard.

2.

While you wait, the body sleeps.
The body wakes. The body will
not eat. The body sips. The body is
hot and cold. The body is
broken. The body is lifted and
set down, again. You can hold
the body. You can kiss the body, but
the body sighs. All day, the body is
failing, the mind failing to
forgive the body for this failure. [ii]

3.

The shadow seems

to stretch beyond

the scene, and where

the ocean meets

the sand, there is

a boat moored,

the silhouette

of someone seated on

the edge facing the

---

ii
Months between appointments, I don't know
how you bear the wait, willing each test
to come back clear. Mint on the sill, how
you held the can's slender spout above
new shoots—deep deep breath, the lip of each.

surf as if it were,

that pale

stroke, coming or

going.[iii]

---

iii
incision closing. Yesterday, we drove
home slowly, the boys falling asleep,
the long trees bending over us,
and each door in my dream opened
into the wrong, brightly lit room.

~ *Blas Falconer*

Kazim Ali is a poet, fiction writer, essayist and translator. His books include four volumes of poetry, *The Far Mosque* (Alice James Books, 2005), *The Fortieth Day* (BOA Editions, 2008), the mixed genre *Bright Felon: Autobiography and Cities* (Wesleyan, 2010), and *Sky Ward* (Wesleyan, 2013). Ali has published two novels, *Quinn's Passage* and *The Disappearance of Seth;* two collections of essays, *Orange Alert: Essays on Poetry, Art and the Architecture of Silence* and *Fasting for Ramadan: Notes from a Spiritual Practice;* and translations of poetry by Sohrab Sepehri and a novel by Marguerite Duras. Recently he edited the essay collection *Jean Valentine: This-World Company* (University of Michigan Press, 2012). In addition to being associate professor of Creative Writing and Comparative Literature at Oberlin College and founding editor of Nightboat Books, Ali is a certified Jivamukti Yoga instructor.

Acknowledgments

The editors are grateful to the following authors, publishers, and journals for permission to reprint previously published work.

Aldrich, Linda, "Deranging Furniture." From *March and Mad Women* (Cincinnati, OH: Cherry Grove Collections, 2012). Reprinted by permission of the author and the publisher.

Beachy-Quick, Dan, "Lines." From *Circle's Apprentice* (Tupelo Press, 2011). Reprinted by permission of the publisher.

Birkelbach, Alan, "Destination." From *No End of Vision* by Alan Birkelbach and Karla K. Morton (Ink Brush Press, 2011). Reprinted by permission of the author and the publisher.

Bosselaar, Laure-Anne, "Parentheses." Appeared in slightly revised form from *The Hour Between Dog and Wolf.* Copyright © 1997 by Laure-Anne Bosselaar. Reprinted with the permission of the author and The Permissions Company, Inc., on behalf of BOA Editions, Ltd., www.boaeditions.org.

Clay, Adam, "Harbor." From *A Hotel Lobby at the Edge of the World* (Milkweed Editions, 2012). Copyright © 2012 by Adam Clay. Reprinted with permission from Milkweed Editions, www.milkweed.org.

Clifton, Lucille, "jonah." From *The Collected Poems of Lucille Clifton.* Copyright © 1972, 1987 by Lucille Clifton. Reprinted with the permission of The Permissions Company, Inc., on behalf of BOA Editions, Ltd., www.boaeditions.org.

Covey, Bruce, "Body & Isn't." From *Glass Is Really a Liquid* (No Tell Books, 2010). Reprinted by permission of the author and the publisher.

Crawford, Stan, "Dog Days." From *Texas Poetry Calendar* (Number 16, 2014).

Dorf, Carol, "Dear Ivar." From *Hip Mama* (Issue 48: The Education Issue, Fall 2011).

Espaillat, Rhina, "Bilingual/Bilingüe." Originally published in *Where Horizons Go* (Truman State University Press, 1998). Reprinted by permission of the author and the publisher.

Espaillat, Rhina, "For My Great-Great Grandson the Space Pioneer." From *Where Horizons Go* (Truman State University Press, 1998). Reprinted by permission of the author and the publisher.

Evans, Anna, "Haikoum." From "Form of the Week 34: The 'haikoum' (and the 'sonnetoum')," online at Lewis Turco's blog, *Poetics and Ruminations: Everything You Ever Wanted to Know about Poetry (and Everything Else) but Were Afraid to Ask.*

Evans, Anna, "Triple Lutz." Previously online at *Tilt-a-Whirl;* also in "Form of the Week 34: The 'haikoum' (and the 'sonnetoum')," online at Lewis Turco's blog, *Poetics and Ruminations: Everything You Ever Wanted to Know about Poetry (and Everything Else) but Were Afraid to Ask.*

Evans, R. G., "Y'all Come Back Now, You Hear." From *Poets Online* (Archive, November 2006).

Glaz, Sarah, "I Am a Number (II)" part 5. From *Talking Writing* (February 2012).

Golos, Veronica, "The Sacrifice of Sarah." From *A Bell Buried Deep* (Story Line Press, 2003; reissued by Tupelo Press, 2014). Reprinted by permission of the author.

Guerrero, Laurie Ann, "Babies Under the Skin." From *A Tongue in the Mouth of the Dying* (University of Notre Dame Press, 2013). Reprinted by permission of the author and the publisher.

Hedge Coke, Allison Adelle, "Eddy Lines." From *Caliban Online* (Number 3).

Hoagland, Tony, "Breaking Up Is Hard to Do." From *Hard Rain* (Hollyridge Press, 2005). Reprinted by permission of the author and the publisher.

Huston, Karla, "Dogma for the Junk Drawer." From *An Inventory of Lost Things* (Centennial Press, 2009). Reprinted by permission of the author.

Katz, David M., "Haikoum for James Dean." First published in *Claims of Home: Poems 1984–2010* (Dos Madres Press, Inc., 2010). All rights to reproduction of the text, quotation, and translation reside with the author.

Kearney, Meg, "First Blow-Job." From *Home By Now,* © 2009 by Meg Kearney. Reprinted with permission of Four Way Books. All rights reserved.

Kearney, Meg, "What It's Like." From *An Unkindness of Ravens.* Copyright © 2001 by Meg Kearney. Reprinted with the permission of the Permissions Company, Inc. on behalf of BOA Editions, Ltd., www.boaeditions.org.

Kennedy, Christopher, "Omphaloskepsis." From *Trouble With the Machine: Prose Poems* (Low Fidelity Press, 2003); reissued in the eBook series (Dzanc Books, 2013). Reprinted by permission of the author.

Keyes, Claire, "You Should Avoid Young Children." From *Adana Literary Journal* (Annual Print Issue Number 1, June, 2011).

Kirby, David, "Broken Promises." From *Big-Leg Music* (Orchises Press, 1995). Reprinted by permission of the author and the publisher.

Kwasny, Melissa, "Nettle." From *The Nine Senses* (Minneapolis: Milkweed Editions, 2011) Copyright © 2011 by Melissa Kwasny. Reprinted with permission from Milkweed Editions, www.milkweed.org.

Laird, Nick, "Epithalamium." From *Go Giant* © 2013 by Nick Laird. Used by permission of W. W. Norton & Company, Inc.

Leche, Christine Dumaine, "Bed." From *Rock Salt Plum Review* (Winter 2006).

Lee, Li-Young, "The Gift." From *Rose,* Copyright © 1986 by Li-Young Lee. Reprinted with the permission of The Permissions Company, Inc., on behalf of BOA Editions, Ltd., www.boaeditions.org.

Lockward, Diane, "You Should Avoid Doctors." From *What Feeds Us* (Wind Publications, 2006). Reprinted by permission of the author and the publisher.

Mathis, Cleopatra, "Canis." From *Book of Dog* (Sarabande Books, 2012). Reprinted by permission of the author and the publisher.

Matuk, Farid, "Of Mule and Deer." From *Between Heaven and Texas,* Ed. Naomi Shihab Nye (University of Texas Press, 2006). Reprinted in *This Isa Nice Neighborhood* by Farid Matuk (Letter Machine Editions, 2010). Reprinted by permission of the author and Letter Machine Editions.

Morton, Karla K. Photo, "Cactus and a Beetle." From *No End of Vision* by Alan Birkelbach and Karla K. Morton (Ink Brush Press, 2011). Reprinted by permission of the photographer and the publisher.

Pound, Ezra, "The River Merchant's Wife: A Letter." By Ezra Pound, original by Rihaku, from *Personae,* copyright © 1926 by Ezra Pound. Reprinted by permission of New Directions Publishing Corp.

Prufer, Kevin, "Churches," © 2013 by Kevin Prufer. From *Churches* (Four Way Books, 2013). Reprinted with permission of Four Way Books. All rights reserved.

Queeney, Courtney, "Back to the Body." From *Filibuster to Delay a Kiss: And Other Poems,* copyright © 2007 by Courtney Queeney. Used by permission of Random House, an imprint of The Random House Publishing Group, a division of Random House LLC. All rights reserved. Any third party use of this material, outside of this publication, is prohibited. Interested parties must apply directly to Random House LLC for permission.

Rader, Dean, "Self Portrait as *Wikipedia* Entry." From *Zyzzyva* (Winter 2011).

Rexroth, Kenneth, "Raccoon." From *Selected Poems,* copyright © 1940, 1956 by Kenneth Rexroth. Reprinted by permission of New Directions Publishing Corp.

Roripaugh, Lee Ann, "origin of tsunami." Forthcoming in *American Poetry Review.*

Sajé, Natasha, "P." From *Vivarium* (Tupelo Press, 2014). Reprinted by permission of the author and the publisher.

Seibles, Tim, "Renegades." From *Buffalo Head Solos.* Copyright © 2004 by Tim Seibles. Reprinted with permission of The Permissions Company, Inc., on behalf of the Cleveland State University Poetry Center.

Silver, Anna Krugovoy, "French Toast." From *The Ninety-Third Name of God: Poems* (Louisiana State University Press, 2010). Reprinted by permission of the publisher.

Smith, Patricia, "A Colored Girl Will Slice You If You Talk Wrong About Motown." From *Granta* online, 26 April 2011; *Shoulda Been Jimi Savannah,* Copyright © 2012 by Patricia Smith. (Coffee House Press, 2012). Reprinted by permission of the author and Coffee House Press.

Smoker, M. L., "Letter to Richard Hugo (1)" and "Letter to Richard Hugo (2)," ©2005 by M. L. Smoker. From *Another Attempt at Rescue* (Hanging Loose Press, 2005). Reprinted by permission of the publisher.

Soli, Sandra, "Dora Evelyn Thaw in Pisa Before Her Husband Commits Murder." From *Poemeleon: A Journal of Poetry* (Volume II, Issue 2, Winter 2007).

Soli, Sandra, "Flying." From *What Trees Know* (Greystone Press, 2007). Reprinted by permission of the author.

Soli, Sandra, "Semi Colon," the second part of "Tri Semi," a three-part poem written with a nod to Dame Edith Sitwell. From *Parody* (Volume I, Issue 1, April 2012).

Stallings, A. E., "The Eldest Sister to Psyche." From *Olives.* Copyright © 2012 by A .E. Stallings. Published 2012 by TriQuarterly Books/Northwestern University Press. All rights reserved.

Stangeland, Joannie, "Signatures." From *In Both Hands* (Ravenna Press, 2014). Reprinted by permission of the author and the publisher.

Sulak, Marcela, "Hebrew Lesson: Avera." From *Fence* (15.2, Winter 2012–13).

Swensen, Cole, "If a Garden of Numbers." From *Ours* (University of California Press, 2008). Reprinted by permission of the author and the publisher.

Tobin, Daniel, "The Avenue," "Brown-Eyed Girl," "Prelude: The Narrows," and "A Scar." From *The Narrows,* © 2005 by Daniel Tobin. Reprinted with permission of Four Way Books. All rights reserved.

Unterecker, John, "Scars," Part 5 of "Hospital." From *Poetry* (June 1977). © John Unterecker, courtesy of Roger L. Conover.

Wee, Rebecca, "Crossings." From *Uncertain Grace,* copyright © 2001 by Rebecca Wee. Reprinted with the permission of The Permissions Company, Inc., on behalf of Copper Canyon Press, www.coppercanyonpress.org.

Weir, John. "The Beautiful American Word 'Guy.'" From *Ploughshares* (Volume 35, Issue 4, Winter 2009).

Williams, William Carlos, "Nantucket." From T*he Collected Poems: Volume I, 1909–1939,* copyright © 1938 by New Directions Publishing Corp. Reprinted by permission of New Directions Publishing Corp.

Worley, Erin Brooks, "Bruxer," "Copacetic," and "Night Shift." From *Ninth Letter* (Volume 2, Number 1, Spring/Summer 2005).

Every effort has been made to trace the ownership of all copyrighted material in this book and to obtain permission for its use.

Index of Contributors

Note: Titles of the poetry writing exercises included in this book are listed in boldface.